◆**ALTERNATIVES** *is a series under the general editorship of Eric S. Rabkin, Martin H. Greenberg, and Joseph D. Olander which has been established to serve the growing critical audience of science fiction, fantastic fiction, and speculative fiction.*

Other titles in this series are:
Bridges to Science Fiction, edited by George E. Slusser, George R. Guffey, and Mark Rose, 1980
The Science Fiction of Mark Clifton, edited by Barry N. Malzberg and Martin H. Greenberg, 1980
Fantastic Lives: Autobiographical Essays by Notable Science Fiction Writers, edited by Martin H. Greenberg, 1981
Astounding Science Fiction: July 1939, edited by Martin H. Greenberg, 1981
The Magazine of Fantasy and Science Fiction: April 1965, edited by Edward L. Ferman, 1981
The Fantastic Stories of Cornell Woolrich, edited by Charles G. Waugh and Martin H. Greenberg, 1981
The Best Science Fiction of Arthur Conan Doyle, edited by Charles G. Waugh and Martin H. Greenberg, 1981
Bridges to Fantasy, edited by George E. Slusser, Eric S. Rabkin, and Robert Scholes, 1982
The End of the World, edited by Eric S. Rabkin, Martin H. Greenberg, and Joseph D. Olander, 1983
Coordinates: Placing Science Fiction and Fantasy, edited by George E. Slusser, Eric S. Rabkin, and Robert Scholes, 1983

No Place Else

Explorations in Utopian and Dystopian Fiction

Edited by

Eric S. Rabkin
Martin H. Greenberg
Joseph D. Olander

Southern Illinois University Press
Carbondale and Edwardsville

Copyright © 1983 by the Board of Trustees, Southern Illinois
  University
All rights reserved
Printed in the United States of America
Edited by Marilyn Davis
Designed by Quentin Fiore
Production supervised by John DeBacher

Library of Congress Cataloging in Publication Data
Main entry under title:

No place else.

  (Alternatives)
  Includes index.
    1. Science fiction, English—History and
criticism—Addresses, essays, lectures.
  2. Science fiction, American—History and
criticism—Addresses, essays, lectures.
  3. Utopias in literature—Addresses, essays,
lectures.   4. Dystopias in literature—
Addresses, essays, lectures.   I. Rabkin, Eric S.
II. Greenberg, Martin Harry.   III. Olander,
Joseph D.   IV. Series.
PR830.U7N6   1983   823'.0876'09372   83-4265
ISBN 0-8093-1113-5

86 85 84 83   4 3 2 1

Contents

Preface

Humankind has created fictions of social perfection at least since Plato's *Republic*. Sir Thomas More gave this thread of intellectual history a name when he called his contribution to it *Utopia*, Greek for *no place*. As time drew out this thread, no place changed, each later writer aware of the work of his predecessors, changing real world conditions suggesting ever new causes for hope and alarm. This volume begins with an introductory essay that tries to discern the common urge toward no place. The subsequent essays each focus on a different and significant work from the last hundred years along the thread. In discussing these central fictions, the contributors see no place from diverse perspectives: the sociological, the psychological, the political, the aesthetic. In revealing the roots of these works, the contributors cast back along the whole length of utopian thought. Each essay can stand alone; together, the essays make clear what no place means today. While it may be true that no place has always seemed elsewhere or elsewhen, in fact all utopian fiction whirls contemporary actors through a costume dance no place else but here.

I

Atavism and Utopia

Eric S. Rabkin

Utopia (Greek for *no place*) belongs to the future. In the pleasant Eutopia (*good place*) of William Morris's *News From Nowhere* (1890), the narrator falls asleep to mystically awaken in the restful twenty-first century; in the monstrous dystopia (*bad place*) of Aldous Huxley's *Brave New World* (1932), the conditioned citizens live out their sterile lives in the sixth century After Ford. In H. G. Wells's *The Time Machine* (1895), the Time Traveller first perceives A.D. 802,701 as a eutopia, "the whole earth had become a garden" (chap. 4), but he later "understood . . . what all the beauty of the Over-world people covered" (chap. 10). When the explicit literary displacement is not from the reader's time but from his place, as in Etienne Cabet's *A Voyage to Icaria* (1839) or Samuel Butler's *Erewhon* (1872), we still understand the practical message of the book to be an exhortation to us readers to mold a better future or avoid a worse one. In its programmatic aspect, utopian literature must belong to the future. After all, if a true utopia had ever really existed, it would still exist today and we would be reading travelogues instead of fictions.

Like all fictions, utopian literature must deal with the values and experiences of its audience. Eugene Zamiatin did not write *We* (1920) for the scientized "Numbers" reported to inhabit his United State any more than Plutarch (fl. ca. A.D. 100) wrote for the implacable infants raised in the romanticized Sparta he associated with Lycurgus. Both these writers, along with Morris, Huxley, Wells, Cabet, Butler and Zamiatin, programmatically address society but dramatically address individual readers, playing on universal hopes and fears, complexes of emotion that arise not from the intellectual contemplation of group alternatives but from the personal experiences of living. Each reader moved by utopian literature is responding intellectually to a vision of the future, but emotionally to a felt memory of his own past.

In the past of all adults, we the corrupt, there is the experience of change that is puberty. Before puberty there was innocence and after it

I

either the experience of oneself as an actively sexual creature or the equally sexual experience of frustration. The story of the Garden of Eden (Gen. 2–3) gives this common bit of personal history a set of mythic symbols. God the Father sets Adam down in a garden, nature regularized, and allows him to name the animals, that is, to further organize nature according to his own point of view. He is forbidden only the fruit of the tree of the knowledge of good and evil. Seeing Adam has no "help meet" (2:20), God creates for him a woman from Adam's rib. The creation of woman is the biological fact on which the story of the Fall rests, the impetus that will necessarily draw Adam away from his filial relationship with the paternal provider/protector. "Therefore shall a man leave his father and his mother, and shall cleave unto his wife: and they shall be one flesh" (2:24). Yet at this stage, "they were both naked . . . and were not ashamed" (2:25). The serpent, almost always a fertility symbol in the Near East and often a phallic symbol at that, convinces the woman to eat the fruit, which she does and which she induces Adam to do. The first consequence of this act is the knowledge of shame (3:7) which indicates to God the primal disobedience. Hence—following the motif of fertility marked by creation, nakedness, the serpent and the fruit—woman, now called Eve, is condemned "in sorrow [to] bring forth children" (3:16) while Adam is condemned to toil over crops: "In the sweat of thy face shalt thou eat bread" (3:19). By their sexually motivated act of self-assertion, according to God, they "become as one of us, to know good and evil" (3:22). Since this knowledge, combined with eternal life, would make people gods indeed, jealous Yahweh must keep them from the tree of life and therefore he expels Adam and Eve from the Garden and sets up "a flaming sword which turned every way, to keep the way of the tree of life" (3:24).

This constellation of symbols—the protecting/providing authority figure, the garden paradise, the calmness of sexual innocence, the advent of sexuality and simultaneously a certain kind of moral knowledge, the expulsion from the garden and the advent of pain, procreation and death—need have no historical basis whatever to still represent dramatically an experience we all feel in our pasts. Other cultures have ordered the symbols somewhat differently, of course. In the *Epic of Gilgamesh* the perfect couple is Ut-napishtim and his wife after the deluge, while the sexual fall is attributed to Enkidu. In Norse mythology the perfectly innocent couple emerge from the world tree Yggdrasil only after the cosmic destruction of Ragnarok. In Hesiod the Golden Age before strife is peopled not with a single couple but with a group who "lived long and virtuous lives, without labour, strife, or the need of law, having all things in common and dwelling safely amid the great abundance of all manner of produce which the earth brought forth of her own accord" (H. J. Rose, *A Handbook of Greek Mythology*, New York, 1959, p. 43). Despite these variations, the wide occurrence of this constellation, its symbolic dramatization of the human fact of sexual awakening and generational strife, and the particularly compelling power of the Bible as a literary source suggest that we can use the story of the Garden and the Fall as a convenient external shorthand for the internal traces of our past. We all know, from personal experience and as the myths remind us, that sexuality and the knowledge of good and evil are destabilizing phenomena. The writers of utopian literature know this as well, and whether they are pointing up a bright future or a dismal one, they know they must deal with the power of sex and they often remind us of the paradise that sex once cost us.

The most common vision of a eutopia, of course, is Eden itself. Wells's Time Traveller sees the whole world as a Garden and the Eloi are "on the intellectual level of . . . our five-year-old children" (chap. 4). Like a pre-Lapsarian Adam, they are "frugivorous" and "indolent." The Traveller felt himself "like a schoolmaster amidst children" and his nights with Weena are spent sleeping. *News From Nowhere* gives us another Eden: "England . . . is now a garden" (chap. 10), a place of innocence. Old Hammond, in extolling his eutopia to the time-travelling William Guest, exclaims, "'At least let us rejoice that we have got back our childhood again. I drink to the days that are!'" (chap. 16).

Often the utopian world is a pastoral one by virtue of the exclusion of technology, as we see in the Savage Reservation of *Brave New World*, the satiric Luddite paradise of *Erewhon*, or the ambiguous upperworld of perfectly asexual and transcendent minds riding in perfect pre-fab bodies in William Hjortsberg's *Gray Matters* (1971). This garden of our past serves as an appealing fictional indulgence of a normal nostalgia for that pre-sexual time when we were protected and provided for, when the demands of our selves were less troubling and when we more willingly followed the patterns set down for us. Utopians have often prized this pastoral equanimity, be it in the Golden Age, Gerrard Winstanley's cooperative Digger's Movement of the mid-seventeenth century, Denis Diderot's glorified Tahiti of the late eighteenth century, the Brook Farm experiment of the nineteenth century, or The Farm of today. That some of these communities have

worked does not at all diminish the fact that part of their appeal is
atavistic, a reversion to a vision of an earlier humankind in closer and
happier relation to necessity and nature and self.

Conversely, we often recognize dystopias for what they are by
virtue of their anti-pastoral, post-Lapsarian nature. Zamiatin's United
State is divided into glassed-in cities, each radically separated from the
others and from nature by its own "Green Wall." *Nineteen Eighty-four*
(1949) is a city book in which George Orwell has Winston Smith
confront nature only in the form of rapacious city-dwelling rats forced
against his face in the dreaded, subterranean "Room 101." Jonathan
Swift criticized Francis Bacon's citified *New Atlantis* (1627) by parody-
ing it as the floating city Laputa the scientists of which seek obviously
useless knowledge and are physically cut off from the land (*Gulliver's
Travels*, bk. 3, 1726). Whether in works of hope or works of warning,
whether in works primarily fiction or works primarily blueprint, writers revert again and again to the old place, the lost Garden, Eden, our
atavistic hope and home.

But there is trouble in paradise, and that trouble is sex. In Fred
Hoyle's story "The Operation,"

> the principal object of the Camps was to shatter the sexual drive of all
> young grown-ups. Joe could see enough of the point of view of "the other
> side" to understand how much of a nuisance sexual drive would be if it
> pervaded the community. It would destroy the crèche system, which
> permitted such careful conditioning of the young. Love would induce
> rivalries that might soon destroy the carefully knit communal life. Sexual
> drive might even cause men and women to become brave, even to resist
> the dominance of the thing in the building without windows. (*Element 79*,
> New York, 1967, p. 138)

Here Hoyle sees sex and love as synonymous, though of course they
need not be as Anthony Burgess horrifyingly shows with Alex's predi-
lection for "the old in-out in-out" (*A Clockwork Orange*, 1962).
Although sex is often associated with love, social disruption occurs not
from sex per se but from love, from the man leaving his mother and
father and other figures of authority and clinging not to his sexual
object but to his "help meet." Although it is not clear whether I-330 is
using sex to coldly manipulate D-503 in *We*, it is clear that D-503 is
finally motivated to his rebellion against the dystopian status quo by
love. As a doctor explains,

> "Yes, it *is* too bad. Apparently a soul has formed in you."
> A soul? That strange, ancient word that was forgotten long ago. . . .
> "Is it . . . very dangerous?" I stuttered.
> "Incurable." (Record 16)

Note that what we readers take as the positive value, the development of a soul, is the atavistic trait reappearing.

In *Anthem* (1946), Ayn Rand has created a collectivized dystopia in which the very word "I" is forbidden. People refer to themselves in the plural because all allowable thoughts are group thoughts. Our hero, Equality 7-2521, has already come to treason by thinking of a particular woman not as a number but as "the Golden One."

> Today, the Golden One stopped suddenly and said: "We love you."
> But then they frowned and shook their head and looked at us helplessly.
> "No," they whispered, "that is not what we wished to say."
> They were silent, then they spoke slowly, and their words were halting, like the words of a child learning to speak for the first time:
> "We are one . . . alone . . . and only . . . and we love you who are one . . . alone . . . and only."
> . . .
> We felt torn, torn for some word we could not find. (Chap. 9)

In this conflicted scene, the effort to reestablish human connection is pictured as a return to childhood and the project just vaguely begun here is the renaming of the contents of the world. The book ends, of course, with our hero and his "help meet" alone in a house in the tamed forest, an atavistic return to Eden.

One way to deal with the disruptive consequences of sex is to make it so frequent and so mechanical that it will not generate any love. That is the object of Zamiatin's "Lex Sexualis": "'A Number may obtain a license to use any other Number as a sexual product'" (Record 5). Huxley literally mechanizes sex in *Brave New World*: "Lenina [returned] from the vibro-vac like a pearl illuminated from within, pinkly glowing." In this dystopia sex must never be allowed to develop into personal attachment: "'You know how strongly the D.H.C. [Director of Hatcheries and Conditioning] objects to anything intense or long-drawn. Four months of Henry Foster, without having another man—why, he'd be furious if he knew'" (chap. 3). When sex is everywhere it shouldn't make much difference. In these mechanized worlds, as in the Garden before the Fall, people know no shame.

A second way to deal with the disruption of sex is suppression. In John Hersey's *My Petition For More Space* (1974), the overcrowded superstate decrees that "it is strictly forbidden for any person, while in accidental or formal proximity with any other person, in waitlines, assemblies, or close passage, to show, offer, signal, or otherwise manifest . . . prurient solicitation . . . lascivious carriage . . ." (P. 5) and so on. When this suppression is dictated from above—by the authority figures—we usually see the narrative world as dystopic. However, when the suppression is natural to the inhabitants of the narrative world we recognize this return to Edenic innocence as intended to be eutopic. Such is the case for Swift's anti-erotic, equiniform Houyhnhnms (*Gulliver's Travels*, bk. 4), an atavistic return to a time even before man was created. The example of the Houyhnhnms suggests a central fact about utopias: a real return to the Garden finally depends on a basic change in human nature.

To explore what such a change might mean, let us move for a moment from the direct consideration of sexuality to a consideration of its mythic concomitant, knowledge. No utopian work tries to proscribe all knowledge for the inhabitants of its narrative world. Even the homogenized population of *Anthem* are taught their collectivist litanies (chap. 1) and, one presumes, these people do know enough to come in from the rain. What they are forbidden is the knowledge of self, the kind of knowledge that leads to the assessment of responsibility, that is, the knowledge that would be necessary for self-assertion and thus potentially for disobedience and shame. To feel shame, one must know that one could make things or do things other than the way they are. Plato's famous banishment of poets from his *Republic* (ca. 380 B.C.) is based in part on the freedom of those concerned with representation to ignore the way things are in favor of the way they might be. The poet "must, apparently, be reproducing only what pleases the taste or wins the approval of the ignorant multitude" (F. M. Cornford edition, New York, 1945, p. 333). This sensuous seduction is no trivial concern. A cornerstone of the Republic is that each person is educated to fulfill the one job for which he is best qualified by native talent, and educated to believe that his functioning in society must be as the doer of that job. Indeed, cohesion in the Republic depends upon every citizen's recognition that he is powerless alone and utterly dependent upon the skills of his compatriots for the maintenance of life in any sort of economy worth the name. But what if a dramatic poet should happen along?

> Suppose, then, that an individual clever enough to assume any character and give imitations of anything and everything should visit our country and offer to perform his compositions, we shall bow down before a being with such miraculous powers of giving pleasure; but we shall tell him that we are not allowed to have any such person in our commonwealth. . . . For our own benefit, we shall employ the poets and storytellers of the more austere and less attractive type, who will reproduce only the manner of a person of high character and, in the substance of

their discourse, conform to those rules we laid down when we began the education of our warriors. (P. 85)

The sensual seduction of imitation is here joined with the poet's miraculous demonstration that things might be otherwise. A person could get god-like ideas. Thus knowledge, like sex, might well lead to individual action, hence disobedient action. If we may take the phrase "a person of high character" to refer to those for whom the proper rules of conduct have become automatic, then the complaint is against deviation from such rules. What Plato wants to re-create in his Republic is another Golden Age in which everyone does what everyone should without external constraints needed to enforce obedience. Thus the planned ignorance of the Republic, though ignorance of a special kind only, is precisely that ignorance needed for an atavistic return to the simpler times of myth, the easier days of youth.

The return to metaphorical youth, this particular manifestation of atavism, is apparent in many utopias. Plato turns his Republic over to father-figures called philosopher-kings. Christianity often describes paradise in terms of child-likeness: "Suffer little children, and forbid them not, to come unto me; for of such is the kingdom of heaven" (Matt. 19:14). In Ray Bradbury's *Fahrenheit 451* (1953), "firemen" burn books so that people will be happy with the pablum poured out to them over the airwaves. In *Leviathan* (1651) Thomas Hobbes argues that there is no natural right, that men should be ruled by the best rulers just as a family should be ruled by the father, and hence he argues for absolute monarchy. In *Childhood's End* (1953) Arthur C. Clarke has his earthlings establish New Athens under the unavoidable protection of the Overlords. In dystopian works like *1984* and *We* the citizenry is forcibly returned to the status of children by fear of the god-like figures of Big Brother and the Well-Doer, both removed, impersonal, implacable protector/providers demanding complete obedience. In *We* this atavistic return is finally made physically permanent by the development of the procedure for the "removal of fancy" (Record 15). At this point, however, we find, as we did with the Houyhnhnms, that the fiction has indulged its atavistic interests by postulating what amounts to a basic change in human nature.

In *Gargantua* (1534) François Rabelais presents the supposedly eutopian Abbey of Thélème which flourishes under the single rule, "Do what thou wilt." We must notice, however, that there is really a second rule, a set of admissions criteria. Judging, for example, by the sumptuous and uniform dress of the inhabitants of the Abbey, we realize that only people of rank, health and money are allowed to join.

These are surely Plato's persons "of high character." That is, the Abbey works as a eutopia because those people who inhabit it have internalized a code of behavior and a set of group values that are pre-designed to work properly. This not only puts them in the position of Adam willingly obedient before the Fall but, since the code disparages sexual jealousy, it allows them to keep their obedience in a sexual world. This set of attitudes may be in some sense plausible for a small and specially privileged class, but the myths of our culture indicate that for most people such freedom exists only in the memory of pre-pubic childhood. In both a straightforward way, then, as well as in its often recognized satiric way, the churchly Abbey was an apt place for Rabelais to situate his ideal society.

A different basic change in human nature is that of Total Breakthrough at the end of *Childhood's End*. In this improbable mass evolution, the *children* of the world form into a group mind of immense power and drift off into space to join with "the Overmind." This is surely humankind's return to childhood and to walking by the right hand of God. Theodore Sturgeon's *Homo Gestalt* in *More Than Human* (1953) achieves similar enlightenment by a basic change in character as does Olaf Stapledon's colony of telepaths in *Odd John* (1935). But to see the possibilities of a eutopia resting on a basic change that eliminates personal jealousies is to recall emotionally life in Eden before the Fall. And even in Eden, as the biblical account makes clear, the mere existence of man and woman together, not children, requires that families break up and re-form, a process that obviously involves social dislocations. To imagine it otherwise is to indulge our nostalgia for a time long past.

In order to test the idea that utopian literature is atavistic in values despite its more obvious future intent, I sought to find a work not obviously set in the future or the past or even displaced in space. Such a work is B. F. Skinner's *Walden Two* (1948), and it confronts atavism head on. When the narrator Burris explains what motivates him finally to convert to Frazier's ideal community, he says that "I could get no satisfaction from atavistic or nostalgic attempts to reconstruct a happier era, and so I contented myself with doing the day's work" (chap. 35). Skinner's book, one may freely grant, is full of schemes and devices that, if followed, might well help a community work its way into a future unlike any past humankind has known. But if one pays close attention, one sees discrepancies between *Walden Two* the program and *Walden Two* the novel. For example, we are told that "the sexes are on such equal terms here that no one guards equality very jealously'" (chap. 8). Nonetheless, we read that "'some of our *women* [emphasis mine] are still engaged in activities which would have been part of their jobs as housewives, but they work more efficiently and happily. And at least half of them are available for other work'" (chap. 8). When the viewpoint characters visit the nursery, the only adults they see are women. Teachers are uniformly referred to by female pronouns. Of course, the espoused equality is perhaps represented by the fact that the *chief* of the Housekeepers is a man. These are not mere slips, I think, but indications that a work like *Walden Two* is in some sense schizophrenic, torn between its existence as a lecture and its existence as a story.

In the last chapter, Burris is talking with Frazier about how to end his account of the community. He suggests

> "a little ambiguity? As a matter of technique."
> "The fact of the matter is," Frazier said, "the end of your personal history doesn't mean a damn, one way or the other. What the reader wants to know is: What was Walden Two really like?"

Frazier is doubtless correct if the reader is interested in assessing Walden Two as a program, but if he is interested in it as a novel then the human dimension is vitally important, centrally important. How the community handles the central problem of sex, for instance, is well known: early marriage, no property rights in people, hence no frustration and no jealousy. But in the *novel* our interest is inevitably tied up with the characters' love lives. The tourists to Walden Two are the working-class Steve and Mary, the upper-class Rodge and Barbara, and the bachelor professors Burris and Castle. The experience of the book, the lecture tour of the program, is enlivened (barely) by our expectation that Steve and Mary will get together and stay at Walden Two while Rodge and Barbara will split up. As in so many romances, our educated literary expectations are indeed fulfilled. But what of the enigmatic Frazier himself? He too is a bachelor and he seems to have a singular fondness for the company of Mrs. Rachel Meyerson. Chapter ten ends with these lines:

> Frazier and Mrs. Meyerson strode off across the lawn in the direction of the Ladder, talking and laughing energetically.
> "By the way," I said to Castle [referring to the image of Walden Two as functioning magically], "I think the Lovely Lady's name is Rachel."
> It was pseudo-wit. I had no idea what I meant.

Now such a line invites suspense. Is Frazier after Rachel? has he guided the construction of Walden Two just for her? will he meet Mr.

Meyerson on the field of honor? will he lash out in frustration and abandon the community he founded? The answer, it turns out, is not in the book. We never find out what Burris might have meant or what Rachel and "Fraze" meant to each other. As a novel, in short, *Walden Two* fails. Frazier's personal answer to the problem of sex is celibacy, apparently, and that is hardly a useful part of a program for an independently thriving community.

I would like to suggest that all utopian romance shares in some degree this schizophrenia. As program it belongs to the future but as novel it pleases us by indulging our atavistic desire for a special kind of orderliness, the simple, calm orderliness found in childhood, a bliss ignorant of sex and ignorant of the full knowledge of personal autonomy. If, as Plato feared, poets attract our attention by virtue of the sensuous pleasures of their imitations, then the seductive interest in utopian literature will always run counter to its programmatic intent. But though this may make us somewhat rein in our estimate of the practical value of utopian literature for shaping the future, it must surely help us recognize the deep psychological use such writing has for us in the present, a consolation for today cast in the forms of tomorrow but borrowed for us from our own personal past.

2

The Coming Race: Hell? or Paradise Foretasted?

B. G. Knepper

Edward Bulwer-Lytton published his utopian novel, *The Coming Race*, in 1871, toward the end of a distinguished career in literature and government. While his reputation in both areas has diminished somewhat, the reputation of *The Coming Race* continues to grow, and its place as a classic of utopian literature seems assured. That place depends, at least in part, upon the skill with which Bulwer-Lytton kept to the modern rule for science fiction, that the advanced technology of an "other" world must be a logical extension of the implications of current scientific knowledge. His use of evolution as the basic fact of human development, of personal fields of force as the mode of mankind's next evolutionary advance, and of electricity as not only the universal structural component of matter, but also as the bridge between body and intellect, fulfills the "rule" and places his work firmly and early in the stream of modern utopian novels.

People living in the 1980s, conditioned for more than a century to think of Victorian times as dull and dowdy, find it difficult to recapture the intense excitement of living during the nineteenth century when Western culture was literally reshaping its world. Yet so it was, in politics, science, and technology (to say nothing, just now, of theology and philosophy), and, in *The Coming Race*, Bulwer-Lytton struggled to resolve the problems, the hopes, and the reservations which occupied the minds of the thinkers and theorists of his time. His task was complicated by the need to present his thinking, as Charles Dickens and George Eliot also did, through the form of the popular novel.

In politics, then, England, as well as much of the rest of Europe, was making a stormy transition from the rule of the rich or the well-bred few to that of the common man, from oligarchy to democracy and thence, in the twentieth century, to socialism. England escaped the worst of the bloodshed which too often marked the changes on the continent, say the German revolutions of 1848, which in their turn grew out of the aborted February Revolution in France, or the ugly affair of the Commune of Paris (1871–73). Still, England had her violent moments, though perhaps none worse than the Battle of Peterloo (Manchester, 1819) which occurred when the yeomanry attacked a peaceable, if illegal, gathering of industrial workers. The massacre resulted in the death of eleven persons and the injury of some four hundred others, a negligible number by continental standards, perhaps, but quite enough to shock England into a determination to find less violent means of settling political differences. Meanwhile, political theories spawned everywhere, the Utilitarians and the Chartists building on the Reform Bill of 1832 and pointing the way toward trade-unionism and socialism, the Utilitarians eventually finding their strongest voices in John Stuart Mill and Herbert Spencer. Mill held that while the old Benthamite theory of pleasure as the central fact of human motivation was correct, it must be modified to recognize quality as well as quantity and to recognize that pleasure is a by-product of useful activity, not a goal in itself. Spencer linked utilitarian ethics to evolution.[1] Such struggles and theories inform much of *The Coming Race*, as does the sense of eventual and inevitably violent social transition which is most powerfully expressed in the dialectic materialism of Marx and Engels.[2]

On a lesser scale, women's rights were much debated during the nineteenth century. Mary Wollstonecraft Godwin produced her *Vindication of the Rights of Women* in 1792. The Chartists embraced the movement and, in 1851, the subject was debated in the House of Lords. In 1869, Mill's *Subjection of Women* appeared. One year later, John Bright moved a bill for women's suffrage in the House of Commons.

The ferment of ideas in the scientific world of the nineteenth century, too, caught Bulwer-Lytton's imagination and he played them off against each other constantly in *The Coming Race*. Among the controversies, perhaps none is more central than that which swirled around the subject of evolution. The earlier notion of teleological evolution, dependent upon will and purpose, demonstrable by design in nature, had been fully established before Bulwer-Lytton was born. It rested, essentially, on the authority of the studies of fossil remains as they relate to geological strata. Those remains indicate the existence of now-extinct life forms, and the teleologist argued that the progressions indicated a design and, therefore, a designer. Among the teleologists may be placed Erasmus Darwin (1731–1802), grandfather of Charles Darwin, and Jean Lamarck (1744–1829), who held that life forms are modified over long geological periods and that the modifications become hereditary, a theory which was widely held and as widely disputed. Later theorists, among them Bernard Shaw, held that purpose is demonstrable in the higher life-forms themselves without there being, necessarily, a connection with an embodied god.

Backers of teleology fought a losing battle against the mechanistic interpretations of the Darwinists who perverted Charles Darwin's theories of selection and survival of the fittest into catch-phrases, not only for biology, but for theology, political science, and even business pursuits as well. With theorists of the magnitude of Sir Charles Lyell, Herbert Spencer, and Thomas Huxley lending their support, it is little wonder that a mechanistic, hedonistic, deterministic view of life battered the teleological one and forced itself upon the consciousness of thinking men like Bulwer-Lytton, creating adherence and opposition not only between groups, but often even within individuals themselves.

Other areas of science were developing rapidly and excitingly. Electricity provides a significant example. The late eighteenth century saw the discoveries of Galvani and Volta. In the nineteenth century, Ohm, Joule, and Kirchoff broke through with discoveries which formed the basis for modern electrical technology. By 1841 Faraday had invented the electric motor, and within ten years the motor had been made practical. While power stations did not exist in Bulwer-Lytton's time, the telegraph certainly did (transatlantic cable, 1866) and medical applications were fairly common, though the X-ray was far in the future (1895).

The borderline between science and quackery in matters electrical was ill-defined. Galvani's theories about electric currents in the body, for instance, set off trains of thinking which have not yet run their course. Electrotherapy became, and remains, standard medical practice. It also became a favorite device for the charlatan. The notion that the body produces fields of force led to the marvels of electrocardiography and electroencephalography. It also led to the not quite so thoroughly demonstrated theories of the personal field of force which can influence that of another person, or which can be a factor in telepathy, or which can be the as yet evolving sixth sense. Cognates with earlier theories of astral bodies and platonic journeys of the soul were easily found and lent new support to the interest of serious

investigator and fraud alike. Bulwer-Lytton was not alone in finding
projections from the demonstrated to the probable to the possible
both interesting and illuminating.

Technology changed the way of life of all Europe in the
nineteenth century, not the least of all in England, which led the way in
the Industrial Revolution. The transatlantic cable has already been
mentioned, but it is a small matter compared with the changes wrought
by the application of steam to mining, factories, and shipping. Steam
travel began in England in 1825, and by the 1850s rail transportation
was completely established throughout western Europe. Steam-
powered industry, manufacturing, and shipping, land and sea, made
England a world power. Still, *The Coming Race* achieves its deepest
interest precisely because scientific principle is emphasized over technical application in an age obsessed with technical innovations. To be
sure, the novel is not free of imaginative technical innovations; much
of its page-to-page interest depends upon them. There are power
transmitters called vril-wands, housework is done by automatons, and
people fly with artificial wings. A superficial reader can easily become
involved with such details to the exclusion of all else. The point is that
Bulwer-Lytton's interest in gimmickry and gadgetry lies in the motives
of the people who develop such things and the effect of those things
upon their developers. Why does one want an ultimate weapons
system, and, once one has it, how does it affect the behavior of its
possessor? Even granting his obvious pleasure in inventing clever,
futuristic machinery, his constantly looking beyond the technology to
its implications for mankind puts Bulwer-Lytton far more in the camp
of Thomas Huxley, Dickens, and Shaw than, say, in that of Thomas B.
Macaulay or even of H. G. Wells.

If one ignores juvenilia and begins with Bulwer-Lytton's novel
Faulkland (1827), and includes work published after his death in 1873,
a conservative estimate of his literary production would include fifty-
three works: twenty-six novels, nine plays, and eighteen other items.
To the massiveness of this output add the great variety of kinds of
writing attempted, and it is no wonder that critical estimates of its
value vary so widely. Bulwer-Lytton has been seen as a serious ex-
plorer of the human condition in its many variations, as a skillful
craftsman working within a well-developed critical theory, and as a
clever entertainer, on the one hand, and on the other, as a hasty
panderer to a vulgar public taste, as a waster of great gifts and talents,
and as a crackpot in wrongheaded pursuit of the least reputable fads

and notions of his time. None of these estimates is without some color of the truth; none catches the whole truth, certainly. The simple fact is that the work is too large and too various to be easily or fairly assessed in any general sense. In addition, only a small portion of the work seems likely to survive as having permanent literary value. Therefore, it seems unlikely that anyone will find it worthwhile to make a definitive study of the entire corpus. What is left, then, and what is alike possible and valuable, are studies of restricted segments of the work made from carefully limited points of view. Such examinations promise rich rewards and will go far toward establishing a sound perspective from which to view Bulwar-Lytton's achievement.

Holding to a narrow focus is, of course, always difficult and sometimes dangerous. It means, largely, that the work itself must be made the center of the critic's attention and that all other intriguing relationships must be either subordinated to it or passed over altogether. The danger is that the critic may lose the larger view, may even be betrayed into prizing narrowness for its own sake. However, if the dangers are skirted, the work comes into view on its own terms, its ideas unclouded by critical preconceptions formed by excursions into biography or by comparisons with the author's previous work. Even consideration of the work's place in literary tradition must, for the moment, be suspended. The work, like a piece of jewelry, a cathedral, or even a race horse, has a heredity and exists within a culture, but it exists, nevertheless, as an individual creation and needs, as a first thing, to be understood as one. It can then be placed easily and accurately in the larger contexts, much understanding having been gained and little lost.

My own first concern with *The Coming Race* was its relationship to Shaw's set of plays, *Back to Methuselah*.[3] My present concern is first to examine the novel in its own right. Having done so, perhaps I can lay to rest at least one of the critical problems surrounding the novel: is *The Coming Race* a utopia or a dystopia? Does it, in short, picture a society which is the best that can be imagined, or one which is unbearably bad? This is the central problem of the story, and getting at it will go a long way toward understanding the book and, perhaps, a good part of the human dilemma as well.

Formal things first. The plot of *The Coming Race* is disarmingly simple and straightforward. In unrelieved chronological order it tells of an experience remembered, a tale carrying a warning of doom for the whole human race. The experience begins when a wealthy young

American, never identified, visits an unnamed mine in an unnamed country.

Almost at once, the American's engineer-companion is devoured by "a monstrous reptile resembling . . . the crocodile or alligator, but infinitely larger."[4] Recovering from the shock, the traveller finds himself in an artificially lit world, on a road surrounded by fields and forests, with buildings in the distance. It is, except for the monster, a pleasant enough place: "The world without a sun was bright and warm as an Italian landscape at noon, but the air less oppressive, the heat, softer" (chap. 3).

Approaching the buildings, Egyptian in nature, but "more ornamental and more fantastically graceful," he meets the first inhabitant; "an indescribable awe and terror" seizes him. He is confronted by a tall being, "tall as the tallest man below the height of giants," shaped like a man, "yet of another race." The creature is winged and carries a metal staff. His face is calm and beautiful, but "of a type of man distinct from our known extant races," and it "roused that instinct of danger which the sight of a tiger or serpent arouses." The traveller believes at once that this being "was endowed with forces inimical to man" (chap. 4). However, when this godlike being places a hand upon the stranger's shoulder and touches him with the staff, all fear is replaced by "a sense of contentment, of joy, of confidence in myself and in the being before me" (chap. 4).

The pair then enter a building, very ornate, having music in the background, birds caged everywhere, and automata for servants. The pair, along with a child, ascend by a lift to a rich apartment where, shortly, the troubled traveller is put to sleep. (chap. 5)

When he awakens he is surrounded by more of these superior beings. In the interrogation which follows, he senses that they are trying to decide whether he should live or die. In the end, he is taken home by the one who first found him, where he is welcomed by the family—a wife, two sons, and a daughter.

At this point the plot separates into several strands and gives place in importance and interest to theoretical and philosophical constructions which are truly the guts of the story. The plot, then, continues to exist mostly to give the traveller, while under the care of several conductors, an opportunity to view various aspects of the underground culture and to compare them with their cognates in the surface culture. This technique of hanging episodes or digressions from a slender thread of plot is no invention of Bulwer-Lytton's, of course, but it allows him to present ideas from several points of view, thus deepening the perspective.

The first plot strand involves the traveller and the being who first discovered him, a minor official called Alph-Lin. Alph-Lin is the primary expositor of his culture's history, art, religion, political science, and technology. The two, while often at odds, are in many ways kindred spirits and tend to act as alter egos for each other. Ultimately Alph-Lin proves unable to protect his guest-student, but he fills the role of guide-protector as long as possible. Thus, it is not for nothing that the traveller refers to him, habitually, as "my host." Alph-Lin acts not only as the entertainer of a guest, but also as the stronger member of a symbiotic pair.

The second plot strand involves the child, Tae, son of the chief magistrate, the Tur. The superior abilities of this child underline the childishness of the traveller who is, after all, a surrogate for all "ordinary" human beings. The two actually play together, and after an initial period of hostility this terrible child, who slays dragons with impunity, becomes a close friend of the traveller, although in some ways the relationship smacks of youthful master and exotic pet. In any case, Tae becomes yet another tutor. In the end, Tae is charged with the duty of killing the traveller, who is not only a dangerous and inferior animal, but a threat to the racial purity of the community. The child, because of his culture's religious conviction that death is only a journey to another life, has no fear of death nor any hesitation to kill any life form which he feels threatens his community. When the traveller learns of all this, he is terrified. He is also touched by Tae's willingness to accompany him in death, a wish which buys time when the child decides to ask his father's permission to kill himself as well as the stranger.

The third plot strand, and possibly the most important one, involves the girl, Zee, daughter of Alph-Lin, and the traveller. As a young female of this advanced race of subterranean giants, Zee is the more powerful of the two. In this topsy-turvy world, women are bigger and stronger than their own men, more intelligent, more aggressive, and, most importantly, more efficient users of vril, the power source which underlies all aspects of their civilization (of which, more later). Oddly, Zee is at once the feminist ideal and the caricature of all feminist ideals. While she, too, is very useful for providing a different perspective from which to measure the ideals of her race, her plot function is rather dreary: she provides the romantic pursuit which is responsible for whatever rising action there is. She is the catalyst which brings on the catastrophe, and her self-sacrifice provides the resolution. More specifically, she woos the traveller as is the custom in her culture, with all the gusto which will become the hallmark of a Shavian heroine, and expects him to display the characteristics of Shaw's womanly woman. The usual complications of the chase are present. Other young women, especially the underaged daughter of Tur, likewise aspire to the traveller's hand, a development which he finds by no means displeasing. Others, however, are horrified at the possibility of intermarriage with a surface dweller, and the traveller's fate is determined. Zee overcomes her jealousy and proposes a way out for the traveller and herself through the old love-and-honor formula. She will sacrifice honor for love and they will leave the colony to establish a version of the rose-covered cottage for themselves. The marriage will be "platonic," that is, it will be "without issue." Sensing at last the traveller's revulsion at the idea of such a marriage, Zee then decides to do the honorable thing, sacrifice her love as well. During the sleeping hours she spirits him away from the community and, using the special powers of vril, she blasts a way back into the mineshaft and restores the traveller to humanity. She blasts the shaft shut again and is heard of no more. The traveller then goes home after uttering a well-considered prophesy about the inevitable destruction of mankind, and the story is over.

The plot, then, is a tenuous thing, depending for whatever effect it may have upon a love theme and a death theme, neither of them very suspenseful. Even allowing for the attractions of fantasy, there is little in the plot itself to account for the popularity of the book in its own time. The digressions, then, as is so often the case in social satire, are more important than the plot, and that assumption will form the basis for their consideration later.

What then of style? Critics have long found this aspect of *The Coming Race* bothersome, possibly because it is to easy to misjudge the book on the basis of its none too impressive plot. However, in his recent book *Bulwer-Lytton: The Fiction of New Regions*, Allen Conrad Christensen argues on the positive side that perceptive readers have always found Bulwer-Lytton's books to have stylistic merit. He writes, "Such figures as Goethe, Carlyle, Mill, Harriet Martineau, Macauley, Dickens, Poe, and Arnold all paid tribute at various times to the serious artistry and intellectual vigor they discerned beneath the surface of his works."[5] This is high praise in general, though of little direct use relative to *The Coming Race* since four of the eight critics died before the novel appeared, three more were nearing the end of

long careers and lives, and only one, Arnold, was still in full career.
Still, if *The Coming Race* is allowed to be one of Bulwer-Lytton's
better works, produced not in his dotage but at the height of his mature
powers, then the evaluation is impressive. In any case, it is a refreshing
change from earlier evaluations which found his style nearly beyond
bearing.

Not all early statements were hostile to Bulwer-Lytton's abilities.
A fairly kind estimate was written in 1858 by J. Cordy Jeaffreson: "He
is entitled to foremost rank amongst writers of *talent*, as distinguished
from writers of *genius*; he is a careful and well-trained artist, deficient
in creative ability."[6]

As I have had occasion to observe elsewhere, Shaw claimed to
have admired *The Coming Race* as a boy, and, in 1887, credited it with
introducing the scientific method in the modern novel. Ten years later
Shaw castigated Bulwer-Lytton as lazy, a man who misused literary
skills to impose very slight scholarship upon the public. The kindest
things he could find to say were that Bulwer-Lytton was a "romantic
humbug," "insincere," and the author of "adventurous schoolboy
romances." Much later, in 1944, Shaw revised his opinion and placed
him among "the greatest poets and most inventive romancers."[7]

Perhaps the strongest plea for viewing Bulwer-Lytton as a serious
artist, as against a commercial boiler of pots, was made by Harold H.
Watts in 1935 in an essay entitled "Lytton's Theories of Prose
Fiction."[8] In it he traces literary theories formulated by Bulwer-Lytton
in 1838 as they appear in the practice of the later novels. Watts credits
Bulwer-Lytton with two notions which cast a great deal of light upon
the techniques employed in *The Coming Race*. One premise is that by
concentrating, in a single focus, the vicious influences of any particular
error in the social system, he (the novelist) will hold up a mirror in
which nations may see themselves reflected. The second is that the
controlling factor of a novel is a great conception (thesis) to which all
else is subordinate or incidental.[9] The first comes close to defining the
purpose of utopian literature; the second fits the catastrophic, evolutionary theme of *The Coming Race*.

On the whole, the style of *The Coming Race* is neither as unread-
able as has often been suggested (see the *Dictionary of National
Biography* entry as an easily available example) nor quite as skillful as
its apologists would have it. Perhaps the view that Bulwer-Lytton was
stuck with the tastes of contemporary popular readers, which demanded a romantic-adventure plot complete with fanciful descriptions
and other fantasy, comes close to the mark. From such a plot, how-

ever, he was free to add the digressions containing the ideas for discussion that are, after all, the heart of the book. Readers are left to cope, as they can, with the puzzling ironies demanded by the genre itself.

How is it, then, that genre study should provide the best answer to the question of whether *The Coming Race* is a utopian or a dystopian work? Consider that the basic characteristic of either form is that an imagined society is compared and contrasted with an existing one. The comparison may be very overt or it may be barely implied. In times during which criticism of church or state is extremely dangerous to the writer, or simply inconvenient, the comparison may well be left to the sharpness of the reader's insight. Theoretically, a simple allegorical comparison, one to one, might be made, such as, I take it, Eugene Zamiatin did in *We*, or George Orwell in *1984*. In practice, things are not so simple and both societies are presented as, to a degree, flawed. Paradoxical as it may seem for a writer to deliberately flaw his ideal society, such flawing is quite useful. The flaws of one society can be used to highlight the flaws or virtues of the other. Moreover, if a utopia is to be convincing, it cannot present a perfect society made up of fallible human beings. No one believes in such things, suspend disbelief as much as one will. Then, too, as a human society, a new society inevitably retains some of the aspects of the old society so that in a utopia or a dystopia there must be a certain amount of trade-off and compromise; increased order and discipline is exchanged for increasing blandness, unrelieved beauty for the highlighting provided by ugliness, and so on. The result is, commonly, that the author sometimes plays the game straight with the reader and sometimes plays it ironically.

The problem is to know when to turn the text upside down and when to take it at face value. For instance, Plato's *Republic* is usually taken at face value. But should it be? How much of the *Republic* is a sneer at Sparta's mindless militarism? Is it possible that even the conception of the reluctant philosopher-king is partly a spoof? If the Greeks must wait for their utopia until such paragons are ready to hand, clearly they must wait forever. Or can one take seriously the astringent sexual puritanism of the "metallic" classes and not smile at the sexual orgy which is their reward for military prowess? Plato's book, no doubt, is to be taken straight much of the time; other parts are either ironic or impossible.

Even Sir Thomas More's *Utopia* has its moments of irony. One example must serve. The notion of prenuptial stripping of the bride and groom for the same sort of physical examination appropriate in the purchase of a horse, a thing in the case of prospective marriage partners at once sensible and outrageous, must seem ironic, unless one is to presume the subtle and urbane More lacked a sense of humor. Jonathan Swift is an altogether tougher nut to crack. *Gulliver's Travels* poses genuinely difficult problems of interpretation. In Book I, Lilliput is England and Blefuscu is France and each is an awful place. No reasonable reader mistakes Lilliput for utopia, and if it is not dystopia, it will do as a substitute. Still, bad as it is, Lilliput has a reasonable system of education for all classes, a boast England will not be able to make with any show of truth for nearly two centuries. Nor are all Lilliputians fools and rogues. In short, with a reduction of vice and folly, and with a few reforms, Lilliput-England could at least approach the condition of a utopia. The irony in Book II is, to a degree, more subtle. Eighteenth-century Europe surely suffers from comparison with enlightened Brobdingnag, but Brobdingnag, for all its abolishing of warfare and its horror at European atrocity, is certainly not an unsullied utopian paradise. The episode about the court ladies at their toilet, or that of the ulcerous beggar, is enough to suggest that human vices and follies are magnified, along with human virtues, in the land of the giants. Book III may be passed over as an unrelieved dystopia. The Struldbruggs, monsters who age progressively but never die, are the proper emblems of ultimate awfulness. Book IV offers endless difficulties. On the surface, it presents the ultimate utopia of the Enlightenment. For the most part, institutions have faded away and only a benevolent society remains, a society formed of horses. These horses, called Houyhnhnms, are contrasted with human society through Gulliver and through the wild human animals called Yahoos, some of whom the Houyhnhnms have domesticated. In Gulliver's view, mankind fails to measure up. In a sense, Houyhnhnmland is utopia, the best society that man can achieve. Had the book started with Laputa, the progression from worst to best would be clear enough. But if the land of the Houyhnhnms is indeed the earthly paradise, it is a strange one. The Houyhnhnms are docile and priggish. Their perfect society is the ultimate in dullness. Consider one of their marriage rules. Each couple is allowed to raise two, and two only, colts—one male, one female. As one colt is as good as another, a swapping custom is established to correct any failure on nature's part to make an even distribution of the sexes. The arrangement may well be humane and sensible. However, it reminds one of the tongue-in-cheek tone of the equally "sensible" arrangements of "A Modest Proposal" which proposed, "reasonably" enough, to establish cannibalism as the solution to Ireland's oversupply of paupers.

It is hardly too much to say that the extreme blandness of a perfect society is one of the most difficult points for the idealist to get over. Shaw's ultimate utopia, presented in *As Far as Thought Can Reach*, is peopled by Ancients who live forever, barring accidents, and who live a life as nearly exclusively intellectual as it is possible to imagine creatures still in the flesh to live. These Ancients explain to their young that their own intellectual experiences are so much more ecstatic than any of the children's sexual adventures that a moment of such pleasure would be more than the children could survive. Contemporary drama critics shared the scepticism of the young about this claim and pronounced adult life in A.D. 31,920, as seen by Shaw, to be unbearable, Shaw's protests of his own sincerity notwithstanding.

Recent critics tend to see *The Coming Race* as dystopian or anti-utopian. In 1965, Geoffrey Wagner described *The Coming Race* as mainly an attack on America, "the new woman," and machine technology. His perception of the satirical intention is certainly accurate, though I can hardly agree that those themes, of themselves, form the central purpose of the book, though they are certainly important elements of it. Even so, Wagner's remark that "Lytton disarms the reader with external satire, then proceeds to get down to business by pushing what seems to him topsy-turvy values *ad absurdum*," is clearly an accurate description of Bulwer-Lytton's method. It also underlines Wagner's identification of the book as no utopia.[10]

In 1971, Hans Seeber published a shortened English version of his longer German article about *The Coming Race*. In it he declared that "by casting his veiled criticism of the inherent dangers of uninhibited utopianism, both political and scientific, in the form of a romance, he fathered a new variety of utopian writing, the anti-utopian novel." For Seeber, the bogeys are Utopian Socialism and scientific materialism. He credits Lytton as being, "in fact, the first writer to emphasize and exploit the contrast between ordinary humanity and inhuman utopian perfection, in terms of narrative treatment."[11]

In 1979, John Weeks provided a slender introduction for a new edition of *The Coming Race*. He observed that the supermen have "little more to do than to contemplate their own perfection" and that the traveller "finds that what seemed at first to be the good life is after all indolent and boring." This language clearly seems to indicate a dystopia. Unfortunately, the thread is not pursued and Week's closing statements muddle the conception of a dystopia. They suggest, instead, that the underground people have established a utopian pattern toward which mankind is, on the whole, happily racing. "In fact," Weeks wrote, "we still haven't quite caught up with the farthest reaches of his [Bulwer-Lytton's] imagination, but we are going that way and gaining fast."[12]

If the novel is taken as a whole and on its own terms, without modification by speculation, however well-supported, about Bulwer-Lytton's attitudes expressed elsewhere in his works about the same or similar topics, it becomes clear that proponents of both the utopian and the dystopian interpretations are right. The home truth of the book is that, take it as you will, evolution is a fact, and that mankind in its present form will be replaced by a superior species—quite likely a hostile one. Thus, the book is a dystopia for the traveller, a truth which does him little credit. He is at once terrified and bored by a world too advanced for him. He sees his own race and culture reflected in those subterranean peoples who failed to evolve and who are doomed. But never does Bulwer-Lytton present the traveller's culture as intrinsically superior to that of the undergrounders. Theirs is presented consistently as a utopia, flawed as a still evolving form must be, but in every way superior. In the end, Bulwer-Lytton does not mince matters. The traveller muses, "The more I think of a people calmly developing . . . powers surpassing our most disciplined modes of force, and *virtues* [emphasis mine] to which our life, social and political, becomes antagonistic in proportion as our civilization advances,—the more devoutly I pray that ages may elapse before there emerge into sunlight our inevitable destroyers" (chap. 29). Just as Shaw's Ancients are unable to appreciate the joys of their terrible parents, and earlier, unevolved people died of awe and discouragement in the presence of the ancestors of the Ancients, so the traveller is unable to bear living in an advanced utopia—though looking back he wonders "how I could have rejected such a love, no matter what dangers attended it, or by what conditions it was restricted" (chap. 29). Romantic balderdash or not, this is not the speech of a character who recalls his lover as a dystopian monster.

Acting on the premise, then, that *The Coming Race* has a dual nature, utopian in the long view, dystopian in the short, the salient features of the book may be examined freshly. The scientific theories need to be dealt with first as they underlie the social ones.

Evolution is the sine qua non of the novel. Earlier discussion distinguished between the Darwinian theory and the older, teleological sort. The distinction is basic to understanding what the work is getting at. At the time Bulwer-Lytton wrote, the Darwinian theories were dominant and their implications were somber. They projected a world which was mechanistic with a vengeance, with the role of will and intellect reduced to the merest of nothings. Chance bound to irresistible cause and effect was everything. While all of this was largely a perversion of Darwin's own theories, it was the popularized Darwinian guff against which Browning and Tennyson, among others, revolted. If *The Coming Race* had been conceived as simply another Darwinian horror story, it would have lost none of its sense of inevitability and doom. It would also have been the unrelieved dystopia it has been so often depicted as being.

But *The Coming Race* is not an unrelieved dystopia. Repeatedly, the text makes it clear that Bulwer-Lytton's master race developed by plan, not accident, and that the mode of development included individual will and racial will plus an implied divine will as well. Consider that, immediately following a passage of the clearest survival-of-the-fittest Darwinism, Zee refers to an ancient legend which held that "'we were driven from a region that seems to denote the world you came from, in order to perfect our condition and attain to the pure elimination of our species by the severity of the struggles our forefather underwent; and that, when our education shall become finally completed, we are destined to return to the upper world, and supplant all the inferior races now existing therein'" (chap. 15). This passage affirms the operation of will and direction, not blind chance. Natural selection is converted from a process of accident to one of education. A second case in point revolves around the nature of vril, the substance which is the source of all the material good and power of the advanced race. The seat of vril lies in a nerve at the base of an enlarged thumb. This nerve, which develops and concentrates the vril, a substance akin to electricity, was not found either in the early ancestors of the upper race or in the contemporary "barbaric" underground races, or, by analogy, in modern human beings. It was, Zee explains, "'slowly developed in the course of generations, commencing in the early achievements and increasing with the continuous exercise of the vril power'" (chap. 16). The power and skill in applying it is, thus, conceived to be hereditarily cumulative and to be the result of will and practice, not of chance. Zee adds that "'in the course of one or two thousand years, such a nerve may possibly be engendered in those higher beings of your own race.'" As to the theory of the descent from frogs, it is indeed the amusing parody of Darwinism it is generally presumed to be. However, when the traveller asks if the theory of "'the origin of your race in the tadpole'" is still recognized, he is put in his place by Zee. Her reply confirms the teleological position and sets the limit for human power:

> "When we know the elements out of which our bodies are composed, elements common to the humblest vegetable plants, can it signify whether the All-Wise combined those elements out of one form more than another, in order to create that in which He has placed the capacity to receive the idea of Himself, and all the varied grandeurs of intellect to which that idea gives birth? The An in reality commenced to exist as An with the donation of that capacity, and, with that capacity, the sense to acknowledge that, however through the countless ages his race may improve in wisdom, it can never combine the elements at its command into the form of a tadpole."

Zee's father then makes the connection between physical and social evolution by remarking that his people "'feel a reasonable assurance that whether the origins of the An [all Subterranean peoples] was a tadpole or not, he is no more likely to become a tadpole again than the institutions of the Vril-ya [the super race] are likely to relapse into the heaving quagmire and certain strife-rot of a Koom-Posh [popular democracy]'" (chap. 16).

The final argument to be advanced here for teleology as the guiding evolutionary concept in *The Coming Race* is provided in a reflective passage by the traveller: "Perfect justice flows of necessity from perfectness of knowledge to conceive, perfectness of love to will, and perfectness of power to complete it" (chap. 14). Besides coming down firmly on the side of will, the words are an astonishing anticipation of Shaw's conception of the prerequisites for social justice, which he articulated in *Major Barbara* and fully elaborated in *Back to Methuselah*, that social justice can occur only when love, intellect, and power are combined, eventually in supermen who will become philosopher-kings.

The scientific validity of the conception of "vril" is of secondary importance to the need in *The Coming Race* for a physical manifestation of the evolutionary process in action. In "vril," Bulwer-Lytton found a power which could be used to exploit the excitement caused by successive discoveries in electricity. While the notion of developing "vril" by a special nerve and transmitting it through a metal wand may strike a modern reader as altogether absurd and corny, it provided a simple, visible concrete object, able to represent a number of abstract notions. From the point of view of *The Coming Race*'s effectiveness as fiction, then, it hardly matters whether Bulwer-Lytton was highly learned in scientific matters or whether the names of distinguished practitioners in many fields (Faraday and Galvani, physicists; Louis Agassiz, naturalist; Lyell, geologist; Robert Owen, social scientist; Descartes, philosopher) which he scatters throughout the book are merely window dressing. Their function as a fictional artifact is to lend an aura of validity to the story as story. Their function vis-à-vis serious social theorizing is to provide apparent authority from contemporary science. The choice of electricity in the form of "vril" was an especially happy one as it provided a simple, yet comprehensive, vehicle for presenting ideas of evolutionary progress.

In the first seriously descriptive passage of *The Coming Race* concerning vril, the traveller mentions magnetism, galvanism, Faraday, mesmerism, electro-biology, and odic force as "the various forms under which the forces of matter are made manifest." He argues further that they "have one common origin . . . [and] are so directly related and mutually dependent, that they are convertible . . . into one another, and possess equivalents of power in their action." The latter point is the basis for a very complicated theory about the interrelation of all things material and spiritual. It leads to the conclusion that once life is created, it continues forever, though translated by death to a different world, and it recalls its progress from stage to stage. Vril is able to interact from one life to another so that the super-race can use it to project their wills into other animate, and even inanimate, bodies and minds and make them behave in whatever way the super-race desires. Thus vril, manipulated through a vril-staff, can power and direct automata, heal the ill, calm the overwrought, or destroy armies and cities at extreme range. So defined, vril is a universal principle which gives its users the powers of gods, at least in the old, Greek sense of gods (chap. 7).

As to social and political theories, *The Coming Race* contains a wealth of ideas treated in great detail. Little more than a sampling can be attempted here, leaving the reader the enormous fun of fully tracing out the details.

The effect of vril on warfare amounts to a profound social and political revolution. War becomes unthinkable in the face of over-whelming power. (Bulwer-Lytton apparently was not cynical enough to envision the twentieth-century use of "limited warfare" in the shadow of the nuclear holocaust.) Imagine a world in which not only nations but individuals possess the power to destroy multitudes at nearly any range. In such a world, strife and violence toward one's fellows must be abandoned, at whatever psychological cost.

Law, too, is a casualty to unlimited individual power in *The Coming Race*. Anarchy, however, does not result, mainly because the habit of restraint is presented as transmissible hereditarily, just as vril itself is. While the habit is being formed, restraint must be enforced by rigid custom. Dissidents have the option of migration and little else. Class distinctions are obviously impossible to maintain. No one can exploit another through superior strength, and vril provides such an abundance of power for agriculture and such other industry as is needed, as well as the automata to run it, that economic exploitation is out of the question. Oddly enough, there are a few individuals who refuse to make even the minimum effort necessary for maintaining themselves. For these, the only suasion possible is a form of ridicule in which the community pretends that such an individual is insane and heaps luxuries upon him until shame brings him to his senses.

Even election to office brings no class privilege to the holder. As in the *Republic*, it simply brings the burden of duty with it, in those few areas in which the community must still be organized, namely light, communications, inventions, and machinery. Light is an obvious need in an underground world. Communications are restricted to other advanced communities, for the most part. Inventions, mostly in the hands of the women of the College of Sages, tend to be vril application research with occasional forays into more esoteric areas. Machinery, curiously, is in the hands of the children, girls until they are sixteen years old, boys until they are twenty. They are in charge of agriculture, housekeeping and border guarding. In the last occupation, their concern is with the possible encroachment of dangerous animals or of the barbaric nations. The children are well paid for their efforts; they earn enough in childhood to support them for the rest of their lives (chap. 19).

Obviously, children capable of destroying prehistoric monsters or the equivalent of modern armies suffer little from excessive parental control. Nevertheless, the family remains a strong institution. This is partly due to an ingrained reverence for life and partly to the conception of society as an extended family. In any case, families stay together until the children achieve adulthood, and the elderly are treated with respect and affection. Such treatment may be made easier with the aged who, despite average life spans of one hundred years and more, stay healthy, vigorous, and financially independent to the end.

Except in sex roles and strength, the sexes are equal. While the reversal of roles and characteristics is great fun, and purportedly based on the principle that in most of the animal kingdom, most mammals aside, the female is the more powerful sex, the reversal functions more as satire than as a serious projection of a real evolutionary tendency (chaps. 9, 10, 15, 26).

At least passing mention should be made of the variety of societies extant under the Earth's surface. All of them exist under the name of An. Only a few have advanced to the possession of vril; they are known as Vril-ya. The lesser An are ranged in a progression of lesser political forms, some of which the Vril-ya have presumably passed through. These forms correspond with those in the *Republic* and to the nineteenth-century European and American models. The bottom of the heap is composed of Glek-Nas. They are democracy run wild, the anarchy which Plato contends is the inevitable tendency of universal democracy. The American Civil War and the revolutions of Europe give color to the theory. Democracy is described as Koom-Posh and is distinguished by "the government of the many, or the ascendancy of the most ignorant or hollow." The satirical intent is clear enough. But the organized anarchy of the Vril-ya must not be confused with either of the imperfect forms; it is the ideal society in which every individual is an aristocrat, a member of Plato's golden class, and a potential philosopher-king (chaps. 9, 15, 18).

Leaving much unsaid about the political and social aspects of the book, especially about its extraordinarily sane and Swiftian religion, I must turn to a consideration of the characteristics it shares with other utopias and dystopias, besides what I have already done in passing. For instance, I suggest that *The Coming Race* must share honors with Francis Bacon's *The New Atlantis* as a prototype of the "scientific" utopia. Like Bulwer-Lytton, Bacon envisioned a society which combined experimental science with the creature comfort of its members. Swift's *Gulliver's Travels* received fairly extensive treatment earlier, but Book III was largely passed over. It will bear examination, however, as Bulwer-Lytton's spoofs are much in the mode of Swift's *Laputa*. Compare the scholars there, for instance, with their penchant for the trivial, with the College of Sages in *The Coming Race*.

H. G. Wells's *A Modern Utopia*, with its world a mirror image of the Earth, except for a population of superior people, shares several features with *The Coming Race*. For instance, each features an evolving society which places a higher value on social virtue than on hedonistic lifestyles. Each is as much a treatise on social theory as it is a novel. They differ markedly in that Wells bases his society on an eighteenth-century norm, mankind at its best, as against Bulwer-Lytton's mankind evolved. Wells's Samurai, nevertheless, see to it that inferior specimens either do not survive or do not reproduce, a bit of genetic tinkering which raises the spectre of totalitarianism gone mad. The similarity to Samuel Butler's *Erewhon*, which appeared one year after *The Coming Race*, has been often noted in the critical literature. The similarity seems to me to be one largely of techniques: Butler produced a dystopia, pure and simple; Bulwer-Lytton a utopia.

William Morris's *News from Nowhere* is a splendid example of another basically anarchistic society, albeit a caring one, seriously put forward as an achievable utopia. In his book, as in Bulwer-Lytton's, institutions have all but faded away, and mankind as extended family has replaced the state. Work has all but vanished, thanks to simplified needs and the development of machinery to do necessary but dull work, so that people, with more leisure than art and handicraft can satisfy, actually compete for whatever meaningful work is left. Evolution toward a super-race is no part of Morris's scheme; he is too much a perfectionist of the Shellyan mode for that. On the other hand, his earthly paradise is unmarred by the same constant, if submerged, threat of violence that Bulwer-Lytton's is.

The relationship of Shaw's work to *The Coming Race* has been glanced at in passing throughout this study. Evolution, awe, and advanced mental powers, far more sophisticated than vril, are but a few of the parallels, a matter I discussed in detail in 1971 in an article entitled "Shaw's Debt to *The Coming Race*."[13]

Finally, Aldous Huxley's *Brave New World*, as a scientific dystopia with a considerable overlay of political and social exploration, will repay comparison with *The Coming Race*. So far as I can determine, *Brave New World* is not based in theory upon teleological evolution, though it certainly implies that, freed from the mind-crushing restrictions of an inhuman, technological, totalitarian society, the human spirit would grow again.

I cannot say with any confidence that *The Coming Race* has had a profound impact upon following writers, Shaw excepted. Along with Bulwer-Lytton's other work, it has mostly languished on library shelves for a century and more. The ideas it contains and the mode of its presentation were hardly unique, even for its day, except in the way in which they were combined; the ideas were "in the air." With the recent revival of interest in his work, and the appearence of at least one new and inexpensive edition, the impact may increase. For my part, I hope it does. Wholly aside from its literary value, or the simple fact that it is fun, I count *The Coming Race* as an important item in the humanist arsenal against despair. The human spirit needs all the weapons it can muster against the hopelessness thrust at it by determinists, mechanists, and assorted totalitarians everywhere. If the human spirit can be coaxed into persisting, perhaps it may at last prevail.

Notes

1. See: Mill, *On Liberty* (1859), *Utilitarianism* (1863); and Spencer, *First Principles* (1862), *The Principles of Biology* (1864–67), and *The Principles of Psychology* (1855).
2. While *The Communist Manifesto* appeared in 1847, it hardly represents the full-blown development of dialectic materialism of *Das Kapital*, the first volume of which did not appear until 1867 and none of which was available in English translation in Bulwer-Lytton's lifetime.
3. "*Back to Methuselah* and the Utopian Tradition" (Ph.D. diss., Univ. of Nebraska, 1967).
4. Chap. 2. I have never been able to discover a definitive edition of *The Coming Race*. The Knebworth edition (London: George Routledge and Sons, 1879; republished Quakertown, Pennsylvania: Philosophical Publishing Co., 1973), possibly comes the nearest to being a standard edition. Since the novel first appeared in 1871 in *Blackwood's*, a variety of authorized and pirated editions have appeared. The most recent and easily available edition to come to my attention is edited by John Weeks (Santa Barbara, Calif.: Woodbridge Pr., 1979). The difficulty, then, of settling on a standard edition accessible to scholar and general readers alike is essentially insurmountable. Fortunately, chapters in *The Coming Race* are very short, and chapter references alone should sufficiently locate passages for all practical purposes.
5. *Edward Bulwer-Lytton: The Fiction of New Regions* (Athens: Univ. of Georgia Pr., 1970), p. x.
6. *Novels and Novelists: from Elizabeth to Victoria*, vol. 2 (London: Hurst and Blackett, 1858), p. 210.
7. "Lectures on Fiction," British Museum Additional MS50699 (1887), ff. 21–22; *Everybody's Political What's What?* (London: Constable, 1950), p. 287; and "From Dickens to Ibsen," British Museum Additional MS50690 (1897), ff. 7–8.
8. *PMLA* 50, no. 1 (Mar. 1935):274–89.
9. Ibid., p. 282.
10. "A Forgotten Satire: Bulwer-Lytton's *The Coming Race*," *Nineteenth Century Fiction* 19 (Mar. 1965):382.

11. "Bulwer-Lytton's Underworld: *The Coming Race* (1871)," *Moreana* 30 (1971):39–40.
12. Weeks, "Introduction."
13. *Journal of Modern Literature* 1 (1971):339–53. See also 1971 *MLA Abstracts*, item. no. 4942.

Selected Annotated Bibliography

Bulwer-Lytton, Edward. *The Coming Race*. Introduction by John Weeks. Santa Barbara, Calif.: Woodbridge Pr., 1979. This book is included for those who want easy access to an inexpensive edition. No claim is made for textual authority.

———. *The Coming Race*. Knebworth edition. London: George Routledge and Sons, 1879. Republished Quakertown, Pennsylvania: Philosophical Publishing Co., 1973. This edition has, perhaps, as good claim as any to the honor of being the definitive edition. Variant readings surely exist between editions. For example, the apparently pirated edition (vol. 2, New York: F. F. Collier, n.d.) mentions Robert Owen as a complete failure as a social experimenter. The Knebworth edition does not—but John Week's edition does. (Weeks gives no hint of the textual sources for his book.) No doubt, collation would multiply instances.

Christensen, Allan Conrad. *Edward Bulwer-Lytton: The Fiction of New Regions*. Athens: Univ. of Georgia Pr., 1976. While this book tends to claim too much on slender evidence, it is still a valuable book and boasts an extensive bibliography.

Jeaffreson, J. Cordy. *Novels and Novelists: from Elizabeth to Victoria*. Vol. 2. London: Hurst and Blackett, 1858. While this book was published well before *The Coming Race*, it is useful as an early estimate which catches the tone of much of the later Bulwer-Lytton criticism.

Kelly, Richard. "The Haunted House of Bulwer-Lytton." *Studies in Short Fiction* 8 (1971):581–87. This article is useful in establishing Bulwer-Lytton's theory that individuals have electrical fields of varying strengths. It also examines the proposition that such fields connect the living world with the spiritual one.

Knepper, B. G. "*Back to Methuselah* and the Utopian Tradition." Ph.D. diss., Univ. of Nebraska, 1967. Chap. 5, "Lytton: Utopia and Evolution," pp. 196–217, compares Bulwer-Lytton's novel with Shaw's play cycle.

———. "Shaw's Debt to *The Coming Race*." *Journal of Modern Literature* 1 (1971):339–53. Abstracted in 1971 *MLA Abstracts*, item no. 4942. This is a fuller treatment of the concerns of the dissertation. Again, the focus is on Shaw, though less exclusively so.

Lord, Walter Frewen. "The Novels of Lytton." *Ninteenth Century* (Sept. 1901), pp. 449–58. The style is old-fashioned and aggressive. I include it as an example of an extreme attack upon Bulwer-Lytton's work. While the work is unfair, the grains of truth hit home.

Lytton, The Earl of, K. G. *Bulwer-Lytton.* London: Morrison and Gibb, 1948. This biography is very readable. While it contains some criticism, it is most valuable as a short overview of Bulwer-Lytton's career.

Seeber, Hans. "Bulwer-Lytton's Underworld: *The Coming Race* (1871)," *Moreana* 30 (1971):39–40. This is essentially an abstract of Seeber's longer German article. On the whole it is heavy-handed and takes the anti-utopian point of view. He sees *The Coming Race* as a warning against "Utopian Socialism" and "scientific materialism."

———. "Gegenutopia und Roman: Bulwer-Lyttons *The Coming Race* (1871)." *Deutsche Vierteljahrsschrift für Literaturwissenschaft und Geistesgeschichte* 45 (1971):150–58. See other comment under Seeber. The German is reasonably easy for those who care to undertake the larger article.

Shaw, Bernard. *Everybody's Political What's What?* London: Constable, 1950.

———. "From Dickens to Ibsen." British Museum Additional MS50690 (1897), ff. 7–8.

———. "Lectures on Fiction." British Museum Additional MS50699 (1887), ff. 21–22.

The Shaw items cover Shaw's shifting attitude toward Bulwer-Lytton's work and contain his acknowledgment of Bulwer-Lytton's influence on his own work. For the general reader, the British Museum MS is hard to come by.

Wagner, Geoffrey. "A Forgotten Satire: Bulwer-Lytton's *The Coming Race.*" *Nineteenth Century Fiction* 19 (Mar. 1965):379–85. This is an article of mixed value. The identification of the Vril-ya with America seems to me far-fetched, though certainly American characteristics furnish part of the material for satire. The thesis that "Lytton, then, was principally objecting to the new woman in *The Coming Race*" is even less palatable. Still, the article is not without weight and value.

Watts, Harold H. "Lytton's Theories of Prose Fiction." *PMLA* 50, no. 1 (Mar. 1935):274–89. The article has more than passing interest as literary criticism. Some of its psychological connections are dated—but it has the real merit of taking a position and arguing for it.

Wolff, Robert Lee. *Strange Stories and Other Explorations in Victorian Fiction.* Boston: Gambit, 1971. Chapter 3 deals with "The Occult Fiction of Sir Edward Bulwer-Lytton." This chapter is interesting mainly to those who see *The Coming Race* as a dystopia. It also traces Bulwer-Lytton's interest in the occult.

3

"The Mirror up to Nature": Reflections of Victorianism in Samuel Butler's *Erewhon*

Thomas J. Remington

> *"The purpose of playing . . . both at the first and now, was and is, to hold, as 'twere, the mirror up to nature: to show virtue her own feature, scorn her own image, and the very age and body of the time his form and pressure."*
> *Hamlet*, III.ii

At first glance, Samuel Butler's *Erewhon*[1] is likely to seem a Victorian oasis to the student of twentieth-century utopian and dystopian literature; the oasis, alas, reveals itself as a mirage in many ways when it is closely examined. To be sure, a critic like U. C. Knoepflmacher can call Butler's imaginary country "an idealized utopia"[2] while Joseph Jones can see the book as a step in the direction of *Brave New World* and *1984*.[3] Nevertheless, the consensus of Butler's published critics is to see him as "a satirist" as opposed to "genuine Utopists,"[4] and sees Erewhon the country—despite its anagrammatic parallel with Thomas More's coinage—as "no utopia."[5] In this case, the consensus is right, unless we recognize that in *Erewhon* Butler stretches the conventional utopian form considerably. *Erewhon* is not an idealized picture of Victorian society at its best or its worst; rather it is a work which holds a mirror up to that society, presenting it recognizably as it is, but in a strangely reversed perspective. It is this aspect of Butler's work which makes it so much richer and more complex than such roughly contemporary and more conventional utopias as Edward Bellamy's *Looking Backward* (1887) and William Morris's *News from Nowhere* (1891).

The most usual touchstone chosen by critics to try *Erewhon*'s value is *Gulliver's Travels*. The comparison was frequent in reviews following the book's publication, and continues to echo through later criticisms by P. N. Furbank, Basil Willey, Joseph Jones, A. E. Dyson, and Robert Philmus.[6] It is important to add that none of these critics claims to see Butler's accomplishment in *Erewhon* as qualitatively equivalent to that of Swift in *Gulliver's Travels*. Knoepflmacher, while noting the frequent comparisons, sees the two works as intentionally different, with Butler's failing "to sustain its satire" (p. 238); and Edmund Wilson makes the comparison between the two works—to *Erewhon*'s disadvantage—by denying the possibility of such a comparison.[7]

But whatever the qualitative judgments one might make, the ways in which *Erewhon* is similar to *Gulliver's Travels* are more telling—and more important—than the ways in which it might be compared with conventional utopian or dystopian fiction, or with modern science fiction, for that matter. Set in neither an ideal future nor an ideal past, *Erewhon*'s imaginary society falls far short of utopian perfection or dystopian horror. Instead, the imaginary country of *Erewhon* is created by Butler as a domain in which he can exercise—to use John F. Harris's term—"the right to twist" (p. 75). In *Erewhon* we know that we are "at once in Erewhon, in England, and in the realm of ideas in Butler's mind," says Ellen Douglas Leyburn in her *Satiric Allegory: Mirror of Man* (p. 95). The title of her study reveals Butler's technique in *Erewhon*, which is basically to chart Victorian society, but with a set of coordinates symmetrically reversed from the conventional ones used by that society. Such a method is, indeed, allegorical, and the oddities of Erewhonian society almost invariably have their exact but opposite counterparts in Victorian England.

But why, then, is *Erewhon* so frequently associated with science fiction in general, and with modern utopian literature in particular? The tendency stems from the fact that, almost accidentally, *Erewhon* touches upon matters which, seen from our contemporary viewpoint, are peculiarly echoic. The effect is quite similar to that which works on the *persona* in Jorge Luis Borges' "Pierre Menard, Author of the *Quixote*." The speaker in that work quotes a passage from Cervantes' classic, and then quotes the same words, verbatim, from *Don Quixote* as it was written in 1934 by Pierre Menard. The seventeenth-century passage "is a mere rhetorical eulogy of history," but Menard, writing the identical passage, is "a contemporary of William James" and his view of history is significantly different from that of Cervantes; his "clauses . . . are shamelessly pragmatic."[8] The twentieth-century reader of *Erewhon* is tempted to cite, not Butler's work, but the *Erewhon* of Pierre Menard—or that of Dennis Jones, Jack Williamson, or Isaac Asimov. The tendency is natural, and may even provoke delight in the book, but it leads us astray from Butler's accomplishment. The clearest example of this tendency relates to "The Book of the Machines" section of *Erewhon*. Erewhonian society has banned all mechanical devices other than those which existed 271 years before the banning act. The reasons for the prohibition, worked out in some detail in "The Book of the Machines," is that machinery, like organic life, is an evolving form; as it grows more complex and specialized, it will eventually surpass mankind, since the evidence shows that its evolutionary speed is greater than that of organic life, and that this speed is accelerating. "There is no security," we are told, "against the ultimate development of mechanical consciousness, in the fact of machines possessing little consciousness now" (chap. 23, p. 223). Further, since animals and plants are in fact the products of a deterministic universe, they can be seen as merely an inferior form of machinery: "A man is the resultant and exponent of all the forces that have been brought to bear upon him, whether before his birth or afterwards. . . . As he is by nature, and as he has been acted on, and is now acted on from without, so will he do, as certainly and regularly as though he were a machine" (chap. 25, p. 245).

These points lead the putative author of "The Book of the Machines" to several conclusions which tickle the consciousness of the reader who comes to them with a knowledge of the main trends in the treatment of technology in science fiction. The "Book" asks rhetorically, "How many men in this hour are living in a state of bondage to the machines? How many spend their whole lives, from the cradle to the grave, in tending them night and day?" (chap. 24, p. 235), and in so asking raises the spectre of Wells's Morlocks, or the inhabitants of the underground city in Fritz Lang's film of *Metropolis*, or Colossus in Jones's Forbin books. The "Book" goes on to prophesy gloomily that men may eventually accept a state of "domestication" under the machines, but grants that many would say that mankind might be well off in such a state, since the machines would be kind governors and masters. Thus it seems to anticipate at once the opposing views of Williamson ("With Folded Hands") and Asimov ("The Evitable Conflict").

Further, a respondent to the author who proposed banning the machines offers further views which seem strangely anticipatory of modern science fiction. This second author views machinery as a simple extension of human bodily powers—suggestive of the cyborg theme. While favoring continued use of machinery, this author also apprehends danger "that the machines would so equalize men's powers, and so lessen the severity of competition, that many persons of inferior physique would . . . transmit their inferiority" resulting in a "degeneracy of the human race" (chap. 25, p. 257). Both Wells's Eloi and the human race portrayed in E. M. Forster's "The Machine Stops" seem anticipated by the suggestion. John Campbell's "Twilight" is only the best known among a multitude of science fiction treatments of the ultimate danger foreseen by this second writer in the "Book": that man could eventually become "nothing but soul and mechanism, an intelligent but passionless principle of mechanical action" (chap. 25, p. 257).

Such touches have led even insightful critics of Butler to argue that "The Book of the Machines" in *Erewhon* had already explored, in a manner that anticipates twentieth-century science fiction at its best, the revolution that machines might bring about when they come fully into their own" (Dyson, p. 134) and that *Erewhon*, along with its sequel, *Erewhon Revisited*, "may be read as an early counterthrust . . . to the unwitting process by which science-technology has been hammered into the tightly clutched implement of the power state until in Thomas Henry Huxley's grandson Aldous and in George Orwell the culmination of protest appeared" (Jones, p. 172). Even Darko Suvin, one of the most knowledgeable of commentators on science fiction, sees the ideas in "The Book of the Machines" as "prefiguring . . . the discussion of reification and machine consciousness in cybernetics."[9]

But such comments are misleading. For Butler, the first author in "The Book of the Machines," the one who succeeded in having the ban on machinery implemented, is a dolt whose application of Darwinism to the mechanical world is readily recognizable as idiocy; as we shall see, unless we recognize this point we miss the main thrust of Butler's satire. At the time that he wrote this section of *Erewhon*,[10] Butler admired Darwin immensely, and was concerned subsequently that his treatment of "mechanical evolution" in the "Book" was mistaken by some reviewers "as an attempt to reduce Mr. Darwin's theory to an absurdity" (preface to 2d ed., p. ix). In defending himself from this speculation, Butler is careful *not* to suggest that there is no absurdity in the argument that machines might evolve, but that the absurdity has to do with the nature of the "Book's" first author's arguments, "a specious misuse of analogy" (preface to 2d ed., p. viii). Butler's sincerity in this matter is substantiated by a letter he wrote to Charles Darwin himself in May 1872, in which Butler asserts that it was his intention to imply "how easy it is to be plausible, and what absurd propositions can be defended by a little ingenuity and distortion and departure from strictly scientific methods."[11] Butler goes on to state in his correspondence with Darwin that the true satirical target of "The Book of the Machines" was Bishop Joseph Butler's (no relation) *Analogy of Religion, Natural and Revealed, to the Constitution and Course of Nature*, written in 1736 (*Memoir*, 1:156). Following this letter, Butler was apparently invited for a weekend visit with Darwin and his wife, and Henry Festing Jones, Butler's biographer, tells us that this visit "seems to have gone off quite pleasantly" (*Memoir*, 1:157).

The point is that there is nothing remotely apocalyptic in "The Book of the Machines"; rather, Butler was posing an argument that was intended to be understood as specious and foolish so that his audience would recognize the absurdity of the arguer. To see the "Book," then, as a prelude to modern science fiction's handling of the "man and machine" motif is akin to finding an anticipation of Apollo 11 in the comment of a lunatic character in a Victorian novel that he intends to fly to the moon; it is also to distort Butler's satire rather grotesquely.

None of this, of course, is to insist that Butler may not have had an influence on the likes of Wells, Forster, Campbell, Williamson, Asimov, or any other science fiction writer; but such influence, if it exists, is likely to be a result of modern misreading of his text. The parallels between "The Book of the Machines" and modern science fiction are accidental at best, and perverted from the text itself of *Erewhon*. Conversely, the *techniques* used by Butler in *Erewhon* (as opposed to the ideas produced therein) *did* have relevance to modern science fiction, and those techniques continue to be used by science fictionists in ways parallel to those in which Butler used them. It is this precise point which Philmus perceptively notes in relating *Erewhon* to *Gulliver's Travels*:

> Although *Gulliver's Travels* is not science fiction, strictly defined, in [some of the work's] details and episodes . . . a technique of presenting science as fiction can be perceived which anticipates the science fiction of later writers. . . . Swift imaginatively transfigures scientific theory and experiment by describing the literal state of affairs that they suggest. This literalizing of the abstract, which tends to enlarge metaphor into myth, does not originate with Swift. But it is a feature in the evolution of science fiction in the nineteenth century most prominent in writers like Samuel Butler. (P. 12)

Philmus's "literalizing the abstract" rather closely resembles Leyburn's view of Butler's use of "satiric allegory," and it certainly applies to *Erewhon*. What needs to be kept in mind is that Butler, like Swift before him, had a good deal of mistrust in the scientific "establishment" and tended to view it in ways not far removed from those presented by Swift in Gulliver's voyage to Laputa.

The basic format of *Erewhon*, like that of *Gulliver's Travels*, involves a trip to an imaginary country. In the case of *Erewhon*, though, the voyage is somewhat more realistic than in Swift's work. Using a sheep station in the New Zealand where he had once lived as the point of departure, Butler describes the journey of the unnamed narrator "over the range."[12] The eventual destiny of the journey is Erewhon itself, where the vast majority of what passes for action (the book has very little plot) takes place. There is nothing physically startling about the Erewhonians; they are simply remarkably handsome human beings who eventually accept the narrator as one of themselves.[13] No technological marvels exist among the Erewhonians; though they had advanced to a Victorian industrial level in the past, they had subsequently rejected machinery. The narrator has no insights or abilities to contribute to the Erewhonians which they would find spectacular, the sole exception being the balloon by which he makes his eventual escape.

As in *Gulliver's Travels*, the point-of-view character is important. He is a rather typical Victorian, reasonably well-educated, but complacent in the values of his own culture. Typically, his entire motivation for the journey is mercenary. His first hope is to find "country" for his own sheep station, but he adds that "even if I did not find country, might I not find gold, or diamonds, or copper, or silver?" (chap. 1, p. 8). His hopes seem exploded on the discovery that the land is inhabited, but he still sees the chance for profit. He concludes the Erewhonians to be the ten lost tribes of Israel and reasons that he himself "might have been designed by Providence as the instrument of their conversion" (chap. 6, p. 52). But even the conversion of the Erewhonians is seen as an undertaking "which, if I can be the first to profit by it, will bring me a recompense beyond all money computations" (chap. 1, p. 1). This idea, in fact, is the impetus for the narrator's revealing his experiences, for in order to evangelize *Erewhon*, he states, "I must possess myself of a considerable sum of money; neither do I know how to get it, except by interesting the public in my story, and inducing the charitable to come forward and assist me" (chap. 1, 1–2). The conversion scheme is returned to in the book's last chapter, which urges the reader to "write at once to the Secretary of the Erewhon Evangelization Company, limited . . . and request to have his name put down as a shareholder" (chap. 29, p. 306). The profit motive is then emphasized by the suggestion that Erewhonians could be conscripted for manual labor, thus insuring the stockholders of "saving souls and filling their own pockets at one and the same moment" (chap. 29, p. 304). In fact, religious and secular matters are continually blended in the narrator's mind, even in casual comments; for example, after a narrow escape, he notes that "as luck would have it, Providence was on my side" (chap. 4, p. 28). To be sure, the narrator is not an evil man; he is merely entirely insensitive to the incongruities of his own thought processes because he is so complacent regarding them. Commercial exploitation and Christianity are conflated in his mind because he is a product of a society in which they are conflated, and his values, with all their inconsistency, are the values of his society. He is, as Butler's close friend and alter ego, Eliza Mary Ann Savage, noted in an early review, "a prig" (*Memoir*, 1:158). As in *Gulliver's Travels*, in *Erewhon* the reader must remain continually aware that all impressions in the book are filtered through the narrator's limited and biased consciousness.[14] The frequent complaints of the book's supposed inconsistencies[15] seem to stem in part from the fact that the narrator himself is inconsistent in his judgments. But in this the narrator reflects his society, and the one paramount consistency in *Erewhon* is that any society—Erewhonian, Victorian, or whatever—*must* be inconsistent.

The basic irony in the book emanates from the narrator's observations that Erewhonian society is logically inconsistent and wrongheaded. Repeatedly he is forced to grant some validity to the Erewhonian system, while continually seeing that other parts of the same system are inconsistent with the ones he admires. But his evaluations are always based on the complacent presumption that the Victorian system in which he was nurtured *is* thoroughly consistent, even though the book makes clear to its audience that such consistency is neither extant nor admirable.

The principal variants between Erewhonian and Victorian society stem from a process of mirror reversals. Just as *Erewhon* itself is an English word spelled backward—or nearly so—and as many Erewhonian names are inversions of English names (Senoj, Nosnibor and Yram, for examples), so Erewhon itself is antipodal to England geographically and culturally.

The first important mirror reversal treated in the book is that of disease and crime. In Erewhon, it is a legal offense to be ill (or even "unfortunate") and offenses are punished with long prison terms, floggings, and hangings—though in recent times the harshness of punishments has been humanely ameliorated. Conversely, moral faults are viewed as matters to be pitied and corrected; a profession of "straightener" exists to aid those who suffer from being thieves, embezzlers, or other sorts of criminals. Critics such as Dyson (p. 126), Knoepflmacher (pp. 230–31), and Kingsley Amis[16] have seen the construction as an attack on English judicial severity, while Hans-Peter Breuer has argued that Butler is, through the Erewhonians, promoting a "rigorously empirical morality" which serves as a scientifically verifiable substitute for conventional religious moral codes.[17]

It should not surprise the reader aware of Butler's "consistency in inconsistency" that both sides are correct. An Erewhonian judge severely sentences a consumptive to a lifetime prison regimen which is certain to increase the sufferer's problems; the judge's stern speech was apparently copied by Butler from an actual Victorian judge's sentencing of a thief (*Memoir*, 1:152). The "Dyson-Knoepflmacher-Amis" view suggests the consumptive's treatment causes the audience of *Erewhon* to recognize the futility of a criminal justice system which punishes social victims by incarcerating them in prisons where their antisocial tendencies will be exacerbated. Breuer responds that Butler "was neither concerned with, nor well-informed about, the judicial code or the treatment of criminals" (p. 317). Instead, drawing on earlier works—including Darwin's—Butler was demonstrating that an enforcement of *natural* morality through the law would, in fact, merely favor those whom nature has endowed with such natural gifts as good health, and would punish those whom nature has treated less kindly by visiting them with disease or misfortune.

However, Breuer seems momentarily to ignore that Erewhonians *do* take conventional moral strictures quite seriously; they merely treat the criminal as we do the diseased—that is, with kindness and sympathy, but with an eye toward curing the problem even if the treatment may be quite painful to the subject. Further, Butler need have been no student of the prisons to have had some idea of the harshness of Victorian penology, since prison reform was an issue in the air of the times. A broad Prison Act had been passed in England in 1865, and an International Congress on treatment of prisoners was scheduled for, and took place in, London in 1873.[18] Attitudes toward prison reform appear elsewhere in Victorian popular literature, as for example in the prison scenes involving Uriah Heep and Littimer in chapter 61 of *David Copperfield*. The 1902 *Encyclopaedia Britannica* article on "Prison Discipline" sounds as if it is citing an oft-repeated truism when it states, "It has been well said that criminals are such by accident or inclination, and that under a perfect system of government they should be spared the one and *cured* [emphasis mine] of the other." But even if one grants that prison reform was likely to have been a familiar, if not seriously studied, subject to Butler, it does not follow that the "crime/disease" inversion is a satiric attack on the Victorian criminal system. Just as there were Victorian prison reformers who wished to view the criminal as victim rather than as perpetrator, so there are reformers in Erewhon "held in great odium by the generality of the public" (chap. 12, 118) who wish to soften the treatment of the diseased. Even though the ill must be imprisoned for the protection of society, these reformers say they should not be harshly punished. The point emphasized is that there is an asymmetry between the Erewhonians' treatment of crime and their treatment of disease, just as there was a similar asymmetry in Victorian society. The one asymmetry is equal to but opposite from the other, and reflects it back to us from a viewpoint not otherwise available. If the reformers in either society are correct, then that society's treatment of crime should be similar to its treatment of disease; both crime and disease should be "cured" and not "punished." Conversely, the Erewhonian judge—paralleling his Victorian counterpart—states that he is "not here to enter upon curious metaphysical questions as to the origin of this or that," and that he will not throw "the only guilt on the tissues of the primordial cell, or on the elementary gases" (chap. 11, p. 107). If his position is correct, and (as Breuer suggests) a harsh natural moral code should apply without regard to victim and perpetrator, then—again—crime and disease should be treated alike, and both should be treated quite harshly. But neither society is logically consistent; each is "oppositely asymmetrical" to the other, and the suggestion is thereby made that the social order is, at its base, inconsistent and irrational.

The asymmetry of the Erewhonian treatment of crime and disease prevents the two elements, taken together, from being conventionally utopian or dystopian. The narrator reveals the value of this reversed perspective when he says, "That which we observe to be taken as a matter of course by those around us, we take as a matter of course ourselves" (chap. 12, p. 112). The new perspective forces us to consider those things we "take as a matter of course." The Erewhonian system is illogical and in some ways unfair—but so is the audience's. Why, then, should the reader object to an alternative system as defensible or as indefensible as his own? The narrator's answer reveals his priggishness, and warns us of our own:

> Of course, according to Erewhonian premises, it would serve people right to be punished and scouted for moral and intellectual diseases as much as for physical, and I cannot to this day understand why they should have stopped short half way. Neither, again, can I understand why their having done so should have been, as it certainly was, a matter of so much concern to myself. . . . Nevertheless I longed to make them think as I did, for the wish to spread those opinions that we hold conducive to our own welfare is so deeply rooted in the English character that few of us can escape its influence. (Chap. 20, p. 191)

The narrator's attitude is reenforced with a vengeance, of course, by his plans for the "Erewhon Evangelizaton Company."

A similar Erewhonian inversion exists in the opposition between the "Musical Banks" and the worship of the goddess Ydgrun (whose name is an anagram for Mrs. Grundy, the personification of conventional social judgment in Thomas Morton's play, *Speed the Plow* [1798]). The Musical Banks, decorated like churches, operate on the basis of a worthless currency in which no one places any trust, but all citizens must participate to some degree in these banks' operation or lose social respectability. Conversely, Ydgrun's rules are those by which society actually conducts itself, though no one is willing to acknowledge openly the power and importance of Ydgrun. Thus the social conventions of the Victorians are apotheosized into an unacknowledged region in Erewhon, while the Victorian church is paralleled with a moribund social institution. Victorian society encourages proper social behavior through Grundyism, but hangs on to the church as an irrelevant appendix; similarly, the social institution of the Musical Banks in Erewhon is a useless appendage to the worship of Ydgrun, whose divinity guides the conduct of her followers, even if they will not openly acknowledge her. Again, there is a fundamental irrationality at the basis of the social order, and the suggestion seems to be that such irrationalities must exist in human societies, even though the particular nature of the irrationality can differ widely from one society to another. Further, we cannot view the Erewhonian system as a utopian ideal or as a dystopian horror compared to our own. It simply differs from ours in specifics, and shares with ours the characteristic of inconsistency.

In his comments on Erewhonian treatment of disease and crime, and in his comments on the Musical Banks and Ydgrun, the narrator's discomfort with the inconsistency and irrationality of the social order in Erewhon becomes clear. And yet, as he discovers more about the society, he is led more and more to the realization that these peculiarities not only *do* exist in all social orders, but they *must* exist for the order's survival.

The Erewhonians hold a belief in the afterlife to be reprehensible, saying that such a belief would cause people to ignore the importance of the present in anticipation of some future reward.[19] However, they do believe that, before birth, individuals have an eternal existence in "The World of the Unborn." Although Erewhonians do not punish criminals, since they deterministically believe all criminals to be such without having chosen, they *do* believe the unborn are responsible for the foolishness and wickedness of their decision to be born. Thus, the Erewhonians have a "birth formula" ceremony which is a valediction to the world of the unborn; the ceremony closely parallels baptism. In this ceremony the infant, through adult representatives who act on its behalf, takes all responsibility for its unfortunate choice to be born, and promises never to hold its parents responsible for any possible results of its own fatal choice. Obviously, the narrator notes, it is outrageous to presume to bind a child to an agreement it is incompetent to make, and thus he ignores the significance of the promises made at baptism, a ceremony in which he places considerable stock. But the Erewhonians "in practice . . . modify their theory to a considerable extent, and seldom refer to the birth formula" (chap. 20, p. 190). Fortunately for the children involved, neither Victorian society nor Erewhonian feels obliged to pursue the tenets of its ritual for infants to a logical conclusion. Pragmatic compromise forces the subsequent ignoring of the birth formula in Erewhon just as (though the narrator fails to see the connection) it does the dismissal of any serious "enforcement" of baptismal promises in Victorian England.

The need for irrationality and inconsistency in society becomes clearer in the treatment of the "Colleges of Unreason." In many ways these colleges are simply parodies of Oxford and Cambridge rather than true reversals. Much of a student's time is spent in the study of "hypothetics" (which, by intention, deal with impossible contingencies) and of the "hypothetical language," an ancient tongue no longer used but still studied and into which even contemporary poetry is translated. But beyond the simple parody, the Colleges of Unreason again represent a reversal from the Victorian norm. Conventional education grants that man has irrational components, and does not wish to repress these human characteristics; conversely, it does seek to guide people into rational channels, with the understanding that humanity needs little training in being irrational. In Erewhon, typically, the picture is reversed. Erewhonian educators feel that "there is hardly an error into which men may not easily be led if they base their conduct upon reason only. . . . People have such a strong natural bias toward [reason] that they will seek it for themselves and act upon it quite as much as or more than is good for them; there is no need of encouraging reason" (chap. 21, p. 209). Reason, for example, would lead people to abolish the Musical Banks, and Erewhonian society requires the absurdity the Banks represent.

The desirability of unreason emphasized in "The Colleges of Unreason" helps to place "The Book of the Machines" in its proper perspective. The problems modern readers have with "The Book of the Machines" stem in part, as I have noted, from the fact that we now see a substance to the first author's concern which Butler did not grant. But they also are a result of the extremely plausible way in which that author presents the scientific logic of his evolutionary argument. In the light of the warning in the preceding chapters against man's natural impulses to be dangerously guided by pure reason, we should be wary of anyone quite so reasonable as that first author.

If one aspect of Butler's philosophy seems consistent throughout his career, it is his strong opposition to dogmatic positions of any sort. As much as anything else, this attitude accounted for the harshness of his antipathy toward Darwinism as he developed his own theory of teleological evolution in later works.[20] In fact, in later letters and notes, Butler is quite explicit in equating the dogma of science with that of religion. In his *Notebooks* we find: "Science is being daily more and more personified and anthropomorphized into a god. By and by they will say that science took our nature upon him, and sent down his only begotten son, Charles Darwin, or Huxley, into the world so that those who believe in him, etc.; and they will burn people for saying that science, after all, is only an expression for our ignorance of our own ignorance."[21] In an 1884 letter he wrote that "science is infested by a lot of false prophets who do nothing but mischief and try to stamp out everything which does not emanate from themselves" (*Memoir*, 1:413); a few days later, to a different correspondent, he wrote, "I am not aware of thinking that men of science are in a conspiracy against me; . . . I have not the faintest idea that there is any greater conspiracy against me than there always is on the part of orthodoxy against unorthodoxy" (*Memoir*, 1:417).

To be sure, the comments on scientific saviors, prophets, and orthodoxy come from a later period than the writing of "The Book of the Machines." But the putative author of the "Book" (he is called a "Professor" at one point—chap. 25, p. 256) is clearly a dogmatist who successfully proposes a ban on machinery because of his concern regarding its evolutionary dangers. Moreover, he writes as a scientist who accepts the idea of evolution; he knows that "there was a time, when the earth was to all appearance utterly destitute of animal and vegetable life" (chap. 23, p. 222), and that "man's body is what it is through having been molded into its present shape by the chances and changes of many millions of years" (chap. 24, p. 242). But as an Erewhonian, and perhaps as a scientist, his concern is with the *future* dangers of evolutionary doctrine (the development of machines superior to man) and not with the implications the doctrine has for the past (that man's ancestors were "lower" forms than himself).[22]

Certainly as an Erewhonian scientist, he is willing to dictate changes in the social order on the basis of his own rational conclusions, and in Butler's view, such an attitude is quite parallel to that of the religious spokesman. Thus, just as Erewhonian social institutions (Musical Banks) are symmetrical reversals of Victorian churches, and Victorian social institutions mirror the Erewhonian worship of Ydgrun, so is Erewhonian scientific dogma balanced against Victorian religious dogma.

The idea is carried to its logical extreme by the fact that another scientific view was offered in opposition to that of the first Professor. This view—that man is a "Machinate mammal" (chap. 25, p. 256)— was probably seen by Butler as more reasonable than the first,[23] but the possible validity of the second author's position is less relevant in *Erewhon* than is the fact that "the other writer was considered to have the best of" the argument (chap. 25, p. 260), and as a result succeeded in imposing his views on the society. Significantly, at the time that the ban on machines was implemented, "the country was plunged into the deepest misery. . . . Civil war raged for many years, and is said to have reduced the number of the inhabitants by one-half." The anti-mechanical party "got the victory," its members "treating their opponents with such unparalleled severity that they extirpated every trace of opposition" (chap. 22, p. 220). Moreover, in destroying their opposition, the anti-machinists used the very machinery they were sworn to oppose, developing several new weapons in the process. The parallels with religious wars—particularly with Christian civil wars in

Western civilization seen from the perspective of a critic of Christianity—seem quite explicit.

Thus the nature of the satiric reversal in "The Book of the Machines" becomes clear: societies tend to accept dogmatic pronouncements, and it matters little if the source of the dogma be theology, science, or something else; the results of pursuing such dogma to its logical conclusion will be disruptive, painful, and, at best, absurd. Breuer touches on this point perceptively:

> Men of science, [Butler] wrote, . . . resemble theologians (*Notebooks*, p. 223); that is, they both deal in the unknowable with a pretense to absolute certitude. But we cannot "self-vivisect ourselves" in respect to the truth-speaking faculty (*Notebooks*, p. 201). These statements, of course, criticize the dogmatism of deification of the nineteenth-century evolutionary science; but they also indicate that Butler was disturbed by the attempts both to circumvent and to eliminate paradox and inconsistency from an understanding of life.[24]

The danger of "attempts . . . to circumvent and to eliminate paradox and inconsistency" is specifically alluded to by Butler in reference to "The Book of the Machines." The success of the first author's opinions perpetrates the horror of civil war, but it could have done worse. As the author puts forth his view, he concludes by urging the destruction of "all improvements that have been made for the last three hundred years." He adds, "Though I should prefer to have seen the destruction include another two hundred years, I am aware of the necessity for compromising" (chap. 25, p. 255). But the followers of such a leader are often less compromising, and the narrator says of the anti-mechanists: "The wonder was that they allowed any mechanical appliances to remain in the kingdom, neither do I believe that they would have done so, had not the Professors of Inconsistency and Evasion [at the Colleges of Unreason] made a stand against the carrying of the new principles to their legitimate conclusions" (chap. 23, p. 222). The reversal, then, is complete; in Erewhon, compromise with doctrine comes from the academic theoreticians of inconsistency, who overcome the popular pressure for logical rigor.

Butler's attack on consistency is continued in "The Rights of Animals" and "The Rights of Vegetables," two chapters which were added to the revised edition of *Erewhon* in 1901. These chapters have been criticized as not contributing to the book, and Leyburn's comments on them are fairly typical. She sees them as "by far the most extended and the most unfortunate additions" to the revised edition, "a sort of appendage to the Book of the Machines." Pronouncing an incident in "The Rights of Animals" "funny enough," she continues:

> It adds nothing to the conception of the Erewhonians or ourselves; and it grows tedious when it is spun out in another chapter giving the evasions of the protective laws for vegetables. These two chapters, the only ones wholly new in the revised edition, lack the spontaneity which is the distinctive quality of the rest of the book; and their position just before Butler leaves the presentation of ideas for the return to physical action in the chapter on Escape gives them a deplorable prominence. The reader must agree with Butler in being sad that the copyright laws compelled him to pad the fresh work of his youth with these rather jaded additions that weaken the allegory. (P. 106)

There can be no question that these two chapters are not as clearly a part of the pattern of reversal as are the other sections of what Leyburn calls the "satiric allegory." In fact, Butler seems to have indicated quite specifically that the substance of the "Rights" chapters is in some ways separate from the rest of his treatment of Erewhonian culture by placing the events of those chapters in the distant past. All other materials in *Erewhon* are part of the "contemporary" culture observed by the narrator, but the events and conclusions in the "Rights" chapters took place *before* the society had adopted its "current" policies regarding sickness, crime, and machinery. The events which transpire in the "Rights" chapter (unlike those in "The Book of the Machines") have no lingering effect on "modern" Erewhonian society; they have long since passed into an irrelevancy as far as the "present age" is concerned. In fact, then, the "Rights" chapters deal with a substantially different Erewhon than does the rest of the book.

This peculiarity raises questions about the "Rights" chapters, for even if Butler's inclusion of them in the revised edition was primarily because of the copyright problems, there seems no apparent reason why the additional material he chose to add should depart so pointedly from the rest of the book. Moreover, the pattern of reversal so clearly at the heart of the earlier version is not strictly adhered to in the "Rights" chapters.

In "The Rights of Animals," an ancient leader of the Erewhonians "who had great influence over them by reason of the sanctity of his life, and his supposed inspiration by an unseen power" (chap. 26, p. 262) succeeded in convincing them to ban the eating of any animal flesh; in "The Rights of Vegetables," a subsequent leader, a "Philosopher" born centuries after the earlier teacher, extends the prohibition on meat to include vegetables as well. This second leader, "though he did not claim to have any communications with an unseen power, laid down the law with as much confidence as if such a power had inspired him. Many think that this philosopher did not believe his own teaching, and, being in secret a great meat-eater, had no other end in view than reducing the prohibition against eating animal food to an absurdity, greater even than an Erewhonian Puritan would be able to stand" (chap. 27, p. 272). Ultimately the dispute over the eating of "fellow creatures" is submitted to an oracle "in which the whole country had the greatest confidence, and to which recourse was always had in times of special perplexity. It was whispered that a near relation of the philosopher's was lady's-maid to the priestess who delivered the oracle, and the Puritan party declared that the strangely unequivocal answer of the oracle was obtained by backstairs influence" (chap. 27, p. 281). The "unequivocal oracle" pays no attention to the moral questions raised regarding the eating of organic tissue; instead, it concludes with the blatantly pragmatic dictum:

> Beat or be beaten,
> Eat or be eaten,
> Be killed or kill;
> Choose which you will. (chap. 27, p. 282)

On the basis of the earlier sections of Erewhon, and particularly on the basis of "The Book of the Machines," we would anticipate some sort of reversal of science and religion as they are treated in Erewhon and in Victorian England, but such does not seem to be the case here. The first Erewhonian teacher, the prophet, seems clearly a religious leader, a point emphasized by his claim to have communication with an "unseen power." As such, though, he merely parodies conventional religious leaders rather than reversing their methods. The case might be made that the second teacher, the philosopher, comes closer to representing a scientific position; he is called a "Professor of botany" at one point (chap. 27, p. 282), and his arguments imply evolutionary theory, since they hinge on the organic similarities among all living things. But his position was developed directly from that of the prophet, and he pays considerable homage to his predecessor in advancing his own arguments. Further, the oracle to whom the case is finally submitted for arbitration is not associated with any scientific (as opposed to religious) power, despite the evolutionary tone of its edict to "be killed or kill."

Since Erewhon had already mocked Victorian religion directly (with the Musical Banks and the birth formula) and indirectly (in "The Book of the Machines"), the "Rights" chapters are particularly disappointing if they not only mar the pattern of reversal set in the rest of the book, but also mar the pattern only, as Leyburn implies, to reiterate previously-treated material.

But while I grant that the "Rights" chapters do not harmonize with the pattern of reversals set in the rest of the book, I also feel that Butler in some way compensates for this problem by placing their materials in a historical past. More importantly, I feel that Butler does raise new materials in these chapters, materials that he had to some extent regretted omitting from the original version.

The one aspect of Victorian social mores which seems notable in its omissions from *Erewhon* is the sexual one. Dyson, particularly, among Butler's commentators, seems conscious of this point. He argues that certain unnamed "faults" to which the narrator casually refers in the early part of the book "no doubt, are sexual" (p. 123) and suggests that in the Erewhonian treatment of disease "Butler *may* be thinking mainly of our treatment of sexual 'crimes,' and the whole trial of the man with pulmonary consumption may have been conceived with this in mind" (pp. 131–32). But Dyson's suggestions are countered to some extent by a letter written by Butler fifteen years after the publication of *Erewhon* in which he states:

> I am aware that the sexual question is of more practical importance than any such as Christianity can be; at the same time till Christianity is dead and buried we shall never get the burning questions that lie beyond approached in a spirit of sobriety and commonsense. It is therefore against superstition, and more especially the Christian superstition, that I have fought to the best of my ability.
>
> But I have got to take the world as I find it and must not make myself impossible. At present I have the religious world bitterly hostile; the scientific and literary world are even more hostile than the religious; if to this hostility I am to add that of the respectable world, I may as well shut up shop at once for all the use I shall be to myself or anyone else. Let me get a really strong position like that of Ruskin, Carlyle, or even Matthew Arnold, and I may be relied upon to give the public to the full as much as they will endure without rebellion; but I will not jeopardise what I believe to be a fair chance of future usefulness by trying to do more than I can. (*Memoir*, 2:49–50.)

The statement suggests two points. The first is that Butler had *not* dealt with the "sexual question" on any conscious level; had it been treated in *Erewhon*—even in the subliminal way that Dyson suggests—Butler would probably have alluded to that treatment in this letter, where he is obviously responding to a friendly query as to why he has not dealt with sex in his published work. The second point is that Butler felt that the "sexual question" *deserved* treatment, but that he was unwilling to treat it as of 1887.

I strongly suggest that it was the previously untreated "sexual question" which accounts in large part for the specific additions made by Butler to the expanded version of *Erewhon* in 1901. Once the prophet's vegetarian strictures were woven into the Erewhonian social fabric, Butler plays with the expedients (such as killing meat animals in "self-defense") taken by Erewhonians to avoid the prohibition. But the greatest burden of the new doctrine fell on the young, and "The Rights of Animals" ends with a story about a young man encouraged for medical reasons ("disease was not yet held to be criminal"—chap. 26, p. 269) to eat meat. After having secretly done so, he found the practice habituating, and was plagued by guilt as a result:

> The poor boy continually thought of the better class of his fellow-students, and tried to model his conduct on what he thought was theirs. "They," he said to himself, "eat a beefsteak? Never." But they most of them ate one now and again, unless it was a mutton chop that tempted them. And they used him for a model as much as he did them. "He," they would say to themselves, "eat a mutton chop? Never." One night, however, he was followed by one of the authorities, who was always prowling about in search of law-breakers, and was caught coming out of the den with half a shoulder of mutton concealed about his person. On this, even though he had not been put in prison, he would have been sent away with his prospects in life irretrievably ruined; he therefore hanged himself as soon as he got home. (chap. 26, pp. 270–71)

One need not even attempt to associate the boy's case with such a specific analogue as, say, Oscar Wilde's to see the implications in it for the Victorian attitudes toward "secret sins." The prophet's restrictions on one carnal appetite are to be paralleled with Victorian Christian attitudes toward another.

Further, this point is amplified in "The Rights of Vegetables," where it is reenforced by Butler's antipathy toward the carrying of a social program to a logical extreme. The old prophet's stricture limited the people's pleasure in eating, but at least it permitted them to survive on food other than meat for several centuries. In this regard, the old man's teachings are like the strictures on sexual activity contained in the New Testament. But the philosopher who followed him centuries later promulgates, as a logical extension of the prophet's position, a doctrine with which people *cannot* live—though, significantly, the "Puritans" attempt to do so. In this regard, the philosopher's teachings can be compared with those of the Manichaeans, Cathari, and Albigensians, who argued that all sexual activity was evil. No society can follow such doctrines and survive, and the edicts of the oracle who condemned the one and of the Church which condemned the others would seem inevitable.

In the aftermath of the oracle's decree, however, Butler comes closer to offering a conventional utopian device than anywhere else in *Erewhon.* Since the decree clearly granted the propriety of eating vegetables, and since the philosopher had so closely tied the rights of vegetables to those of animals, "though the Puritan party made a furious outcry, the acts forbidding the use of meat were repealed. . . . Even the Puritans, after a vain attempt to subsist on a kind of jam made of apples and yellow cabbage leaves, succumbed to the inevitable, and resigned themselves to a diet of roast beef and mutton, with all the usual adjuncts of a modern dinner-table" (chap. 27, p. 282). Thus, the condemnation of the philosopher's "heresy" by the oracle results in a rejection even of the old prophet's position—a more favorable outcome, from Butler's perspective, than had resulted in Christianity's rejection of such heresies as Albigensianism. The dietary strictures are completely ignored in Erewhonian society as the narrator observes it, and it would seem reasonable to see such a result, from Butler's perspective, as indeed a utopian ideal.

But this idealized case is the exception in *Erewhon.* If the book is to be considered as a description of a utopia, it must be under an expanded definition of the term from the conventional one, for Erewhonian society is, in general, neither better nor worse than our own; it is merely different in ways that give us a new perspective on the world in which we must live, one which helps us to recognize its foibles and inconsistencies.

When the narrator makes his escape by balloon in the last chapters, he returns home essentially unchanged—or so his hopes for the Erewhon Evangelization Company would lead us to believe.[25] But by holding the mirror of Erewhonian society up for us to see, the narrator unconsciously (and Butler quite consciously) has shocked our own social complacency, and the Victorian confidence that the system to which we are used must be the right and logical system. This reflecting technique which Butler uses is anticipatory of modern science fiction in a much more substantial way than are the accidental parallels so often cited from "The Book of the Machines." One has only to turn for examples to the portrayals of alien societies, of alternate societies—neither ideal nor horrifying, but "twisted" and thereby different—in works as diverse as (say) Ursula LeGuin's *The Left Hand of Darkness*, Larry Niven's *Ringworld*, or Gordon Dickson's *The Alien Way*. *Erewhon* anticipates such works in startling our complacency and forcing us to recognize the possibility of entirely different sets of social values, sets which are neither better nor worse than, but merely alternative to our own. The value of such a work, as Robert Scholes has noted, is that "it forces us to think about what is and what may be" and its "final joy . . . comes not from the departure, nor even from the trip itself, but from the return," when (quoting T. S. Eliot) we "'arrive where we started / And know the place for the first time.'"[26] Scholes's observation holds quite precisely for *Erewhon*; the narrator himself may be unchanged by his experience, but when we return with him we recognize our own world with its accidents and contingencies much more clearly than when we started.

Notes

1. The publication history of *Erewhon* is somewhat complicated. The book, the only one of Butler's to achieve even limited commercial success in his lifetime, was first published anonymously in 1872. In a second edition in the same year, Butler acknowledged his authorship and made some comparatively minor revisions. In 1901, at the time he published the sequel, *Erewhon Revisited*, Butler also published a revised edition of *Erewhon*. In his preface to the revised edition, Butler explained that several parts of the original *Erewhon* had grown out of earlier journalistic publications. He added that he had considerably expanded *Erewhon* in the revision, primarily to insure a renewal of copyright. The majority of these additions comprise "The Rights of Animals" and "The Rights of Vegetables" which I discuss below. These revisions are discussed by Lee E. Holt in "Samuel Butler's Revisions of *Erewhon*" (*Papers of the Bibliographical Society of America* 38 [1944]:22–38) and in his *Samuel Butler* (New York: Twayne, 1964), p. 143, and by Ellen Douglas Leyburn in *Satiric Allegory: Mirror of Man* (New Haven: Yale Univ. Pr., 1956), pp. 103–6. Daniel F. Howard's "Samuel Butler" in *Victorian Fiction: A Second Guide to Research*, ed. George H. Ford (New York: Modern Language Association, 1978) notes: "A new scholarly edition, using the basic text revised by Butler in July 1872 (after the first publication in March 1872) and giving variants from the 1901 edition and the manuscript separately, is being prepared by Hans-Peter Breuer and Daniel F. Howard for publication in 1978" (p. 291). This edition will be of enormous

value to Butler scholars but, even though its publication has been announced in *Books in Print*, the edition is not available from the publisher and I have been unable to consult it. (This text was finally published by the University of Delaware Press in 1981, but too late for it to be taken into account in this essay. There are, however, a few points in the introduction to the Breuer and Howard text that anticipate some of my arguments below, as when *Erewhon* is pronounced "a fine statement of the ambiguities inherent in Victorian life"—p. 24—and a work "much closer to the nonsense sense of Lewis Carroll's looking-glass world than to that of conventional satire—p. 27.) The usually preferred text for all of Butler's works is the Shrewsbury edition (1923–26), but in the case of *Erewhon*, as Howard notes, there is little reason for preferring it over other texts. Since the Shrewsbury edition was issued in limited numbers, I have chosen in this paper to cite the Modern Library edition (New York: 1927, and frequently reissued). Citations will include chapter numbers for the benefit of those with other editions, and will be followed by page citations of the Modern Library text.

2. *Religious Humanism and the Victorian Novel: George Eliot, Walter Pater, and Samuel Butler* (Princeton: Princeton Univ. Pr., 1965), p. 239.

3. *The Cradle of Erewhon: Samuel Butler in New Zealand* (Austin: Univ. of Texas Pr., 1959), p. 172.

4. John F. Harris, *Samuel Butler, Author of "Erewhon": The Man and His Work* (New York: Dodd, Mead, 1916), p. 72.

5. Holt, *Samuel Butler*, p. 38. The subject of *Erewhon*'s "non-utopianism" is also discussed in W. G. Bekker, *An Historical and Critical Review of Samuel Butler's Literary Works* (New York: Russell and Russell, 1964), p. 150.

6. Bekker offers several examples of these reviews from 1872 (pp. 110–11 n.); Furbank, *Samuel Butler (1835–1902)*, 2nd ed. (Hamden, Conn.: Archon Books, 1971), p. 7; Willey, *Darwin and Butler: Two Views of Evolution*, 1959 Hibbert Lecture (New York: Harcourt Brace, 1960), p. 61; Jones, p. 156; Dyson, "Samuel Butler: The Honest Sceptic," *The Crazy Fabric: Essays in Irony* (London: Macmillan, 1965), p. 112; Philmus, *Into the Unknown: The Evolution of Science Fiction from Francis Godwin to H. G. Wells* (Berkeley and Los Angeles: Univ. of Caifornia Pr., 1970), p. 12.

7. "The Satire of Samuel Butler," *The Triple Thinkers: Ten Essays on Literature* (New York: Harcourt and Brace, 1938), p. 212. (The Butler essay was dropped from later editions of *The Triple Thinkers*.)

8. In *Ficciones*, trans. Anthony Bonner (New York: Grove Pr., 1962), p. 53.

9. *Metamorphoses of Science Fiction: On the Poetics and History of a Literary Genre* (New Haven and London: Yale Univ. Pr., 1979), p. 166.

10. In the preface to the revised edition, Butler notes that an article, "Darwin among the Machines," published in 1863, was the basis for the "first author's" comments in "The Book of the Machines," and that, therefore,

this was the first part of *Erewhon* to be composed. A second article, written shortly after the first, served as the basis for the "second author's" views (we know this latter work to have been "Lucubratio Ebria," which was published in 1865). Thus, in substance, "The Book of the Machines" was the first part of *Erewhon* to be composed.

11. Henry Festing Jones, *Samuel Butler, Author of "Erewhon" (1835–1902): A Memoir*, 2 vols. (London: Macmillan, 1920), 1:156. This work will subsequently be cited as *Memoir*.

12. *Over the Range* is the subtitle of *Erewhon*. In *Erewhon Revisited*, we discover that the narrator of *Erewhon* was named George Higgs.

13. The narrator's blond hair and blue eyes make him remarkable from the Erewhonian viewpoint; fair features are rare, though not unheard of, in Erewhon.

14. Almost alone among Butler's recent critics, Dyson recognizes the importance of this point, pp. 121–24.

15. Holt summarizes and quotes from several reviews that castigated *Erewhon* for inconsistency, pp. 46–47. More recently, A. Dwight Culler has noted similar difficulties in his "The Darwinian Revolution and Literary Form" in *The Art of Victorian Prose*, ed. George Levine and William Madden (New York: Oxford Univ. Pr., 1968), pp. 234–35.

16. Afterword to the Signet edition of *Erewhon* (New York: New American Library, 1960), p. 236.

17. "The Source of Morality in Butler's *Erewhon*," *Victorian Studies* 16 (1973):317–28.

18. *Encyclopaedia Britannica*, 1888 ed., s.v. "Prison Discipline."

19. This view is the opposite of that in More's *Utopia*, where we are told that all religions were permitted freedom in Utopia except those which denied an afterlife. If one denied an afterlife, the Utopians presumed he would have no reason not to behave evilly now, since he would have no fear of punishment after death. (More's treatment of this question is in the last chapter of the second book of *Utopia*.)

20. These works would include, in particular, *Life and Habit* (1877), *Evolution, Old and New* (1879), *Unconscious Memory* (1880), and *Luck or Cunning, as the Means of Organic Modification?* (1886).

21. *The Notebooks of Samuel Butler*, vol. 20 of *The Shrewsbury Edition of the Works of Samuel Butler*, ed. Henry Festing Jones and A. T. Bartholomew (London: Jonathan Cape; New York: E. P. Dutton, 1923–26), pp. 346–47. The *Notebooks* were published in 1926 as the last volume in the series.

22. It is worth noting that the "past/future" reversal implied in the Erewhonian view of afterlife and pre-existence seems to be carried out in "The Book of the Machines" as well. "The Erewhonians say that we are drawn through life backwards" (chap. 19, p. 180). Thus, despite his clear recognition of man's evolutionary past, the first author in the "Book" is quite willing to ignore its implications. He writes: "I shrink with as much horror from believing that my race can ever be superseded or surpassed [by

evolving machines], as I should do from believing that even at the remotest period my ancestors were other than human beings. Could I believe that ten hundred thousand years ago a single one of my ancestors was another kind of being to myself, I should lose all self-respect" (chap. 25, p. 255). The point may be that, just as Victorian religionists seemed to shy from the idea of evolution because of what it said of man's past, and to ignore the implication that man would continue to evolve in the future, so the Erewhonian scientist, focusing only on the future implications of evolution, is able to ignore what the theory says about his own past.

23. In the preface to the revised edition of *Erewhon*, Butler says that this second view "led me to the theory I put forward in 'Life and Habit'" (p. xi).

24. "Samuel Butler's 'The Book of the Machines' and the Argument from Design," *Modern Philology* 72 (1974–75):382.

25. This point might seem obscured by the fact that George Higgs in *Erewhon Revisited* is identified as the narrator of *Erewhon*, and Higgs's views are considerably different in the later book from the narrator's in the earlier one. But it is also clear in the author's preface to *Erewhon Revisited* that that book was not envisioned at the time that the concluding chapters of *Erewhon* (which include the narrator's evangelizing scheme) were written.

26. *Structural Fabulation: An Essay on Fiction of the Future* (Notre Dame and London: Univ. of Notre Dame Pr., 1975), p. 104.

4

Zamiatin's *We*

Gorman Beauchamp

> There are books of the same chemical composition as dynamite. The only difference is that a piece of dynamite explodes only once, while a book explodes a thousand times.
>
> Zamiatin

In 1920 the Czech writer Karel Čapek was completing a play that would provide the world with a new word and a new nightmare: the play was *R.U.R.*, the word was *robot*, and the nightmare was of man's destruction by his own machines. Faced with the imperatives of modern technology, writes one critic of Čapek's play, man must either "give way to the machine, or he himself must become a machine."[1] While Čapek in *R.U.R.* portrays the former alternative, Eugene Zamiatin in *We*, written in the same year, presents the latter: the projection of a futuristic society that transforms man himself into a machine, a human robot. *We* is not only Zamiatin's most important work, but is arguably the most effective of all the dystopian depictions of the technological abolition of man.[2]

The dystopian novel, in formulating its warning about the future, fuses two modern fears: the fear of utopia and the fear of technology. If, as Zamiatin's fellow *émigré* Nicholas Berdyaev claims, in that passage made famous as epigraph to *Brave New World*, twentieth-century society is moving toward utopia, then it is doing so through the agency of modern technology. The utopian ideations of the past, that once seemed impossible of historical actualization, appear in our century not only possible, but perhaps inevitable, given the increasing array of techniques for social control made available by our science. As these venerable idola—Plato's *Republic*, say, or Tommaso Campanella's *City of the Sun* or Etienne Cabet's *Voyage to Icaria*—threatened, in modernized form, to replace the societies they had criticized, the image of utopia loomed more ominous, its darker implications for human freedom and initiative more apparent. What could be entertained on paper with detachment proved more disturbing when projected or practiced on flesh-and-blood subjects. Having himself lived through, and supported, a revolution of utopian aspirations, Zamiatin early on perceived its pernicious consequences—a decade before the rise of Stalin—and portrayed them with prophetic insight: so prophetic, indeed, that the Soviet regime has never allowed his novel to be published in Russia. But the satire in *We* is inclusive of much more than a specific regime or a particular revolution: it comprehends modes of thought, millennial expectations, chiliastic dogma, a mechanistic *Weltanschauung* that have come increasingly to characterize Western culture and of which Soviet Marxism is only one manifestation, albeit an important and portentous one.[3]

So resonant is *We* with the complex ideological struggles of the nineteenth and early twentieth centuries that to isolate even the most salient influences in the intricate tapestry of the novel is no easy task. Still, Zamiatin seems to draw most explicitly on four ideological sources which can be divided, two and two, as the antagonistic and protagonistic positions in his dystopian dialectic.

The Antagonists: The Grand Inquisitor and Frederick Taylor

Over the United State depicted in *We*, a glass-enclosed city separating its strictly regimented inhabitants from the natural world, hovers the oppressive spirit of the Grand Inquisitor, Feodor Dostoevsky's cryptopolitical spokesman for utopian authoritarianism. His heretical betrayal of Christianity, ironically presented in the parable of Ivan in *The Brothers Karamazov*, has become the inflexible orthodoxy of the United State; and he is reincarnated in Zamiatin's figure of the Well-Doer, the godlike ruler who takes all freedom into his own hands and offers a mindless contentment in its place. From the Grand Inquisitor, through the Well-Doer, stems that line of spokesmen for dystopia that runs from Mustapha Mond in Aldous Huxley's *Brave New World* and O'Brien in George Orwell's *1984* to the Darling Dictator of L. P. Hartley's *Facial Justice*, Captain Beatty of Ray Bradbury's *Fahrenheit 451* and Wei of Ira Levin's *This Perfect Day*. In his rejection of the benevolent tyranny of the Grand Inquisitor, Zamiatin must be counted among Dostoevsky's most ardent followers. But if the Grand Inquisitor (cum the Well-Doer) is the perverted god of Zamiatin's negative utopia, Frederick Winslow Taylor is his prophet. Taylor, the father of scientific management, plays a role in *We* analogous to that of Henry Ford in *Brave New World*: the exponent of a philosophy of industrial efficiency that reduces man to an appendage of his machines. In *We* Zamiatin meshes utopian social theory with the principles of scientific management, the Grand Inquisitor with Frederick Taylor, as the ideological antagonists of his satire.

The apologia of the Grand Inquisitor embodies arguments, ironically but not inaccurately, for a paternalistic *Führerprinzip* that both sums up and anticipates a pervasive impulse of the utopian imagination. From Plato's philospher-kings, Campanella's Hoh, and Francis Bacon's Fathers of the House of Solomon to the scientific elites of H. C. de Saint-Simon and Auguste Comte, the Samurai of H. G. Wells, Lenin's Central Party, and B. F. Skinner's behavioral engineers, the benevolent dictator who will control men's destinies for them has been a hallmark of authoritarian utopias. The rationale for the utopian abrogation of individual freedom, for the imposition of a ruling elite on the weak and muddled mass of mankind nowhere receives starker articulation than in the words of the Grand Inquisitor; but brutal as his diagnosis of the human condition is, it only makes overt the assumptions that lurk, draped by benevolence, in the subtext of utopia.[4]

Chief of these assumptions holds that man cannot cope with freedom: "Nothing has ever been more insupportable for a man and a human society," the Grand Inquisitor declares, "than freedom." He will willingly relinquish it for security, for contentment, for bread. "No science will give them bread so long as they remain free. In the end they will lay their freedom at our feet, and say to us, 'Make us your slaves, but feed us.'"[5] Though Ivan's parable is ostensibly a religious allegory, the Grand Inquisitor speaks not really of a church but of a state, not of a spiritual priesthood to guide men, but of a secular elite to rule them. In rejecting Caesar's coercive sword, Christ erred—argues the Grand Inquisitor—in wanting man's free love, in demanding of him conscious moral choice between good and evil. "Nothing is more seductive for man than his freedom of conscience, but at the same time nothing is a greater torture. . . . [You] burdened the spiritual kingdom of mankind forever with its sufferings." Consequently while the few great spirits have lived in imitation of Christ, the masses of mankind have been crushed under the burden of their dreadful freedom, too weak to bear moral responsibility. "By showing [man] so much respect, You acted as though You had ceased to have compassion for him, because You asked too much from him. . . . Had You respected him less, You would have asked less of him." Man is weak, rebellious, childish, craving not free choice but security. Thus, concludes the Grand Inquisitor, "We have corrected Your work":

With us everybody will be happy and will neither rebel nor everywhere
destroy each other any more as they did under Your freedom. . . . We
shall show them that they are weak, that they are pitiful children, but that
childish happiness is the sweetest of all. . . . Yes, we shall set them to
work, but in their leisure hours we shall make their life like a child's
game, with children's songs, choruses and innocent dances. . . . And they
shall have no secrets from us. . . . and we will have an answer for
everything. And they will be glad to believe our answer, for it will save
them from the great anxiety and terrible agony they now endure sup-
plying a free, individual answer.

In the Grand Inquisitor's philosophy are to be found the informing principles of Zamiatin's United State. Its citizens rejoice in their
non-freedom, in their childlike yielding to omnipotent authority.
"Why is the dance beautiful?" muses the novel's narrator. "Answer:
because it is *unfree* movement. Because the deep meaning of the dance
is contained in its absolute, ecstatic submission, in the ideal of non-
freedom."[6] Or again: "It is pleasant to feel that somebody's penetrating eye is watching you from behind your shoulder, lovingly guarding
you from making the most minute mistake, from the most minute
incorrect step" (p. 63). The eye over the shoulder belongs to the
Bureau of Guardians, the Well-Doer's secret police who monitor and
correct any deviation from the state's norms. So deeply has D-503—
the narrator—internalized these norms that the rumor that some of his
fellow citizens seek "liberation from the beneficial yoke of the State"
horrifies him:

Liberation! It is remarkable how persistent human criminal instincts are!
I use deliberately the word "criminal," for freedom and crime are as
closely related as—well, as the movement of an aero and its speed: if the
speed of an aero equals zero, the aero is motionless; if human liberty is
equal to zero, man does not commit any crime. That is clear. The way to
rid man of criminality is to rid him of freedom. (P. 34)

These passages illustrate Zamiatin's filiation with Dostoevsky in the
articulation of a proto-totalitarian social theory that permeates his
dystopia: the Grand Inquisitor, then, is one antagonist. But the language of the narrator suggests the second antagonist, an ultra-
technocratic rationalism for which Frederick Taylor stands as
Zamiatin's synecdoche.

Early in the novel, D-503 describes the daily regimen of the
Numbers, as the citizens of the United State are designated:

> Every morning, with six-wheeled precision, at the same hour, at the same
> minute, we wake up, millions of us at once. At the very same hour,
> millions like one, we begin our work, and millions like one, we finish it.
> United into a single body with a million hands, at the very same second,
> designated by the Tables, we carry the spoons to our mouths; at the same
> second we all go out to walk, go to the auditorium, to the halls for Taylor
> exercises, and then to bed. (P. 13)

This passage provides not only the novel's first reference to Taylor but
an encapsulation of the effect of Taylorism extended throughout an
entire society. From the publication of his *Principles of Scientific
Management* in 1911, Taylor's system for the structuring of industrial
operations enjoyed a considerable vogue in both the United States and
Europe, particularly in the years immediately after World War I. In his
first months in power Lenin strongly endorsed Taylorism as the best
means of enhancing Soviet economic power. "The Soviet Republic
must at all costs adopt all that is valuable in the achievements of
science and technology in this field," he wrote. "We must organize in
Russia the study of teaching of the Taylor system and systematically
try it out and adapt it to our purposes."[7] Himself a naval engineer and
faculty member of the Saint Petersburg Polytechnic Institute,
Zamiatin clearly recognized the appeal that Taylorism made to the
emerging technocratic elite of the Soviet Union, eager to consolidate
its political revolution with an industrial one.

Beyond its promise of increased industrial capacity, however,
Zamiatin saw that Taylorism embodied basic utopian ideals, only
expressed in new terminology; indeed, were Plato or Cabet or Edward
Bellamy—or the Grand Inquisitor—transported to the twentieth century, he would have found a kindred spirit in Frederick Taylor. For
Taylor had adapted to the factory the model of the organic, conflict-
free society—hierarchically structured, with strict division of labor and
the reduction of individuals to cogs in a rationally regulated machine—
that marked utopias in the Platonic tradition. Zamiatin, in turn, recon-
verts the factory model into a social one, drawing out the dystopian
implications of commitment to a purely rational efficiency.

The popularity of Taylor's system owed much to its promise of
obviating labor-management conflict: the increase in production that
it promised would mutually benefit all parties, who would thus have
common, not antagonistic interests. The credo of scientific management he summarized as: "Science, not rule of thumb. Harmony, not
discord. Cooperation, not individualism."[8] The techniques whereby
these results would be achieved are too complex to concern us here,

except to note those most germane to *We.* Time was, literally, of the essence to Taylor; he would have agreed with Lewis Mumford that "the clock, not the steam-engine, is the key of the modern industrial age," that "the clock is not merely a means of keeping track of the hours, but of synchronizing the actions of men."[9] Synchronization is the key to Taylorism. "Now, among the various methods and implements used in each element in each trade," he explains, "there is always one method and one implement better than any of the rest. And this one best method and best instrument can only be discovered or developed through a scientific study and analysis of all the methods and implements in use, together with accurate, minute motion and time study" (p. 25). The best method of production, that is, is the most efficient, and the most efficient is the quickest: the clock becomes the arbiter, indeed the model, for human activity. The Tables of Hours that regulate minutely the lives of Zamiatin's Numbers only extend Taylor's "task charts" to the whole of social existence.

Each operation in Taylor's system is minutely calculated for the worker by management; he is to follow it step by step, without thought, without question. Since the "science" that underlies even the simplest mechanical task, Taylor claims, "is so great and amounts to so much that the workman who is best suited actually to do the work is incapable . . . of understanding this science" (p. 41), he must learn to obey his superiors unhesitatingly. Taylor makes explicit the authoritarian basis of his system: "It is only through *enforced* standardization of methods, *enforced* adoption of the best implements and working conditions, and *enforced* cooperation that this fastest work can be assured. And the duty of enforcing the adoption of standards and enforcing this cooperation rests with management alone" (p. 83). *Mutatis mutandis*, the Grand Inquisitor could be speaking. The regimen of the Numbers is a fusion of his philosophy and Taylor's techniques. "I see others like myself," writes D-503, " . . . movements like mine, duplicated a thousand times. . . . I see myself as part of an enormous, vigorous, united body; and what precise beauty! Not a single superfluous gesture, or bow, or turn. Yes, this Taylor was undoubtedly the greatest genius of the ancients. . . . How could they write whole libraries about some Kant and take only slight notice of Taylor, of this prophet who saw ten centuries ahead?" (pp. 31–32).

Little in *The Principles of Scientific Management* depends on high technology, on the machine per se; rather it details the application of engineering systems to human behavior, specifies the means for converting man himself into a machine. While the *mise en scène* of *We* is replete with futuristic trappings—glass houses, helicopters, bugged streets, space ships, psychosurgery—Zamiatin is less concerned with the hardware of technology than with its *mentalité*. With Taylorism as his specific target, he anatomizes what Jacques Ellul will later term *technique*, the equation of rationality with efficiency, standardization, and mechanical order. Ellul concludes, "Technique transforms everything it touches into a machine";[10] in *We*, technique touches everything.

In the sociomachia of his dystopia, then, Zamiatin establishes as his coantagonists utopian social theory, as redacted by the Grand Inquisitor, and the scientific management of Frederick Taylor, which symbolizes the *reductio ad absurdum* of the technological world-view. The techniques of the latter made the reification of the former appear only too possible to Zamiatin, who at a propitious moment in history fused these elements into a fictive projection of a nightmare future when man had been transformed into a machine, an efficient, obedient, mindlessly content robot incapable of freedom. Or almost incapable: for a band of rebels makes one last stand against the utopian technique of the United State. In them are embodied the protagonistic values of Zamiatin's novel—freedom, spontaneity, fancy, the individual's own foolish will.

The Protagonists: The Underground Man and the Anarchists

Just as Dostoevsky provided, in the figure of the Grand Inquisitor, one antagonistic force for *We*, so in *Notes from Underground* he provides a figure whose arguments against utopian authoritarianism and technocratic mechanization are echoed distinctly by the rebels against the United State—I-330, R-13, even D-503 in his awakened or "sick" state: indeed, if the Well-Doer is a reincarnation of the Grand Inquisitor, D-503 is clearly an avatar of the Underground Man. In addition, just as Zamiatin fuses arguments from a literary source with those from a sociohistorical source—the Grand Inquisitor with Taylorism—in establishing the thesis in his dialectic, so in establishing its antithesis he unites the literary anarchism of the Underground Man with the theories of the historical Anarchists that Russia so plentifully bequeathed to a reluctant Europe throughout the latter part of the nineteenth century. Michael Bakunin is the representative figure here, symbolic, like Taylor, of a world-view contesting for dominance in the modern age; as such, his anti-statist, anti-authoritarian, anti-technocratic stance dominates Zamaitin's dystopia. *We* is, in its ideological stance, clearly anarchistic.

Notes from Underground launches a polemic against the technocratic utopianism of the mid-nineteenth-century *raznochintzi* or so-called Nihilists, whose ideas were disseminated most widely in the soddenly didactic novel of N. G. Chernyshevsky, *What Is To Be Done?* Chernyshevsky argues for a theory of "rational egotism," a belief that people invaribly act from selfish motives, but that, once they are enlightened by science, the selfish and the rational will become identical: to know the good will be to do the good. Creating a "rational" environment thus becomes the first priority of the *raznochintzi*, for once society is scientifically structured, man could not act unreasonably if he wanted to, since to do so would violate his basic (selfish) nature. The result will be utopia—a utopia, as presented in the famous Fourth Dream of Vera Pavlovna, like the Crystal Palace of 1851: "Glass and steel, steel and glass." In this Crystal Palace everyone is happy, rational, moral; machines do all the work: the millennium has arrived on the wings of scientific determinism and the hedonic calculus.[11]

The notion that man will inevitably act according to rationally calculated advantage strikes Dostoevsky's Underground Man as both absurd and pernicious. Nothing in human history, he protests, supports the claim that man will ever learn to live by reason alone, or even wants to: instead, he seeks to follow his "own foolish will!"

> Man everywhere and always . . . has preferred to act as he wished and not in the least as his reason and advantage dictated. Why, one may choose what is contrary to one's own interests, and sometimes *positively ought* (that is my idea). One's own free unfettered choice, one's own fancy, however wild it may be, one's own fancy worked up at times to frenzy— why that is the very "most advantageous advantage" which we have overlooked, which comes under no classification and through which all systems and theories are continuously being sent to the devil.

The Nihilists contended that man "does not really have caprice or will of his own and that he never had it, and that he himself is something like a piano key or organ stop" played by external environmental forces in accord with the inexorable physical laws of nature. "Consequently we have only to discover these laws of nature," the Underground Man mocks, "and man will no longer be responsible for his actions and life will become exceedingly easy for him. All human actions will then, of course, be tabulated according to these laws, mathematically, like tables of logarithms up to 108,000 and entered in a table." Faced with this possibility, he asserts, foolishly willful man would rebel in any way he could: "If you say that all this, too, can be calculated and tabulated, chaos and darkness and curses, so that the mere possibility of calculating it all beforehand would stop it all, and reason would reassert itself—then man would purposely go mad in order to be rid of reason and have his own way!" In this passage are discovered the sources of both the Tables of Hours of *We* and the rebellious Numbers' obdurate reaction against its stultifying rationalism: If this be reason, cries D-503, then "all must become insane; we must become insane as soon as possible!" (p. 147).

For the Underground Man the Crystal Palace signifies not the true culmination of man's desires, but a prison that encloses him in its rigid system of reason: utopia raises a wall, and the Underground Man rejects all walls. Zamiatin, who sets his nightmare dystopia in the glass-walled Crystal Palace of Chernyshevsky's fantasy, echoes this rejection. The Green Wall that separates the United State from the natural world is one of Zamiatin's central symbols throughout the novel, palpable evidence of utopia's denial of freedom; thus it becomes the target of the rebels who conspire to destroy the Green Wall "and all other walls, so that the green wind may blow over all the earth, from end to end" (p. 145). In this creative/destructive act, as in all their anti-utopian program, Zamiatin's protagonistic rebels appear clearly as the ideological descendants of Dostoevsky's Underground Man.[12]

Thus when D-503 awakens from his utopian torpor to discover the Underground dimension of his own personality, this "sickness" conveys the novel's positive values. These are the values of the heretic, of the nay-sayer to all orthodoxies, of Zamiatin himself. Repeatedly in his essays, Zamiatin affirms that "the world is kept alive by heretics," that "heretics are the only (bitter) remedy against the entropy of human thought."[13] If, in his praise of the heretic as the exemplar of anarchic freedom and creative energy in a world of stultifying systems, Zamiatin shows himself the spiritual heir of the Underground Man, he also demonstrtaes his filiation with the political Anarchists, particularly with Bakunin, who, like Zamiatin, resolutely rejected the imposition of all orthodoxy, all system on life.

Bakunin was hardly a systematic—or even a very consistent—thinker; his actions not infrequently contradicted his theories;[14] yet, for all his inconsistencies, he was a figure possessed of prophetic insights, who in his struggles with Marx for control of the International not only identified the most damaging propensities of his opponent's character and doctrines, but also predicted accurately the despotic course that Marxism would take. "The most fatal combination that could possibly be formed," he warned, "would be to unite socialism to absolutism; to unite the aspiration of people for material well-being... with the dictatorship or the concentration of all political and social power in the State.... We must seek full economic and social justice only by way of freedom. There can be nothing living or human outside of liberty, and a socialism that does not accept freedom as its only creative principle... will inevitably... lead to slavery and brutality."[15] Here and in his numerous reaffirmations of this basic credo that revolution must always create, never deny, liberty, Bakunin most clearly anticipates Zamiatin's own sociopolitical views. Even the romantic rhetoric, charged with metaphors of apocalypse, adumbrates the idiom of *We* and of Zamiatin's essays. "Revolution requires extensive and widespread destruction," Bakunin asserts, "a fecund and renovating destruction, since in this way, and only in this way, are new worlds born." Or again: "Let us put our faith in the eternal spirit which destroys and annihilates only because it is the . . . eternally creative source of life. The urge to destroy is also a creative urge."[16] This same heretical faith in creative destruction, excesses and all, informs Zamiatin's anarchic world-view.

In particular, he shares with Bakunin two motifs that figure centrally in *We*: a dread of technocratic tyranny and a celebration of Satanic rebellion against the enforced perfection of paradise. In the century when science was assuming the status of a new religion and scientists enjoyed unrivaled prestige, Bakunin's was one of the few voices raised against the potential for tyranny that science and scientists posed; he foresaw and decried the rise of technocracy. Suppose, he suggests in *God and the State*, in a scenario of social Taylorism with Baconian overtones,

> a learned academy, composed of the most illustrious scientists, were charged with the lawful organization of society, and that, inspired by the purest love for truth, it framed only laws in absolute harmony with the latest discoveries of science. Such legislation, I say, and such organization would be a monstrosity.... [A] society which obeyed legislation emanating from a scientific academy, not because it understood its rational character but because this legislation was imposed by the academy in the name of science which the people venerated without comprehending it, would be a society not of men but of brutes.[17]

Such a state as Bakunin hypothesizes here describes precisely the United State in *We* where the rule of scientific rationalism results not in autonomous individuals capable of thinking for themselves, but in the sheeplike Numbers, parroting slogans of reason and science that they do not understand. It is the old paradox of Plato's *Republic* in which the great majority of men must rest content with *eikasia* while the handful of philosophic rulers alone achieve *noesis*. Under such an authoritarian system as science would impose, Bakunin contends, "the State becomes the patrimony of the bureaucratic class and then falls—or, if you will, rises—to the position of a machine."[18] This perception of the state as a bureaucratic machine is graphically realized in Zamiatin's dystopia.

Throughout much of the nineteenth century the mythic figure that embodied revolutionary aspirations was Prometheus, the rebellious fire-bringer: Marx himself employed the mythic Titan for this symbolic purpose. But for others—Pierre Joseph Proudhon, for example— Satan proved the truer archetype for the individual in rebellion against tyrannical authority. Bakunin was of Satan's party: he believed that the instinct to revolt—*lèse majesté*—made up one of the basic "moments" in the development of humanity, and thus he pays homage to Satan as the original rebel, enemy of the God-State, true friend of human freedom. His version of the Fall of Man is a *felix culpa* with a distinctly unorthodox twist: "To entice man to eat of the forbidden fruit of the tree of knowledge, God had but to command him: 'Thou Shalt Not!' This immoderation, this disobedience, this rebellion of the human spirit against all imposed limits, be it in the name of science, be it in the name of God, constitutes his glory, the source of his power and of his liberty."[19] This ironic inversion of the Myth of the Fall, with all its value signs reversed, provides the central structural metaphor of *We*. In his own ironic redaction of Genesis, Zamiatin pits the antagonistic forces sketched above—the utopian political theory of the Grand Inquisitor and the mechanistic social order of Taylor, meshed in the image of the United State as neo-Eden with the Well-Doer as the new Jehovah—against the protagonistic forces represented by the Underground Man and Bakunin: anarchism, heresy, the "sinful" quest for freedom and knowledge. Significantly, the rebellious Numbers of *We* are called the *Mephi*, followers of Mephistopheles. In dystopia, where the state claims the omniscience and omnipotence of God, the Party of Satan becomes the only hope of those who resist becoming robots.

The Mythos and the Myth

In its narrative structure, *We* is a log or series of Records of D-503, begun as a testimonial to the perfect order of the United State. As the designer of the spaceship *Integral*, whose mission "is to subjugate to the grateful yoke of reason the unknown beings who live on other planets, and who are still perhaps in the primitive state of freedom" (p. 3), he intends his log to convey to them what "we" think: "*We*, therefore, shall be the title of my records" (p. 4). When the reader first encounters him, D-503 is seemingly a well-adjusted Number, worshipful of the Well-Doer, content in his glass cubicle under the watchful eyes of the Bureau of Guardians, moving effortlessly in the clockwork rhythm of the regimen set by the Tables of Hours. For the few Private Hours in the week, he has an assigned sex partner, 0-90; but the Private Hours represent the one remaining defect in the design of the state, due for elimination in the final "celebration of *all* over *one*, the *sum* over the *individual*" (p. 44). Otherwise, the Well-Doer's in his heaven and all's right with the United State: no change in the social order is conceivable, the petrifaction of paradise reigns. "The ideal (it's clear) is to be found where nothing *happens*," writes D-503, but then "something *happened* to me" (p. 24). What *happens* to him is I-330.

In the dystopian novel there must be, as Irving Howe notes, a flaw in the perfection of the perfect.[20] I-330, a strangely enigmatic Number, who appears to D-503 "like an irrational component of an equation that you cannot eliminate" (p. 10), represents the flaw in the United State's perfection. She seduces D-503, literally and figuratively, away from his loyalty to the Well-Doer by awakening in him the sense of his instinctual, animal self—a sexual self-awareness that, Zamiatin implies, is the strongest source of man's individualism. Whether or not Zamiatin had read Freud, he invests the conflict in *We* with a decidedly Freudian substructure: that is, he motivates D-503's revolt against the rationalism of utopia by positing in his protagonist a subconscious, irrational-erotic drive that surfaces to consciousness through the sexual temptations of I-330.[21] The eternal seductress beneath the drab Unif, I-330 has charms that prove stronger than the state's mathematical formulae. She tempts D-503 to sexual disobedience, and he falls: "Suddenly her arms were around my neck . . . her lips grew into mine, even somewhere much deeper, much more terrible" (p. 53).

The experience proves shattering:

> I became glass-like and saw within myself. There were two selves in me. One, the former D-503, Number D-503; and the other. . . . Before, that other used to show his hairy paws from time to time, but now that whole other self left his shell. The shell was breaking. (P. 54)

The other (unconscious) self emerging from the shell that civilization had constructed around it now begins to dream, a phenomenon symptomatic among the Numbers of mental disorder. And, indeed, by the utopian standard of the United State, D-503 has become "sick."

> I *felt* myself. To feel one's self, to be conscious of one's personality, is the lot of an eye inflamed by a cinder, or an infected finger, or a bad tooth. A healthy eye, or finger, or tooth is not felt; it is non-existent, as it were. Is it not clear, then, that consciousness of oneself is sickness? (P. 121)

The question is, of course, ironic, since D-503's "sickness," like that of the Underground Man, constitutes for Zamiatin the human essence, that which separates man from the robot. And sexuality he presents as the force that liberates consciousness, frees man from the utopian state's repression of his instincts, and gives rise to his individualism, his imagination. "I know that I have imagination," the post-lapsarian D-503 realizes, "that is what my illness consists of. And more than that: I know that it is a wonderful illness—one does not want to be cured, simply does not want to!" (p. 78).

What I have described so far of the *mythos* or plot of the novel will have suggested the myth that underlies it: Zamiatin is ironically rehearsing the Myth of the Fall. His *dramatis personae* are the cast of Genesis, with their value signs reversed: D-503 is Adam, I-330 is Eve, and the Well-Doer Jehovah—an identification made explicit in the description of his appearance on the Day of Unanimity: "This was always the most magnificent moment of our celebration: all would remain sitting motionless, joyfully bowing our heads under the salutary yoke of that Number of Numbers" (p. 134) as "He descend[ed] to us from the sky, He—the new Jehovah—in an aero, He, as wise and lovingly cruel as the Jehovah of the ancients" (p. 131). Indeed, Zamiatin has the poet R-13 (secretly a Mephi) spell out, with conscious irony, the parallel between Eden and the United State.

> That legend referred to us of today, did it not. Yes. Only think of it for a moment. There were two in paradise and the choice was offered to them: happiness without freedom or freedom without happiness. No other choice. . . . They, fools that they were, chose freedom. Naturally, for centuries afterward they longed for fetters, for the fetters of yore. . . . For centuries! And only we found the way to regain happiness. . . . The ancient god and we, side by side at the same table! We helped god to defeat the devil definitely and finally. It was he, the devil, who led people to transgression, to taste pernicious freedom—he, the cunning serpent. And we came along, planted a boot on his head, and . . . squash! Down with him! Paradise again! We returned to the simple-mindedness of Adam and Eve. (P. 59)

But this Adam and Eve, true to prototype, reject the security of paradise for the dangerous knowledge of good and evil. The rest of *We* is the tale of their rebellion.

I-330's motive for rebellion is overtly political: a leader of the Mephi, she is dedicated to the overthrow of the Well-Doer, to the collapse of the United State, to the destruction of the Green Wall. Through her, Zamiatin voices his own anti-utopian, anti-rationalistic, anti-mechanistic attitudes. She combines a faith in cultural primitivism with a Bakuninesque attachment to apocalyptic anarchy, that creative desire to destroy the mechanical order of utopia in the hope of freeing the Numbers for a fuller, more natural existence.[22] Beyond the Wall lives a race of "savages," the antithesis of the denatured Numbers within it; they represent, I-330 tells her lover, "'the half we have lost,'" the instinctual half without which the purely intellectual man is incomplete: "'these two halves must be reunited'" (p. 152). The reintegration of the Numbers with nature constitutes the Mephi's program.

Under the sexual spell of I-330, D-503 becomes a rebel for reasons of passion rather than of politics; his treason is that of a man blindly following his heart. "I want to be with I-330. I want her every minute, every second, to be with me, with no one else. All that I wrote about Unanimity is of no value. . . . For I know (be it sacrilege, yet it is the truth) that a Glorious Day is possible only with her and only when we are side by side" (p. 130). She has, in fact, robbed him of his reason; after spending an ecstatic night with I-330, he struggles to rationalize his confused sensations: "Of course it is clear that in order to establish the true meaning of a function one must establish its limit. It is also clear that yesterday's 'dissolution in the universe' taken to its limit is death. For death is exactly the most complete dissolution of self in the universe. Hence: $L = f(d)$, love is the function of death" (p. 127). Such a "reasonable" conclusion would leave a healthy Number no alternative but to reject the fatal allure of love—as D-503 tries spasmodically to do, for he is a reluctant rebel. But, "the horror of it is that even now, when I have integrated the logical function, when it becomes evident that the function contains death hidden within it, still I long for it with my lips, my arms, my heart, with every millimeter." (p. 127). Eros aroused in him, D-503 is no longer a healthy Number; he will sacrifice everything, Adam-like, for his obdurate Eve.

He agrees to turn over to the Mephi the *Integral*, to be used to destroy the Wall and topple the Well-Doer. But their plans for the spacecraft fail, thwarted by the Gestapo-like Bureau of Guardians, and even though they manage to breach the Wall and foment an uprising, it too appears doomed to failure at the novel's end. D-503 is captured by the Guardians and forced to undergo the Great Operation, a kind of lobotomy by X-ray, that leaves the Numbers "perfect . . . mechanized." His "fancy" thus removed, D-503 reverts to perfect Numberhood: docile, content, unable to feel love for any but the Well-Doer, again a smoothly functioning cog in the machine state. Sitting beside the Well-Doer, he watches blankly as I-330 is tortured to death: "When they began pumping the air from under the Bell she threw her head back and half-closed her eyes; her lips were pressed together. This reminds me of something. She looked at me, holding the arms of the chair firmly. She continued to look until her eyes closed" (p. 218). He cannot remember who she is, but is convinced that her death is right, "for reason must prevail." The Great Operation, the United State's "final solution," has rendered further rebellion impossible in this glass and steel new Eden; D-503's has been man's last disobedience.

The single grace note in the novel's pessimistic conclusion comes, faintly, from o-90, who, in violation of the state's "maternal norms," has conceived a child by D-503 and fled beyond the Wall to give it birth. Her natural primitivism—centered in the womb, in the nurturing instinct of a mother—thus manages a modest victory over utopia, which from Plato on has shown a marked hostility toward mothers. As with the "proles" in *1984*, whatever hope the novel holds lies with the primitives, with the savages beyond the Wall who have escaped the yoke of Reason.

Style and Symbol

The artistic attraction of *We*, apart from its ideological message, resides in the innovative style of the novel and the use of a complex of symbols derived from science through which Zamiatin conveys his humanistic world-view. The old realism of the European novel and its permutation in Socialist Realism he found moribund and inadequate for the modern age; the century of Einstein and the airplane demanded a new and revolutionary *form* of art, which he discovered in the "sociofantastic novels" of H. G. Wells, where are found "side by side, mathematics and myths, physics and fantasy, blueprints and miracles, parody and prophecy, fairy tales and socialism."[23] This amalgam, which Zamiatin called fantastic realism, describes his own style as much as that of Wells.

Comparing his technique (somewhat inaccurately) to that of the French Impressionists, Zamiatin sought to replace the academic realism of minute, mundane detail with the vivid, bold imagism of the unique perception:

> The old, slow, creaking descriptions are a thing of the past; today the rule is brevity—but every word must be supercharged, high-voltage. We must compress into a single second what was before in a sixty-second minute. And hence, syntax becomes elliptic, volatile. . . . The image sharp, synthetic, with a single salient feature—the one feature you will glimpse from a speeding car. The custom-hallowed lexicon has been invaded by provincialisms, neologisms, science, mathematics, technology.[24]

The style of *We* is precisely so: swift, elliptical, volatile, impressionistic, supercharged, kaleidoscopic. And, ironically, this attack on the technocratic mentality of the modern age crackles with the language of technology.

One demanding challenge for the fabulist inventing a future world involves imagining a language appropriate for the altered social conditions he envisions. The most successful responses to this challenge are the Newspeak of *1984*, the nadsat of *A Clockwork Orange*, the linguistic *tours des forces* of Stanislaw Lem, and the technocratese of Zamiatin's Numbers. "Every intervention of technique," Ellul writes, "is, in effect, a reduction of facts, forces, phenomena, means and instruments to the scheme of logic."[25] In *We* Zamiatin demonstrates the reduction wrought by technique on language: emotions are expressed in equations, feelings are formulated as syllogisms, reactions are rendered in mathematics, and thought itself becomes coextensive with logic. Indeed, Zamiatin manages to create the illusion of a language of almost complete dehumanization, a language appropriate for robots.

The creation of this language for his dystopian state poses, however, another challenge. "The more nearly absolute a social order claims to be," writes Robert Philmus, "the more absolutist and compulsive its demands for unanimous assent becomes. . . . Hence, utopia insofar as it pretends to be 'ultimate' aspires toward closure, whereby alternative ideas of order would be, if not unthinkable, at least inexpressible. The 'closed society,' in other words, can afford to tolerate only a language of assent."[26] Since the United State has evolved just such a language of assent and thus rendered any other impossible, the problem becomes how to express heretical ideas at all in this medium. Zamiatin solves this problem convincingly by generating from within the mechanical-mathematical matrix of his robotic discourse metaphors of irrationality, individualism and rebellion.

One of the two most important of these metaphors is the negative or irrational number, $\sqrt{-1}$.[27] As D-503 begins to realize that he is not a mere mechanism, but a man of flesh and blood, of hot passions and fierce desires, he remembers an event from his school days when the teaching machine had first introduced the class to irrational numbers:

> I remember I wept and banged the table with my fist and cried, "I do not want the square root of minus one; take the square root of minus one away!" This irrational root grew into me as something strange, foreign, terrible; it tortured me; it could not be thought out. It could not be defeated because it was beyond reason.
>
> Now, that square root of minus one is here again. I read over what I have written and I see clearly that I was insincere with myself, that I lied to myself in order to avoid seeing that square root of minus one. (P. 37)

As a result of this moment of introspection, as he faces the truth that he had hidden from himself, D-503 decides against informing on I-330 to the Guardians for her dangerous deviations. Thus he himself becomes, in Zamiatin's almost Metaphysical pun, an irrational Number, acknowledging the $\sqrt{-1}$ lurking in him "beyond reason." Through this mathematical symbol Zamiatin expresses analogically his perception of the mysterious depths of human nature and, furthermore, provides D-503 a means for affirming his instinctive desires in the very utopian rhetoric that would deny them.

For his second central metaphor, Zamiatin turns to thermodynamics. "'Don't you as a mathematician know,'" I-330 challenges D-503, "'that only differences—only differences—in temperature, in thermic contrast make for life? And if all over the world there are only evenly warm or evenly cold bodies, they must be pushed off! . . . in order to get flame, explosions!'" (p. 163). I-330 attributes the evenly lukewarm bodies of utopia to a process of psychosocial entropy. The conflict of energy and entropy becomes for Zamiatin the basic metaphor or model not only for all physical life, but for all social life as well. "'There are two forces in the world,'" I-330 says, "'entropy and energy. One leads into blessed quietude, to happy equilibrium, the other to the destruction of equilibrium, to torturingly perpetual motion. . . . [T]he Christians worshiped entropy like a God. But we are not Christians'" (pp. 153–54). In his most famous essay, "On Literature, Revolution, Entropy, and other Matters," Zamiatin poses the contrast between these two forces that structure the myth and the *mythos* of *We*:

The law of revolution is red, fiery, deadly, but this death means the birth of a new life, of a new star. The law of entropy is cold, ice blue. . . . When the flaming, seething sphere (in science, religion, social life, art) cools, the fiery magma becomes coated with dogma—a rigid, ossified, motionless crust. Dogmatization in science, religion, social life or art is the entropy of thought. What has become dogma no longer burns. . . . And if the planet is to be kindled into youth again, it must be set on fire, it must be thrown off the smooth highway of evolution: this is the law.[28]

Zamiatin's use of entropy as a social metaphor is perhaps initially misleading to the reader familiar with the Second Law of Thermodynamics, on which the concept of entropy is based. The First Law of Thermodynamics states the principle of the conservation of energy, or in Clausius's formulation: "Die Energie der Welt ist constant." But the Second Law holds that "Die Entropie der Welt stebt einem Maximum zu"—the entropy of the universe pushes toward a maximum. Entropy—or disorder—will increase for any process, and thus all processes lead to an increase in disorder, a constant reduction of the amount of energy available. The term "disorder" may confuse when Zamiatin characterizes utopia, the ne plus ultra of social order, as entropic; but the following elaboration of the concept may help to clarify his particularistic use of it: "The condition of maximum entropy, toward which the universe moves, is the one in which all energy has been dissipated and has been equalized throughout the universe so that there are no temperature or utilizable energy differences anywhere."[29] This Heat Death (as Lord Kelvin first called it) Zamiatin considered an inescapable consequence, in the social sphere, of the utopian will to calm perfection, "where nothing *happens.*"

Since, however, as one writer puts it, "the Second Law of Thermodynamics promises an inexorable downhill march to statistical heat-death,"[30] Zamiatin's use of this metaphor may still seem puzzling. When the implications of entropy filtered down to the general consciousness, they occasioned a rash of *fin de siècle* jeremiads from such non-scientists as Henry Adams, Max Nordau and (somewhat later) Oswald Spengler: "What the myth of Götterdämmerung signified of old, the irreligious form of it, the theory of Entropy, signifies today."[31] The most familiar literary image of entropy *in extremis* appears in Wells's *The Time Machine*, at the farthermost point of the Time Traveller's journey where the Earth is frozen and the sky is black. But Zamiatin, with a Bergsonian vitalism, denies the *inevitability* of entropy, at least of social entropy, just as the Underground Man denies the inevitability of the equation $2 \times 2 = 4$. Hostile Soviet critics have pronounced the energy/entropy metaphor of *We* "a dead, empty scheme,"[32] but, like Dostoevsky's absurdist affirmations, it represents (at least) an imaginative triumph of human will over the stone wall of determinism, natural or social. And it manages to do so in the language of the enemy.

Notes

1. William E. Harkins, *Karel Čapek* (New York: Columbia Univ. Pr., 1962), p. 85.
2. Mark Hillegas, *The Future as Nightmare: H. G. Wells and the Anti-Utopians* (New York: Oxford Univ. Pr., 1967), p. 99, comments that "the anti-utopian tradition after Wells pivots on *We*." While Zamiatin's work ranks in importance with *Brave New World* and *1984*, Irving Howe, for one, finds it artistically superior to either of them. See "The Fiction of Antiutopia," in Howe's *The Decline of the New* (New York: Harcourt, Brace and World, 1970), pp. 73–74.
3. Christopher Collins, *Evgenji Zamjatin: An Interpretative Study* (The Hague: Mouton, 1973), p. 40, states, "In *We* Zamjatin was writing a novel about the central problem in modern Western civilization, not a novel specifically about the Soviet Union." While this claim is entirely true, Collins tends, in his otherwise excellent study, to discount the plenteous satire directed against the Soviet Union that the novel *does* contain. (For instance, the physical description of the Well-Doer is obviously based on Lenin, as Orwell's of Big Brother is on Stalin.) But for placement of *We* in literary and historical contexts broader than that of anti-Soviet satire, see Howe, "The Fiction of Antiutopia," pp. 66–74; George Woodcock, "Utopias in Negative," *Sewanee Review* 64 (1965):81–97; Eugene Weber, "The Anti-Utopia of the Twentieth Century," *South Atlantic Quarterly* 58 (1959):440–47; Chad Walsh, *From Utopia to Nightmare* (New York: Harper and Row, 1962), pp. 92–114 et passim; and Robert C. Elliott, *The Shape of Utopia* (Chicago: Univ. of Chicago Pr., 1970), pp. 84–101. I have dealt with *We* in this larger context in several previous essays, particularly in "Utopia and Its Discontents," *Midwest Quarterly* 16 (1975):161–74.
4. For an elaboration of the argument that I have been able only to limn here, see my essay, "The Anti-Politics of Utopia," *Alternative Futures* 2 (1979):49–59, which includes references to the major discussions of utopian political theory.
5. The citations from "The Legend of the Grand Inquisitor," as well as those from *Notes from Underground*, are taken from the edition of both these works (along with other related pieces) by Ralph E. Matlaw (New York: Dutton, 1960). Because the "Legend" and part 1 of *Notes* are relatively brief and the editions of both works so numerous, I have not included page

numbers after quotations. In *The Brothers Karamazov*, the Grand Inquisitor episode is found in part 2, book 4, chapter 5.

6. *We*, trans. Gregory Zilboorg (New York: Dutton, 1952), p. 6. Subsequent
   page references to this edition are included parenthetically in the text.

7. Quoted in Charles S. Maier, "Between Taylorism and Technocracy:
   European Ideologies and the Vision of Industrial Productivity in the
   1920's," *Journal of Contemporary History* 5 (1970):51. This essay provides a wealth of information of the impact of Taylorism in Europe, but
   for a more detailed discussion of its impact in the Soviet Union, see E. H.
   Carr, *The Bolshevik Revolution, 1917–1923*, vol. 2 (New York: Macmillan, 1952), pp. 108–15.

8. *The Principles of Scientific Management* (1911; rpt. New York: Norton,
   1967), p. 140. Subsequent page references to this edition are cited parenthetically in the text.

9. *Technics and Civilization* (New York: Harcourt, Brace and World, 1963),
   p. 14.

10. *The Technological Society*, trans. John Wilkinson (New York: Vintage,
    1964), p. 4.

11. The currently available version of *What Is To Be Done?* in English—trans.
    Benjamin R. Tucker, rev. and abr. Ludmilla B. Turkevich (New York:
    Vintage, 1961)—is severely truncated and, inexplicably, omits "Vera
    Pavlovna's Fourth Dream," generally regarded as the culminating vision
    of the novel. Fortunately, Matlaw includes this episode in his edition of
    Notes from Underground. For the significance of this book, see Joseph
    Frank, "N. G. Chernyshevsky: A Russian Utopian," *The Southern Re-
    view*, n.s. 3 (1967):68–84; and N. G. O. Pereisa, "Chernyshevsky's *What
    Is To Be Done?* As a Statement of Socialist Utopia," *Rocky Mountain
    Social Science Journal* 9 (1972):35–44.

12. For further discussion of Zamiatin's debt to Dostoevsky, see Robert L.
    Jackson, *Dostoevsky's Underground Man in Russian Literature* (The
    Hague: Mouton, 1958), pp. 150–57; and Patricia Warrick, "The Sources
    of Zamiatin's *We* in Dostoevsky's *Notes from Underground*," *Extrapola-
    tion* 17 (1975):63–77.

13. Such statements occur repeatedly throughout Zamiatin's essays, which
    have been translated and edited by Mirra Ginsburg, *A Soviet Heretic:
    Essays of Yevegny Zamyatin* (Chicago: Univ. of Chicago Pr., 1970). The
    two I cite come from "Tomorrow," p. 51, and "On Literature, Revolu-
    tion, Entropy, and Other Matters," p. 108. For a thorough discussion of
    Zamiatin's view of the heretic as apostle of freedom, see Judith M.
    Garson, "The Idea of Freedom in the Works of Yevgeni Zamyatin," in
    Columbia Essays on International Affairs, ed. Andrew Cordier (New
    York: Columbia Univ. Pr., 1968), pp. 1–24.

14. Isaiah Berlin, "Herzen and Bakunin on Individual Liberty," in *Russian
    Thinkers*, ed. Henry Hardy and Aileen Kelly (London: Hogarth Pr.,
    1978), pp. 82–113, has recently stressed—indeed, overstressed—all the

weaknesses of Bakunin as a thinker, while minimizing his virtues. For more balanced accounts of his thought and influence, see Sam Dolgoff, "Introduction," *Bakunin on Anarchy* (New York: Knopf, 1972), pp. 3–21; George Woodcock, *Anarchism* (Cleveland: World Publishing Co., 1962), pp. 143–87 et passim; James Joll, *The Anarchists* (New York: Grosset and Dunlop, 1966), pp. 84–113; and Franco Venturi, *Roots of Revolution*, trans. Francis Haskell (New York: Grosset and Dunlop, 1966), pp. 129–86 et passim.

15. Quoted in Dolgoff, p. 4.
16. Quoted in Dolgoff, p. 14; quoted in Woodcock, p. 151.
17. *Bakunin on Anarchy*, p. 227.
18. *Bakunin on Anarchy*, p. 318.
19. Quoted in Dolgoff, p. 6. Cf. *Bakunin on Anarchy*, p. 317: "Forbidden fruit has such an attraction for men, and the demon of revolt, that eternal enemy of the State, awakens so easily in their hearts when they are not entirely stupified, that neither the education nor the instruction nor even the ownership of the State sufficiently guarantees its security. It must still have a police, devoted agents who watch over and direct . . . the current of people's opinions and passions." The relevance of this observation to *We* is patent.
20. Howe, p. 73.
21. For a more detailed discussion of the Freudian dimensions of the Myth of the Fall, see my essay "Of Man's Last Disobedience: Zamiatin's *We* and Orwell's *1984*," *Comparative Literature Studies* 10 (1973):285–301. See also Zamiatin's essay "Paradise," in *A Soviet Heretic*, pp. 59–67. For other discussions of mythic elements in *We*, see Richard A. Gregg, "Two Adams and Eve in the Crystal Palace: Dostoevsky, The Bible, and *We*," *Slavic Review* 24 (1965):680–87; Christopher Collins, "Zamjatin's *We* as Myth," *The Slavic and East European Journal* 10 (1966):125–33; and Alexandra Aldridge, "Myths of Origin and Destiny in Literature: Zamiatin's *We*," *Extrapolation* 19 (1977):68–75.
22. I have dealt with this motif in dystopian fiction, including *We*, more extensively in my essay "Cultural Primitivism as Norm in the Dystopian Novel," *Extrapolation* 19 (1977):88–96.
23. "H. G. Wells," *A Soviet Heretic*, p. 270.
24. "Literature, Revolution, Entropy," *A Soviet Heretic*, p. 111. See Irving Howe, "The Idea of the Modern," in *Literary Modernism* (Greenwich, Conn.: Fawcett, 1967), pp. 19–21.
25. *The Technological Society*, p. 79. For a fuller discussion of some of the points I make here, see my essay "Future Words: Language and the Dystopian Novel," *Style* 8 (1974):462–76.
26. "The Language of Utopia," *Studies in the Literary Imagination* 6 (1973):64.
27. Robert Russell, "Literature and Revolution in Zamyatin's *My [We]*," *Slavonic and East European Review* 51 (1973):43, notes that Zamiatin

balances his mathematical images with animal ones. Thus the counterpart of $\sqrt{-1}$ is D-503's "hairy paws," the atavistic reminder of his animal nature. See also John J. White, "Mathematical Imagery in Musil's *Young Törless* and Zamyatin's *We*," *Comparative Literature* 18 (1966):71–78.

28. "On Literature, Revolution, Entropy, and Other Matters," *A Soviet Heretic*, p. 108.

29. D. Stanley Tarbell, "Perfectibility vs. Entropy in Recent Thought," *Science/Technology and the Humanities* 1 (1978):104.

30. Monroe Beardsley, quoted in Rudolf Arnheim, *Entropy and Art* (Berkeley, Los Angeles, and London: Univ. of California Pr., 1971), p. 12.

31. Spengler, *The Decline of the West*, trans. Charles F. Atkinson (New York: Modern Library, 1965), p. 220.

32. For the reaction of Soviet Critics to *We*, see Vasa D. Mihailovich, "Critics on Evgeny Zamiatin," *Papers on Language and Literature* 10 (1974):324–26.

5
Olaf Stapledon's *Last and First Men*
Eugene Goodheart

Olaf Stapledon's reputation is something of an anomaly. Stapledon was a philosophical writer who did not think of himself essentially as a writer of science fiction. Yet serious writers and readers of science fiction regard him with awe. Basil Davenport says typically that he is "one of the few creative intelligences that have ever tried the medium."[1] Writers and thinkers of the distinction of Bertrand Russell, C. S. Lewis and H. G. Wells wrote of Stapledon with admiration. Arthur C. Clarke speaks of his influence on his own work. And Davenport provides us with a catalogue of Stapledonian themes that have entered the mainstream of science fiction: "the mutant who is both a prodigy and a monster; the superman who is not the oppressor of *Homo Sapiens* but his potential savior and actual victim; alien intelligences which are not even animal; controlled evolution and artificial brains." And yet (to complete the anomaly) Stapledon is virtually unknown outside the field of science fiction. I do not intend here to solve the mystery of Stapledon's reputation, though in the course of a consideration of his masterwork *Last and First Men* (1930) I hope to shed some light upon it.

We might begin with the preface to *Last and First Men*.

> Yet our aim is not merely to create aesthetically admirable fiction. We must achieve neither mere history, nor mere fiction, but myth. A true myth is one which, within the universe of a certain culture (living or dead), expresses richly, and often perhaps tragically, the highest admirations possible within that culture. A false myth is one which either violently transgresses the limits of credibility set by its own cultural matrix, or expresses admirations less developed than those of its culture's best vision. This book can no more claim to be true myth than true prophecy. But it is an essay in myth creation.[2]

The imaginative freedoms taken by Stapledon in *Last and First Men* make one wonder what "the limits of credibility" are. If Stapledon's own imagination is evidence of what is possible within *our* cultural imagination, there is virtually no limit to what man can imagine his future to be. If *Last and First Men* is to read as "future history" and not as myth as it should be, then the reader will be endlessly troubled by the question of credibility, for the "limits of credibility" are constantly and violently transgressed in Stapledon's refashionings of both the human intelligence and the human body through the eighteen incarnations of "man" before his ultimate demise. By "myth" I understand Stapledon to mean an imaginative or narrative embodiment of ideas and ideals, both positive and negative, by which men can judge their actual condition and prospects.

The most striking fact of Stapledon's imagination is its fantastic expansion of time. The human adventure occurs through billions of years and within our solar system. We are witness to the emergence of numerous species of men (often radically dissimilar in shape and in intellectual character, though linked together by a concept of intelligence), whose adventures occur on several planets of the solar system (Earth, Venus, Mars and Neptune). In *Star Maker*, Stapledon extends his imagination to other galaxies, producing, as it were, a new kind of galactic consciousness. The particular excitement of *Last and First Men*, however, is temporal rather than spatial. In order to overcome temporal distances and domesticate the future for the contemporary reader, Stapledon admittedly strains credibility by making his narrator "an inhabitant of the remote future . . . communicating with us today." The introduction of such a narrator is justified by the capacity of the Eighteenth Man to enter telepathically into the consciousness of people who lived in the past. This power is presented in the context of an extended and moving meditation on mortality, to which I will return. But it should be noted here that Stapledon's bold decision to introduce a narrator from the remotest future is necessary to the unfolding of Stapledon's "argument."[3]

The immediate effect of the expansion of the time sense is to produce an alteration in our cultural perspective. Before that effect is achieved, Stapledon gives us a compressed "future history" of our own era. The opening chapters read like political journalism, in which Stapledon extrapolates tendencies in world politics from contemporary situations. Writing in 1930, Stapledon begins with "the European War," called at the time "The War to End War."

> At the outset a tangle of motives, some honorable and some disreputable, ignited a conflict for which both antagonists were all too prepared, though neither seriously intended it. A real difference of temperament

between Latin France and Nordic Germany combined with a superficial rivalry between Germany and England, and a number of stupidly brutal gestures on the part of the German Government and military command, to divide the world into two camps; yet in such a manner that it is impossible to find any difference of principle between them. During the struggle each party was convinced that it stood for civilization. But in fact both succumbed now and again to impulses of sheer brutality, and both achieved acts not merely of heroism, but of generosity unusual among the First Men. For conduct which to cleared minds seems merely sane, was in those days to be performed only by rare vision and self-mastery.

The terms of political understanding do not take us very far. Motives are "dishonorable" or "disreputable." The difference between France and Germany is temperamental or racial: *Latin* France and *Nordic* Germany. Of a subsequent war between England and France, the narrator speaks of the "subtle [racial] difference in mentality" between the two countries, making a stereotypic distinction between "French sensualists and English hypocrites." Countries make unprincipled, "stupidly brutal" gestures, each country believing mistakenly that it stands for civilization. The "dialectic" of history as Stapledon's narrator understands it is epitomized by the false peace that follows the European War: dawning vision versus incurable blindness; higher loyalty versus compulsive tribalism. The Eighteenth Man seems to be a startingly simpleminded moralist.

But it may not be simplemindedness as much as the effect of perspective. The Eighteenth Man knows our world within a billion year perspective. What seems to us as inevitability or at least as causally determined sequences of events may be no more than foolish choices or accidents. "Save for a number of most untoward accidents, to be recorded in due course, the party of peace might have dominated Europe during its most dangerous period; and through Europe, the world." It may appear that anyone who allows accident to play a large role in his understanding of history is naive. Or it may be—as I think Stapledon intends—that such an understanding exists on the other side of sophistication. Our familiar historicist or determinist understandings of history may be no more than the illusion of First Men, still ignorant of the larger destiny of mankind. Moreover, one must understand what Stapledon means by accident. Accident is a function of the quality or level of intelligence that characterizes mankind at any given moment. "With either a little less bad luck or a fraction more of vision and self-control at this critical time, there might never have occurred that aeon of darkness, in which the First Men were presently to be submerged. For had victory been gained before the general level of mentality had seriously begun to decline, the attainment of the world state might have been regarded, not as an end, but as the first step toward true civilization." Stapledon is primarily interested in the changing quality of intelligence through "history." He is not concerned with understanding conditions under which intelligence prevails or declines. Another way of putting it is that Stapledon is what might be called an "intelligential" determinist.

Which is not to say that Stapledon is not at times a shrewd observer of the political scene. In judging the tendency of Russian socialism, he achieves something close to prophecy. Falling under the influence of "Western, and especially American, finance, Russia becomes materialist." And Stapledon foresees the end of our present civilization in a "very serious oil famine." But note that Stapledon does not try to understand the political or economic conditions in which the oil famine developed or the conditions which make one outcome or another probable. The oil famine "could have been overcome if the intelligence of the race" had not "so deteriorated that it could no longer cope with such a crisis."[4]

In rapid order, war follows war: between France and England, Russia and Germany, Europe and America (Europe is destroyed by America), America and China. The result is an Americanized planet and the foundation of the First World State. In a curious episode, Stapledon presents his version of the fantasy which impels America toward world domination. During negotiations between American and Chinese heads of state on a Pacific Island, a beautiful Polynesian woman appears as a temptress both to the American and the Chinese. It is not so much his sexual appetite as his lust for power that arouses the puritanical American president, who wins the Polynesian beauty. The result of their coupling is the creation of the First World State. In his fine monograph on Olaf Stapledon, Jack Kinnaird argues persuasively that the seeds of destruction of the First World State are to be found in the creation of the First World State. "Without a spiritual basis in true will to community," the state will be undone by a "perversion of sexuality and its consequent undermining of intelligence." Kinnaird goes on to speak of "mass-sublimations of sexual desire in an official world-religion of ritualized flight [aviation], and in other practices that reflect a fatal confusion of human vitality with technological prowess and compulsive ego assertion."[5]

The immediate cause of the decline of the first world-civilization is "the sudden failure of the supplies of coal," and the cause of this failure is aviation, which Stapledon sees not to be a genuine human need, but a ritual system, supported by the "prestige of science." Stapledon gives a mythic embodiment to the ritual flights. The flying aristocracy promises "the release of the secret of divine power," which, of course, fails to materialize. But the decline of civilization is not to be attributed to a single cause. Stapledon provides us with several heresies and perversions, which betray human intelligence: humanitarianism, which permits the unwholesome members of the species to survive; the adoration of instinct at the expense of intellect, and the adoration of intellect at the expense of instinctual energy.

The theme of flight is, of course, essential to Stapledon's cosmic imagination. It is both part of its narrative necessity (eventually man will have to get from one planet to another in order to escape the demise of Earth) and emblem of the freedom and power of human intelligence and imagination. But there is in Stapledon's imagination a countervailing tragic awareness, which constantly dramatizes the hubris of flight. Thus in the first Dark Age of the First Men, the landscape is characterized by the debris of "ancient residential pylons, flying mansions," mute testimony of a mighty doomed civilization and an adumbration of tragic overreachings to follow.

If tragedy is the result of a failure of human intelligence and if human intelligence needs time to develop and mature, it would seem logical that one solution to the problem would be to increase the span of human life. It would also seem possible to achieve this result in the post-Darwinian world. The increase of the life span could be the result of artificial as well as natural selection in man's unending progressive adaptation to the conditions of existence. The possibility of increasing the life span is a major theme in the work of George Bernard Shaw, a contemporary of Stapledon. Shaw, of course, was a Lamarckian and consequently anti-Darwinian. Like Stapledon, Shaw focused on the genetic endowment rather than the environment. The saving power, if there is to be salvation, is intelligence. Stapledon's First Men achieve a doubling of the life span. Other species will even reach to the possibility of immortality. The Patagonian civilization, which is, so to speak, the last gasp of the first world-civilization, represents a perversion (albeit an attractive one) of the effort to slow the process of aging. The Patagonians attempt to *arrest* the process and their god appropriately is the [Divine] Boy who Refused to Grow Up. The Cult of Youth with its adoration of beauty and its sexual vigor dramatizes not so much the capacity of the Patagonians as their unrealized aspiration. "Though in a sense it was an expression of their own culture, it was an expression upon a plane of vitality to which very few of them could ever reach." In an ironic turnabout, the Divine Boy renounces his message of vitality ("the first step is to outgrow this adulation of life itself, and this cadging obsequiousness toward Power") and is himself tried and executed for sacrilege. Arrested in a state of permanent immaturity, unable to believe either in the values of an earlier time or in the possibility of progress, the Patagonians go into rapid decline. Volcanic eruptions, caused by a mischievous monkeying with machinery in mines (appropriately the expression of youthful anger against parental authority), effectively destroy the Patagonians. The end of the civilization of the First Men quickly follows.

With the demise of the First Men we are properly launched into a fantastic region in which new species emerge and decline.[6] Though the character and atmosphere of the work change radically, Stapledon, as I have already suggested, anticipates in the early chapters the alteration produced in our cultural perspective. Our view of history (whatever variations exist within it) is still largely determined by the Idea of Progress. This was even truer in Stapledon's time than in ours. Events are seen as forming a chain which generates the impression of inevitability. It is an irony of the Idea of Progress that it has made people feel as if they were imprisoned in a sequence of events over which they have no control. In speaking of accidents, unrealized possibilities, disasters that could have been averted, Stapledon (the narrator) is clearly trying to liberate the historic sense from the prison-house of inevitability. Men have choices, Stapledon is saying. To be sure, the choices are conditioned by environment and the mental and physical limitations of human beings at any given time. In expanding the time sense in which differently constituted species are allowed to emerge, Stapledon means to alter the sense of limitation, not, one should quickly add, eliminate limitation itself: that would be doing both the impossible and the undesirable. Like a scientist in a laboratory, Stapledon alters conditions (introduces variables) so that we can perceive what the possibilities of human life are. When Stapledon says in his preface that he means to remain within the limits of credibility, I think that he is speaking of his commitment to a view of men situated within the conditions of existence. Stapledon never violates the logic of those conditions—though the variety of possible conditions exceeds our normal experience. But then we are not usually privileged to enjoy the perspective of billions of years of experience.

The "experimental" character of Stapledon's imagination is evident in his presentation of the rise of the Second Men. The environment, altered by volcanic eruptions, becomes temperate and favorable to the appearance of new species. There are few dangerous animals; meat, fruit and timber are plentiful. Stapledon speaks of "an epidemic of biological variations" many of which are extremely valuable. The Second Men are gigantic; their feet lose their separate toes and "become more efficient instruments of locomotion." "Their eyes were large, and often jade green, their features firm as carved granite, yet mobile and lucent." The Second Men are a production of Nature, repeating and excelling the original cave-dwellers. Their life span is increased to about two hundred years, with a corresponding change in the times of pregnancy, puberty and maturity. Their strong sexual appetite includes an "erotic appreciation of the unique physical and mental forms of all kinds of living things." This increase in erotic capacity is connected with an instinctive communalism (a "native aptitude for cosmopolitanism"), but the communalism is never abstract, never at the expense of an appreciation of the individuality and diversity of personality. The Second Men are utopian creatures, combining two capacities that had been "unattainable ideals" for the First Men: "the power of wholly dispassionate cognition, and the power of loving one's neighbors as oneself, without reservation." "Natural Christians," the narrator calls them.

Yet Stapledon constantly qualifies his admiration for the Second Men by an awareness of what they have not achieved, an awareness shared by the Second Men themselves. They "were oppressed by the brevity of human life, and the pettiness of the individual's achievement in comparison with the infinity round about him." It is, of course, true that short of immortality and the capacity for ambiguity, men will always experience the brevity and pettiness of their lives. This is the tragic condition of human life. It is also a valuable and necessary condition, as men learn when the possibility of immortality is available to them. The conviction of the value and necessity of mortality is strengthened, paradoxically, in the realization of the potentialities that exist within the limits of the human condition.

The Second Men are troubled by a sense of the incomplete community of the race. And they conceive the utopian ambition of remaking human nature so that it would be possible to "knit" the community into one mind through "each unique individual's telepathic apprehension of the experience of all his fellows." It is left to the Fifth Men to achieve this telepathic power. The destruction of the Second Men is brought about by an invasion from Mars. (Stapledon's great rival in science fiction was, of course, Wells.) The introduction of the Martians is an accident from the human point of view, but it is not imaginatively gratuitous. The economy of the Martians illustrates precisely that capacity for telepathic communication that the Second Men wish to achieve. Moreover, it reveals the price paid for telepathy: a loss of individual self-sufficiency in the units that compose the jelly-like mass of the Martian community. Ironically, Martian telepathy does not extend to the Second Men, so the Martians' super-individuality becomes a kind of communal selfishness, which results in the destruction of both their own community and that of the Second Men. Unable to recognize the "worth . . . of minds other than [their own] minds," the Martians seek to destroy the Second Men. Universal destruction is achieved by biological warfare initiated by the Second Men, who lose their sanity under the enormous pressure of the Martian armies which pour forth from the home planet. Though the Martians are not a benign presence in the book, Stapledon does not exhibit the usual xenophobia in science fiction about people from other planets.

The allegorical implication for contemporary nationalism and world peace is clear enough, but Stapledon is not simply writing political allegory. He is, I think, making a dramatic statement about the parochialism or provincialism of contemporary ideas of the human. Here it might be useful to invoke Nietzsche, who also sought modes of being not customarily thought of as human, but which represent new possibilities of life for human beings. Stapledon's imagination unfolds within this over-reaching mode. The remnant of the Second Men becomes the basis for the emergence of the Third Men. The human series that Stapledon presents is no simple progress. Catastrophic interruptions cause losses and forgettings. The Third Men do not stand on the shoulders of the Second. They are more cunning than intellectual, more practical than theoretical. Their interests are aesthetic and religious rather than scientific. But the Third Men do represent "progress" in the project of remaking human nature.

Utopian thought is generally unembarrassed by the project of remaking human nature. Dystopian thought, on the other hand, dramatizes the cost incurred: its threat to the given, the natural, the very idea of the human. Though his speculation is essentially within the utopian mode, Stapledon has what might be called a dystopian sensitivity to the perversions in the process of remaking men. As we shall see, the Fourth Men are a monstrous outcome of this project, though Stapledon's presentation of the pathos of their condition suggests his resistance to the dystopian mode. But Stapledon's utopianism is profoundly qualified by his tragic awareness. He is attracted to the adventure of remaking, but he craves at the same time the resistances which make the remaking difficult. He wants both the experience of radical transformation and that of resistance and limitation. Stapledon's utopianism occurs within a tragic universe. This is as it should be, because radical change and limitation are utterly interdependent. Stapledon's characteristic vision is to be found in the following passage about the Third Men.

> The Worship of Life, as agent or subject, was complemented by worship of environment, as object to life's subjectivity, as that which remains ever foreign to life, thwarting its enterprises, torturing it, yet making it possible, and, by its very resistance, it was said, was the most vivid apprehension of the sacred and universal Object.

The Fourth Men constitute a warning to those who regard the project of remaking human nature as unproblematically benign. They are "Great Brains," for whom life is purely intellectual activity. Their bodies are artifically created to be mere instruments of the intellect. Thus the brain was "twelve feet across," and the body "was reduced to a mere vestige upon the undersurface of the brain." The monstrous "organism" is really a factory to support the exercise of intellect. "A self-regulating pump, electrically driven, served it as a heart. A chemical factory poured the necessary materials into its blood and removed waste products, thus taking the place of the digestive organs and the normal battery of glands etc. etc." The Fourth Men do achieve mastery of the laws of the material universe. "The Great Brain"—without genuine sympathy for "the petty troubles" of the people it rules—does, however, manage through an exact knowledge of behavioristic psychology to govern with tact the emotional race of Third Men (who spawned the Brain).

Yet it becomes clear that the Fourth Men are deficient in intellectual capacity as well as in their physical and emotional capacities, for their intellectual life is compromised by the absence of a genuine physical and emotional existence. They have, for instance, no appreciation for the limitations of life, a consequence of life in the body. Stapledon appreciates the necessary intimacy of body and mind. Oddly enough, he bestows this self-critical understanding on the Fourth Men themselves, who come to realize that the form of transcendence that they represent was a mistake and therefore needs to be transcended. It is, I think, a symptom of the abstractness of Stapledon's imagination to make the Fourth Men finally so innocuous in their horror and so understanding of their own deficiencies. If the intellect needs the body and the emotions for a truly human exercise of intelligence, it could not itself generate the self-critical sensitivity Stapledon confers upon it.

In making the Fifth Men, the Fourth Men try to be guided by a conception of a natural type. Appropriately, they work on the surviving specimens of the Third Men. The Fifth Men constitute one of the few triumphant achievements of *Last and First Men*. The narrator says that their highest achievement "lies wholly beyond the comprehension of those for whom this book is intended." This, of course, is exaggeration. As one reads the narrator's account, Marx's dream of a society of abundance comes to mind. "The vast economic routine of the world-community was carried on by the mere touch of appropriate buttons." This freedom from economic necessity becomes the opportunity for the "energy of the race . . . to seek recreation in its many admirable sports and arts." There are relatively few traces of Stapledon's involvement in left-wing societies and movements. Wherever Stapledon's imagination brings forth a Marxist-seeming idea, it is usually the result of the intersection of the logic of his imagination with Marxism. Stapledon is a writer of originality rather than a borrower.

What finally distinguishes the Fifth Men is the tonality of their lives: a richness of perception, feeling and intelligence far exceeding anything that the world has previously known. And this is accomplished in great part by the exercise of the telepathic power originally appropriated from the Martians.

> One result of the general "telepathic" facility of the species was that speech was no longer necessary. It was still preserved and prized, but only as a medium of art, not as a means of communication. Thinking, of course, was still carried on largely by means of words; but in communication there was no more need actually to speak the words than in thinking in private. Written language remained essential for the recording and storing of thought. Both language and the written expression of it had become far more complex and accurate than they had ever been, more faithful instruments for the expression and creation of thought and emotion.
>
> "Telepathy" combined with longevity and the extremely subtle brain-structure of the species to afford each individual an immense number of intimate friendships, and some slight acquaintance actually with the whole race. This, I fear, must seem incredible to my readers, unless they can be persuaded to regard it as a symptom of the high mental

development of the species. However that may be, it is a fact that each person was aware of every other, at least as a face, or a name, or the holder of a certain office. It is impossible to exaggerate the effects of this facility of personal intercourse. It meant that the species constituted at any moment, if not strictly a community of friends, at least a vast club or college. Further, since each individual saw his own mind reflected, as it were, in very many other minds, and since there was a great variety of psychological types, the upshot in each individual was a very accurate self-consciousness.

This may be the feature of the culture of the Fifth Men that is beyond comprehension. Or rather it defies our usual comprehension of it. Telepathy in the political sense has usually meant mind-control. In Eugene Zamiatin's *We* and George Orwell's *1984* we are given visions of the totalitarian uses of telepathy so powerful as to frighten us from even speculating about its possible benign uses.

Of course, Stapledon's experiment precludes the conditions which would make totalitarianism possible. The very psychobiology of the Fifth Men excludes the possibility of their achieving gratification from a totalitarian exercise of telepathy. Still, one may wonder about the losses in personal relationships and in human activities incurred by telepathic consciousness. If speech is no longer necessary, what kind of art would arise without living speech as its raw material? What of the pleasures of distance, difference, otherness, even solitude? Would telepathy be flexibly, discriminatingly applied? One is reminded of Rousseau's fantasy of a transparency which would overcome all obstacles to communication and all opportunities for concealment. And we know what paranoid motivation lies behind such a fantasy. I am aware that I am mixing considerations of present and future consciousness. But I would insist nevertheless that despite the device of a narrator from the remote future a contemporary consciousness invented the book.

Stapledon's use of telepathy is inspired when he connects it with the theme of immortality. The Fifth Men achieve a life span of fifty thousand years, but refuse the possibility of immortality, which they feel "would lead to spiritual disaster." As a compensation for mortality, they develop a telepathic gift for entering fully into the lives of people who lived in the past. The narrator characterizes it mystifyingly as an experience of eternity. Telepathic experience of the past has its risks: "Those, who in the course of their voyaging in the past, encountered regions of eternal agony, came back distraught." But the voyage is worth the risks. The Fifth Men achieve a community in a dimension at once temporal and eternal, which both enriches them and (most difficult for First Men to comprehend) revives and enriches the consciousness of those who have died. The subchapters "The Cult of Evanescence" and "Exploration of Time" within the chapter "The Last Terrestrials" are at once fascinating and mysterious. One feels that Stapledon is on the frontier of occult speculation and has not achieved full articulateness. What Stapledon means to suggest, it seems to me, is the possibility of an experience of the past beyond what we ordinarily understand by the words *memory, recollection, remembrance*. Those who have lived in the past are revived by those in the present, not simply appropriated to present purposes. The past for us is always a re-creation of the present. Telepathy makes possible the rehabilitation of the past as present in the terms of the past. Though Stapledon obviously does not have the historian's enterprise in mind, the telepathic power would be the envy of every historian.

A question arises about the losses incurred in the achievement of telepathy. Telepathy, in Stapledon's understanding, assumes the existence of a past apart from the changing life of that past in the succession of presents that constitute history. If the past is a chameleon, its reality or truth is not simply elusive or unascertainable, it may have no existence. But the changefulness of the past (our capacity even to forget the past) may also constitute its power to energize and differentiate the present. Perhaps Stapledon means to suggest that the price of telepathic capacity is too high when he shows that despite "the almost perfect order" of the Fifth Men, they fall into despair because of their empathic experience of past misery. (Subsequently, in their life on Venus, the telepathic capacity becomes the source of cancer. The narrator remarks that "human tissues had never perfectly assimilated the Martin units" which were the means of "telepathic communication." Stapledon's psychogenic symbolism is clear enough.) The changefulness of the past is a function of the freedom of man to achieve new presents, new futures.

But the Fifth Men are not allowed to remain immersed in their "social melancholy." Despite their mastery of cosmological science, the Fifth Men are surprised to discover an unanticipated change in the lunar orbit produced by telepathic disturbances of the electromagnetic field of the planet. The change in orbit presages the end of terrestial existence. Now the Fifth Men must devote their efforts to space travel and to the making of another planet in the solar system habitable. Venus is the first step in man's solar migration. The chapter on the Last Terrestials concludes with a description of the necessary preparation of Venus to make it habitable for men. The preparation (oxidizing through electrolysis the atmosphere of Venus) tragically involves the destruction of the native fauna of Venus. Stapledon is forever reminding us of the costs of these Faustian enterprises.

The theme of flight achieves its fullest expression in the presentation of the Seventh Men, who transcend mechanical flight and become bird men. The narrator describes the life of these creatures as of one of extraordinary intensity both in pleasure and in pain. They are aerial artists, each engaged in "ceremonial ballet with sky darkening hosts of his fellows." So intense is their sensuous and aesthetic sense of the universe that while in the air even the prospect of the experience of death becomes the occasion for exhiliration. On the ground, "[the bird men] would be overwhelmed with grief." The price of their intense aesthetic life is the loss of interest in scientific and intellectual pursuits. Since science has lost all useful function for them, they no longer need it—that is, until biological changes require scientific understanding. By that time it is too late to preserve the bird men. As the bird men decline, a new policy is formulated. A group of deformed infants, with no chance for aerial life, is trained to do biological research. Predictably, these "brilliant cripples," as the narrator calls them, experience both envy and contempt for their aerial progenitors and eventually master and eliminate the bird men. The "dialectic" here recapitulates in somewhat different terms the relationship between the Third and the Fourth Men.

Though life on Venus is of longer duration than life on Earth, it too is threatened by destruction. The Eighth Men detect signs of the freezing of Venus. After an abortive plan to migrate to Mercury, they decide to make the journey to Neptune, the planet potentially most hospitable to men. (One can already see the logic which will compel Stapledon to contemplate man's journey to other galaxies.) Again, as in the case of Venus, the Eighth Men must prepare Neptune for human life. Ether vessels and vegetation are sent; a process of the automatic annihilation of matter to create a supply of energy for warmth is rediscovered. Neptune will be man's last habitation. It is the scene of ten more species of men, who reveal an even greater diversity than those on Earth and on Venus. "They range from the instinctive animal to modes of consciousness never before attained." Stapledon passes quickly over the history of Neptune, pausing briefly to mark some unusual or distinguishing feature of a particular species. Thus in the fifteenth human species "unaided nature . . . produced that highest form of natural man which she had produced only once before." "The

Fifteenth Men set themselves to abolish five great evils, namely, disease, suffocating toil, senility, misunderstanding, ill-will." The cosmic process, however, intervenes in the form of a strange and beautiful supernova, whose radiation will ultimately destroy the sun and all the planets. Kinnaird incisively notes the symmetry between "man's fate" and "the cyclical cosmic process." He cites the beautiful sentence: "Man is a fair spirit whom a star conceived and a star kills." To see man as a manifestation of cosmic process is, of course, to absolve him from the responsibility for his own survival. The vision is tragic rather than moral.

The Last Men are last in the chronological sense. They exist in a universe that cannot sustain the life of the race forever. This is the tragic condition of human life. But they are also last in a utopian sense—of having realized human potentiality. Realization, for Stapledon, consists in the development of "a super mind," a collective or communal consciousness, which does not entail the suppression of individuality and diversity. The Eighteenth Men revive the power of telepathy, but they avoid the pitfalls of Martian telepathy, "in which the racial mind of Mars had failed to transcend the minds of the Martians." The mediating activity between individual and group life is sexual intercourse, which is often polymorphous. "Occasionally there is a special kind of group intercourse in which during the actual occurrence of group mentality, all the members of one group will have intercourse with those of another." Stapledon's pre-Marcusan or pre-Brownian audacity is somewhat neutralized by the pedestrianism of his prose.

It is telepathy that has made possible the narrative device by which the Last Man speaks to us, the First Men. No longer simply the power of passive participation in the experience of past minds, the Eighteenth Men have now achieved the power of influencing past minds. What does this mean? Stapledon's provisional imagination does not conceive a series of inevitable events. What happens in his book may happen. Its provisionality functions as an influence, both as a spur to emulation and as a deterrence. Stapledon proposes a variety of men, who in their partial development as intellectual beings or instinctual creatures suggest by contrast what the path of full humanity is. And then in his imagination, the Fifth and Eighteenth Men in particular, he conceives of a fully developed, fully articulated human life, in its personal and communal aspects. But even these fulfillments are conditioned by a tragic awareness of the "pitiless universe."

And yet there is what Nietzsche called "the eternity of the phenomenon," the permanent energy of existence that expresses itself in Stapledon's work as the music of the spheres, the great symphony of life. Stapledon's language does not avoid banality. But there is a genuine note of ecstasy and doubt in the concluding paragraphs of the book.

> Great, and terrible, and very beautiful is the Whole; and for man the best is that the Whole should use him.
>
> But does it really use him? Is the beauty of the Whole really beautiful? And what is beauty? Throughout all his existence man has been striving to hear the music of the spheres, and has seemed to himself once and again to catch some phrase of it, or even a hint of the whole form of it. Yet he can never be sure that he has truly heard it, nor even that there is any such perfect music at all to be heard. Inevitably so, for if it exists, it is not for him in his littleness.
>
> But one thing is certain. Man himself, at the very least, is music, a brave theme that makes music also of its vast accompaniment, its matrix of storms and stars. Man himself in his degree is eternally a beauty in the eternal form of things. It is very good to have been man. And so we may go forward together with laughter in our hearts, and peace, thankful for the past, and for our own courage. For we shall make after all a fair conclusion to this brief music that is man.

The vision belongs to the last of the Last Men, a youth with all the gifts of his civilization, born "with the power to withstand the tempest of solar energy longer than the rest of us" and yet without illusions about the destiny of his race. He, more than anyone else, is ready for the end. *Last and First Men* concludes with his voice, a voice which tries to fix the moment of eternity in the tragic transience of all created things.

Stapledon's claim that he means to create a myth rather than mere history or fiction is a fair one. But myth, after all, depends upon the power to make fictions, which in turn requires powers of characterization, imagination and language, all of which are deficient (not absent) in his work. There is a kind of cosmic (?) imagination (it is difficult to find the exact language for it) of which Stapledon has a superabundant share. This imagination serves him as an inventor of myth. And he is a maker of myth rather than a philosopher in the sense that his gift is for telling the story of an idea rather than analyzing it. But this gift is combined with an essayistic rather than a fictional impulse. I suspect that the solution to the mystery of his reputation has something to do with this combination of gifts. His stories are fertile sources of ideas about men, of interest to people of humanistic philosophical interests

as well as to writers and readers of science fiction, but they are deficient
in the fictional concreteness and stylish felicity which give authority to
works of imagination.

Notes

1. Preface to *The End of Time: The Best of Olaf Stapledon*, ed., Basil Davenport (New York: Funk and Wagnalls, 1953), p. 111.
2. All references to *Last and First Men* are from the Dover edition, 1968. This
   edition also contains *Star Maker*.
3. An appropriate term since the book is an "essay" in myth creation. I would
   want, however, to preserve the epic sense of "argument."
4. I will inconsistently refer to the narrator and Stapledon, who—strictly
   speaking—are not one and the same, simply because, despite my admiration for Stapledon's invention of the device of having the story narrated by
   the Eighteenth Man, I see no difference between the quality of Stapledon's intelligence and that of the narrator.
5. *Olaf Stapledon: A Reader's Guide* (West Linn, Oregon: Starmont, 1982).
   Kinnaird's monograph is the first full-length study of Stapledon's work.
6. Stapledon is known to have read J. B. S. Haldane's *Possible Worlds* (1927),
   perhaps for scientific inspiration and support for his mythical speculation.
   I am not prepared, however, to judge its scientific credibility.

6

On *Brave New World*

William Matter

In an interview with a representative from the *Paris Review*, Aldous Huxley once commented that he began *Brave New World* as a parody of H. G. Wells's *Men Like Gods*.[1] But the novel thus initiated as a simple parody was altered and broadened by the creative process until, in 1932, Huxley published his masterpiece of dystopian fiction—an incisive, satiric attack upon twentieth-century man's sometimes ingenuous trust in progress through science and mechanization. *Brave New World* warns the reader that "perfection" of the state entails absolute social stability, and social stability entails the effacement of personal freedom. The pleasantries of Obstacle Golf, scent organs, sex-hormone chewing-gum, and other mindless diversions garishly mask the loss of the individual's right to feel.

The novel is set in the distant future, specifically 632 years After Ford. As the Huxleyan chronology indicates, conventional religious worship has been replaced by the celebration of Henry Ford, whose assembly lines greatly advanced progress through mechanization. Symbolically, the top portion of the cross has been removed to form the sign of the T—in honor of Ford's Model T. This change is indicative of the high esteem Huxley satirically accords to science and the machine in his society. The reader sees many such "improvements." For example, the story begins as the Director of Hatcheries and Conditioning escorts a group of students through the Central London Hatchery. The official explains the modern processes employed to produce children. Embryos, he tells the students, are created scientifically. Women who are not freemartins (sterile) donate ova to the state. The eggs are put in expertly prepared test tubes which provide an artificial environment better than mother herself. A withdrawal is made from the sperm bank, and life begins before the watchful eyes of the supervising workers. Children are not born in this new world; they are decanted. In fact, the word "mother," as a symbol of past decadent social structures, is considered to be horribly vulgar. The family unit in

Brave New World has been dissolved because love, a dangerously powerful emotion, may threaten the security of the state. By establishing eugenic control and doing away with the family, Huxley adheres to a utopian tradition first espoused in Plato's *Republic* and followed by later utopian thinkers.

And the family in Huxley's futuristic society is indeed defunct. Viviparity has been replaced by a procedure known as "Bokanovsky's Process": "One egg, one embryo, one adult—normality. But a bokanovskified egg will bud, will proliferate, will divide. From eight to ninety-six buds, and every bud will grow into a perfectly formed embryo, and every embryo into a full-sized adult. Making ninety-six human beings grow where only one grew before. Progress."[2] Standardized humans are thereby produced in "uniform batches" (p. 6). Individuality must be repressed because it invites a malleable social structure. By providing identical physical attributes for as many as ninety-six different people, Bokanovsky's Process serves as an extremely important instrument of social stability. As in the *Republic*, which provided Huxley with a model of the authoritarian utopia, stability in A.F. 632 is frightfully important. The same techniques Ford used for the mass production of automobiles have finally been applied to people.

As soon as the developing embryo is taken from the test tube, it is subjected to a series of chemical treatments that govern its continued physical and mental development. If the product resulting from the union of science and nature is fortunate enough to be an "Alpha," his future is promising. But even if his mental and physical structure is deliberately retarded so that he will have an intellect and a physique most suitable for repetitious, menial tasks, he feels no anger toward society. Each child is subjected to several years of psychological conditioning reminiscent of Plato's "necessary lies" and Pavlov's classical conditioning experiments with dogs. An object is presented to the child and paired with disturbing noises and electrical shock. Soon the infant learns to associate his fear of strident sounds and pain with the object: "Books and loud noises, flowers and electric shocks—already in the infant mind these couples were compromisingly linked; and after two hundred repetitions of the same or a similar lesson would be wedded indissolubly. What man has joined, nature is powerless to put asunder" (p. 23). Other training sessions are devoted to making the child happy with his social position; the secret of happiness and virtue, the reader learns, is "liking what you've *got* to do. All conditioning aims at that: making people like their unescapable social destiny" (p.

17). Plato also employs a less sophisticated kind of conditioning to reconcile people to their distinct social destinies.

In *Brave New World* the principle of hypnopaedia is used for this purpose. A sleeping child is exposed to hours of whispered messages which reinforce class distinctions: "Alpha children wear grey. They work much harder than we do, because they're so frightfully clever. I'm really awfully glad I'm a Beta, because I don't work so hard. And then we are much better than the Gammas and Deltas. Gammas are stupid. They all wear green, and Delta children wear khaki. Oh no, I *don't* want to play with Delta children" (p. 31). Thus infants are decanted, in Plato's terms, with constitutions of gold, silver, brass, or iron. Opportunity for the Alpha is golden, but for the dwarfed Gamma it is iron at best. Because of Bokanovsky's Process and hypnopaedia, the physical and psychological characteristics of lower-caste children are unvexed by individual differences. Like residents in many other utopias, they are clothed in identical uniforms. People are not only stable, they are products—like electric knives and vacuum cleaners.

After the Director explains the process of decanting and conditioning to the students, one of the ten World Controllers talks to them about a usually forbidden subject—history. Before Ford, he tells them, people believed in an omnipotent being known as "God." Then Ford, or Freud as he frequently preferred to be called, developed new theories of psychology, sexual behavior, and mechanization. As his ideas were gradually adopted, the antiquated concepts of motherhood, love, family living, and monogamy were abandoned. The thought of "Home Sweet Home," in fact, has become repugnant to Huxley's society. Speaking to the students, the Controller does his best to characterize that effete idea. "'Home, home—a few rooms, stiflingly over-inhabited by a man, by a periodically teeming woman, by a rabble of boys and girls of all ages. No air, no space; an understerilized prison; darkness, disease, and smells'" (pp. 41–42). In order that the students might fully grasp the agonizing implications of "home," the official continues his description: "'And home was as squalid psychically as physically. Physically, it was a rabbit hole, a midden, hot with the frictions of tightly packed life, reeking with emotion. What suffocating intimacies, what dangerous, insane, obscene relationships between the members of the family group!'" (p. 42). The Controller's powerful condemnation of the family unit and of emotion is strictly in the tradition of Plato, Lycurgus, Tommaso Campanella, and many other utopists. In A.F. 632, as in the upper class of the *Republic*, the social danger of unrequited love is avoided because "every one belongs to every one else" (p. 46). The family unit encourages ideas of "mine" and "not mine" and breeds strong emotions. Passions, in many utopian societies, are considered dangerous to stability and therefore antagonistic to the public good. The Controller stresses this idea to the students: " 'No pains have been spared to make your lives emotionally easy—to preserve you, so far as that is possible, from having emotions at all' " (p. 51).

In continuing the discussion of emotion and the family group, the Controller indicates that even before Ford there were a few exceptions to the generally odious home life. He mentions a much more pleasant scene that took place at one time among the "uncivilized" people of Samoa, on islands off the New Guinea coast: " 'The tropical sunshine lay like warm honey on the naked bodies of children tumbling promiscuously among the hibiscus blossoms. Home was in any one of twenty palm-thatched houses' " (p. 44). The idea of multi-homes—Mutual Adoption Clubs, Huxley later calls them—reappears in an expanded form in his utopian novel, *Island*.

Many thematic points found in *Brave New World* germinate in Huxley's philosophy and appear in a positive form in his *Island*. But *Brave New World* describes what Huxley fears may be man's future. He seeks to warn his readers that "utopia" must be avoided. For example, Huxley views the theory of planned obsolescence with profound displeasure; but both children and adults in A.F. 632 are conditioned to believe that "ending is better than mending" (p. 59). The Controller does not approve any toy for distribution to the public unless it contains at least as many moving parts as the most complicated toys on the market. In that way, toys become obsolete very rapidly, and the demand for new and more complex forms of entertainment is always high. Here Huxley satirizes late nineteenth-century utopists like Edward Bellamy and Wells rather than the classical utopist who wishes to avoid luxury and material possessions. Thus it is apparent, even early in the novel, that the repetition of trite phrases from conditioning exercises, the inescapable togetherness, and the scientific "advances" are not intended by the author as goals toward which society should strive. By propounding a philosophy abhorrent to free men, Huxley shows his readers that the creative spirit—the right to think and act as individuals—must be forfeited if mankind follows his machines into utopia.

Huxley's beliefs subtend his brave new society, but he allows a few characters to experience moments of sanity even in A.F. 632. Some isolated individuals do not agree that as long as Ford is in his flivver all is well with the world. Bernard, an unusually small Alpha-Plus with eccentric habits, does not deem credible the assertion that "when the individual feels, the community reels" (p. 110). His highly typical and very "pneumatic" companion, Lenina, regards his rather unorthodox ideas as curious in the extreme. Talking about contemplating the sea alone, without the distraction of other people, Bernard confides: "'It makes me feel as though . . . I were more *me*, if you see what I mean. More on my own, not so completely a part of something else. Not just a cell in the social body. Doesn't it make you feel that, Lenina?'" (p. 106). But Bernard's blasphemies succeed only in making Lenina cry: "'It's horrible, it's horrible . . . and how can you talk like that about not wanting to be a part of the social body? After all, every one works for every one else'" (p. 106). The same spirit of working for the state while ignoring one's individuality—a spirit that pervades the atmosphere of utopias by Plato, More, Campanella, Cabet, Bellamy, Howells, Wells, and others—is patently manifest in *Brave New World*. The "normal" member of society can neither accept nor understand Bernard's desire to be more than a single cell in a large social body.

It is one thing to actively seek isolation as Bernard sometimes does, but it is quite another thing to find that a sense of alienation constantly and involuntarily invades one's happy moments. When Bernard and Lenina travel to the "Savage Reservation" in America, they encounter a peculiar young man named John who is atypical of reservation inhabitants. The Indians on the reservation are dark-skinned; but John, like the visitor to Erewhon and the unhappy primitivist in Wells's *A Modern Utopia*, is fair-skinned and blond. He is different from the Indians in another respect, too. He is the son of a Beta-Minus from the outside world. His mother somehow forgot her contraceptives and exercises and became pregnant. She was stranded on the reservation and thus forced into viviparity. John, whom the civilized world outside the reservation calls the "Savage," does not fit within the society of the reservation. He is what Colin Wilson calls an "outsider."[3] The question of death bothers John. Like the existentialist, he sees that there is only one short step between the frightening, incomprehensible life of an outsider and the eternal quiet of nonexistence.

His hopes for happiness increase, however, when Bernard promises to take him from the reservation out into the brave new world. Through his mother's glowing accounts of life in civilized society, the Savage has learned about a euphoric drug called *soma*, throw-away clothes, music from synthetic plants, decanting, and many other modern advances in technology and social theory. He has also learned about life from a volume of Shakespeare's works, and he is anxious to escape the reservation to discover how accurately Shakespeare describes the human character. But when John actually gains entry into "civilized" society, he is surprised and distressed by what he finds. There is no love as there is in Shakespeare; no one is allowed to be an individual. After seeing a large group of ugly, terrifying, identically dwarfed factory workers, John repeats Miranda's words with a very Huxleyan note of satire: "'O brave new world that has such people in it'" (p. 191). He cannot understand a society which prefers Obstacle Golf to the dignity of man.

The people of England find John intensely interesting but equally confusing and frequently laughable. Bernard, whose social status has dramatically increased due to his association with John, parades him from one party to another until isolation seems a desirable goal. The question of death again becomes important to the Savage when he learns that his mother is dying. He is troubled because death means very little in A.F. 632. Children are conditioned to it: "Every tot spends two mornings a week in a Hospital for the Dying. All the best toys are kept there, and they get chocolate cream on death days. They learn to take dying as a matter of course" (p. 195). Individuals are considered useful to the state even after death, since phosphorus recovered in the process of cremation helps plants grow. The Savage, though, reacts quite differently to the idea of death. When his mother expires in a *soma* stupor, John rebels against the new world: "He woke once more to external reality, looked round him, knew what he saw—knew it, with a sinking sense of horror and disgust, for the recurrent delirium of his days and nights, the nightmare of swarming indistinguishable sameness" (p. 250). He preaches against the evils of *soma* to a group of Deltas about to get their weekly supply: "'Don't you want to be free and men? Don't you even understand what manhood and freedom are?'" (pp. 254–55). The Savage's battle against *soma* and society is, of course, hopeless. The Deltas have been conditioned not to know what real freedom is. Reacting to this wild stranger, the befuddled men in khaki riot, and John is arrested. He is taken to the leader of the society, Mustapha Mond, who is one of the ten World Controllers. The philosophical debate between the Savage and Mond which ensues is, perhaps, the most important thematic point in *Brave New World*.

John is distressed because there is no concept of God in the new world. Mustapha Mond answers that "'God isn't compatible with machinery and scientific medicine and universal happiness. You must make your choice. Our civilization has chosen machinery and medi-cine and happiness'" (p. 281). Science has, in fact, taken Huxley's civilization to the extreme position of making unhappiness a crime against the social body. Even scientists have been forced to make concessions for the sake of stability. Referring to a contemporary attitude Huxley regards as foolish, Mond states: "'It's curious . . . to read what people in the time of Our Ford used to write about scientific progress. They seemed to have imagined that it could be allowed to go on indefinitely, regardless of everything else. Knowledge was the highest good, truth the supreme value; all the rest was secondary and subordinate'" (p. 273). Mond points out that science's good work must not be undone by unlimited research. An uncompromising devo-tion to knowledge and truth is harmful to stability. In this conversation between Mond and the Savage, Huxley condemns uncontrolled mechanization as dangerous even to the generally detestable society of *Brave New World*; he underlines the naiveté of writers who believe that science in utopia can go unchecked. Practical, controlled mecha-nization is the god of Huxley's perverse society, with Ford as the reigning deity.

The Savage does not care for talk of science and predestined happiness. He prefers the nobility and sacrifice of Shakespeare's world. He cannot accept any philosophy based upon hedonism and the social good. Life in this new world, he feels, is meaningless; there is nothing "brave" about it. To the Savage, the civilized infantility is "not expensive enough" (p. 189). John wants to feel intensely, to test the boundaries of his emotional faculties, and to live life fully. He seeks experiences involving pain and danger. The criticism of utopia which Huxley voices here is plain. The utopist generally makes every provision to be certain the inhabitants of his perfect world do not undergo disturbing emotions. Utopian writers like Plato and Cam-panella attempt to banish emotion altogether. The Savage, however, regards the experience of pain and sorrow as a valuable counterpoint to happiness. Such experiences are not possible in Mustapha Mond's world. The Controller makes this point very clear:

> "And if ever, by some unlucky chance, anything unpleasant should somehow happen, why there's always *soma* to give you a holiday from the facts. And there's always *soma* to calm your anger, to reconcile you to your enemies, to make you patient and long-suffering. In the past you could only accomplish these things by making a great effort and after years of hard moral training. Now, you swallow two or three half-gramme

tablets, and there you are. Anybody can be virtuous now. You can carry at least half your mortality about in a bottle. Christianity without tears—that's what *soma* is." (p. 285)

The Savage refutes Mond's philosophy: " 'But I don't want comfort. I want God, I want poetry, I want real danger, I want freedom, I want goodness. I want sin' " (p. 288). Denied the aspects of life which he regards most essential, John decides that he must escape from society. He retreats to a deserted lighthouse and there claims the right to rebel against society by punishing himself for his real and imagined sins. Even at the lighthouse, however, he is not safe. His odd actions draw a large crowd of curiosity seekers. John concludes that he can never find peace in this new world. One morning he is found hanging in the lighthouse with his feet revolving slowly from the north to the east and then back again—like a Hamlet who is but mad directionally.

Before his suicide John discovers that there is an enormous difference between the description of utopia and utopia in fact. He remembers the stories his mother told him about "that beautiful, beautiful Other Place, whose memory, as of a heaven, a paradise of goodness and loveliness, he still kept whole and intact, undefiled by contact with the reality of this real London, these actual civilized men and women" (p. 241). The Savage's comment underlines a central theme in *Brave New World*. While the fiction of a perfect world is interesting, one should be mindful of reaching that utopia—of the very concept of progress; for, once in the "ideal" commonwealth, the individual may find a wide disparity between his dreams and reality. Utopianism, Huxley feels, "runs the risk of becoming ruthless, of liquidating the people it happens to find inconvenient now for the sake of the people who are going, hypothetically, to be so much better and happier and more intelligent in the year 2000." [4] One should live for the present—the "here and now" Huxley calls it in *Island*—rather than aiming one's sights toward some future perfect that progress will provide. John's discovery that the Other Place must censor art, restrain individuality, do away with love, and prohibit innovation in order to maintain stability reminds him that the myth and the reality of utopia are very different indeed.

The reality of utopia, to Huxley, is "appalling." [5] In *Brave New World* he attacks the classical view of the ideal commonwealth and denounces "the horror of the Wellsian Utopia." [6] Science and mechanization are the focal points of his attack upon Wells, but it is important to note that Huxley is also reacting to a lengthy tradition in utopian thought. Campanella's *The City of the Sun* is perhaps the first work in the utopian tradition to cast the natural sciences and the idea of scientific progress in a leading role.[7] Valentin Andreae's *Christiano-polis*, too, stresses the importance of scientific progress.[8] More significant to the equation of happiness and scientific advance, though, is Francis Bacon's fragmentary *New Atlantis*. Glenn Negley and J. Max Patrick observe that "under the influence of Bacon, Gott paid some attention to scientific experimentation in his *Nova Solyma*, and Winstanley wrote what is probably his finest prose passage in praise of science. In 1660, *New Atlantis Continued* by R. H. was devoted to adulation of monarchy and glorification of the possibilities of science. Thenceforth nearly all utopias paid some attention to the importance of science in a perfected society."[9] Campanella, Andreae, and Bacon created ideal commonwealths which—with the help of science—they felt were actually capable of realization. In the cases of Campanella and Andreae, the literary utopias were related to projects attempted later in an effort to establish the earthly paradise.[10] Trust in scientific knowledge was essential in their plans to build a better world.

The industrial revolution had an enormous effect upon nineteenth-century utopias. Traditionally, luxury had been an evil to be avoided in utopia since it softens society and breeds discontent. Vast increases in man's ability to produce goods, however, promised luxury for everyone. The utopian dreams of the nineteenth-century thinker were, for the most part, very materialistically oriented. Cabet's *Voyage to Icaria* is a good example of the utopia heavily imbued with industrial progress, invention, and materialism. The importance of science is also demonstrated by the wonders of "vril" in Edward Bulwer-Lytton's underground utopia, *The Coming Race*. And of course Bellamy expresses almost unbounded enthusiasm for industrialization in *Looking Backward*.

Certainly not all nineteenth-century utopias stressed industrialization. One noteworthy exception is William Morris's *News from Nowhere*, which uses the agricultural community as the basis for future society. Still, there is a natural progression from Bacon's *New Atlantis* through the age of industrialization to the work that most directly influenced Huxley, Wells's *A Modern Utopia*. While this work is a significant consideration of and addition to the utopian tradition, it has been most influential, perhaps, because writers like Eugene Zamiatin, Huxley, and Orwell view such a utopia as a distasteful extension of a tradition too heavily laden with authoritarian principles and unrealistic trust in the perfectability of mankind. That trust is clearly expressed by the central character in Wells's utopia: "The plain message physical science has for the world at large is this, that were our political and social and moral devices only as well contrived to their ends as a linotype machine, an antiseptic operating plant, or an electric tram-car, there need now at the present moment be no appreciable toil in the world, and only the smallest fraction of the pain, the fear, and the anxiety that now makes human life so doubtful in its value."[11]

Science and mechanization are the focal points of Huxley's disagreement with Wells, but the ideas of necessary stability, unity, and totalitarian rule come from traditions established by the *Republic*. The social conventions and controlling regulations in *Brave New World* are as fixed and immovable as those in Plato's work. The means used to achieve this sense of stability are also frequently similar. The eugenic techniques in A.F. 632 are far in advance of the improvements practiced by the guardians, but in both *Brave New World* and the *Republic* the rulers see a need for genetic control. Both works incorporate "necessary lies" as a means of controlling the individual and therefore increasing the stability of society. Both works banish strong passions as dangerous and keep the true artist from expressing himself in public. As the Savage notes, the silly, sensual dramas of the "feelies" do not approach *Othello* in artistic merit. The World Controllers, like Plato's guardians, insist that what is "good" for society is not necessarily good art. Plato and Huxley's Controllers diverge most noticeably on the question of money and luxury. Plato will have neither in his Republic, while mechanization and science demand that Mustapha Mond have both.

Huxley's society is close to those of Wells and Bellamy in the insistence upon luxury and pleasure. In Bellamy's *Looking Backward*, the individual may find any number of delightful diversions on which he can spend his credit. Wells's modern utopia, too, is full of wonderful luxuries derived from science. Huxley's happy people can while away the idle hours—and much of their time is idle—with Centrifugal Bumble-puppy, Musical Bridge, or the feelies.

While *Brave New World* contains frequent satiric references to gifts from science which enhance man's intellectual vacuity (scent organs, *soma*, Obstacle Golf, etc.), there is very little science-fiction gadgetry in the novel. Huxley explains this omission in the foreword to the 1946 edition: "The theme of *Brave New World* is not the advancement of science as such; it is the advancement of science as it affects human individuals. The triumphs of physics, chemistry and engineering are tacitly taken for granted. The only scientific advances to be specifically described are those involving the application to human beings of the results of future research in biology, physiology, and psychology" (pp. ix–x). Clearly, Huxley's biological innovations, considering recent discussions of cloning and genetic engineering with test tube babies, are reasonably close at hand. While modern science fiction tends to favor bionics to eugenics, the physiological and psychological conditioning procedures which prescribe social happiness in A.F. 632 are increasingly possible.

Another popular element of science fiction found in *Brave New World* is the Wellsian world war. Often, Wells requires that a battle between science and the old order take place before utopia can be established. Huxley does not believe that war is the way to utopia. His interest in pacifism would never allow him to entertain such a consideration seriously. He satirizes Wells's concept in *Brave New World* and more completely in *Ape and Essence*. In the former work an official's callous description of the Nine Years' War sardonically implies a criticism of Wells's attitude toward war. The reader learns that "the explosion of the anthrax bombs is hardly louder than the popping of a paper bag" (p. 56). Other devices of war result in "an enormous hole in the ground, a pile of masonry, some bits of flesh and mucus, a foot, with the boot still on it, flying through the air and landing, flop, in the middle of the geraniums—the scarlet ones; such a splendid show that summer!" (p. 56). The dreadful utopia of A.F. 632, one discovers, came about as a result of a war, and the destruction of that war is described with the same unfeeling disregard for human life that accompanies the candy doled out on death days.

Huxley may have also borrowed the idea of a blond savage from *A Modern Utopia*. In Wells's novel the savage is an unhinged dissenter, but Huxley regards him as a spokesman for the lost nobilities of society. He shows the reader what must happen when the Noble Savage reaches utopia. The Indians on the Savage Reservation are as primitive as Montaigne's cannibals, but they are much less happy. They have lice in their hair and sometimes disagreeable temperaments. The Savage Reservation is, in many respects, "hardly less queer and abnormal" than the world outside of its boundaries (p. viii). For example, Linda's sojourn into primitivism does not leave her unscarred. John's mother was once an attractive woman; but life on the reservation, away from synthetic society, turns her into an odious caricature of the woman she once was. Her wrinkles, blood blisters, and broken teeth serve as an unspoken testimony to the rigors of primitive life. Huxley's vivid description of Linda's "sensual" stride ably projects her unfortunate appearance: "Linda advanced into the room, coquettishly smiling her broken and discoloured smile, and rolling as she walked, with what was meant to be a voluptuous undulation, her enormous haunches" (pp. 178–79). The primitivist's utopia is obviously not Huxley's alternative to the brave new society.

Huxley describes another concept of utopia that is best reflected, perhaps, in Morris's *News from Nowhere*. The essentially ruler-less agricultural and industrial community made up of superior men and women is not, according to the results of the Cyprus experiment, a realistic picture of utopia. When the Savage insists that all people should be Alphas, Mustapha Mond cites an experiment conducted in A.F. 473:

> "The Controllers had the island of Cyprus cleared of all its existing inhabitants and re-colonized with a specially prepared batch of twenty-two thousand Alphas. All agricultural and industrial equipment was handed over to them and they were left to manage their own affairs. The result exactly fulfilled all the theoretical predictions. The land wasn't properly worked; there were strikes in all the factories; the laws were set at naught, orders disobeyed; all the people detailed for a spell of low-grade work were perpetually intriguing for high-grade jobs, and all the people with high-grade jobs were counter-intriguing at all costs to stay where they were. Within six years they were having a first-class civil war. When nineteen out of the twenty-two thousand had been killed, the survivors unanimously petitioned the World Controllers to resume the government of the island. Which they did. And that was the end of the only society of Alphas that the world has ever seen." (Pp. 267–68)

According to Mond, stability is essential to a happy society. There could be no stability on Cyprus because there was no social hierarchy; there were no men with hearts of gold, silver, brass, or iron. Without Gamma-Minus machine minders, the community reels.

Another important aspect of social stability in Huxley's world is the absence of history and the vacuity of language. Long ago the World Controllers decided that society must cut itself off from its depressing past when motherhood was in flower. One of the most inspired phrases of Ford is that "history is bunk." The great writers and historians of the old world concerned themselves with man's struggles, his cravings, his failures, and his successes. Such emotions would shake the foundations of the new society. In a like manner, emotive language would injure the social cell. The World Controllers appear to agree with Whorf's theory of linguistic relativity, which suggests that people who have no words to express antisocial sentiments cannot think antisocially.[12] John does not learn to hate Popé until Shakespeare gives him the necessary words. Helmholtz feels that he has the power to write good literature if he only had the words. He states: "'I'm thinking of a queer feeling I sometimes get, a feeling that I've got something important to say and the power to say it—only I don't know what it is, and I can't make any use of the power. If there was some different way of writing . . . '" (p. 82). When Lenina desires to express an uncommonly powerful emotion, she recites the most passionate lines at her command, thereby voicing the poetry of a linguistically deprived language: "'Hug me till you drug me, honey . . . kiss me till I'm in a coma'" (p. 231). The frequent repetition of infantile clichés contrasts very sharply with the language of Shakespeare which John often recites. The people of Huxley's society cannot understand John's strange words; they have no historical, social, or linguistic base that relates to such language. As Jerome Meckier observes, in *Brave New World Revisited*, Huxley "insists on the precise use of language as a safeguard against societies such as that of *Brave New World*."[13]

Huxley's interest in language is also reflected by the naming games he plays—games which remind the reader of similar linguistic witticisms in More's *Utopia* and Samuel Butler's *Erewhon*. Hints of socialist and communist philosophers appear in the names of Polly Trotsky, Sarojini Engels, and Bernard Marx; the name "Lenina" bears a close resemblance to "Lenin." A decorative container for contraceptives in *Brave New World* is called a "Malthusian Belt."[14] One of the leading newspapers is *The Fordian Science Monitor*. Even the grand old clock in London is "Big Henry." The concept of the burning cross has become the "Charing T," and the reader may cringe a bit when he discovers that a great northern hotel is called the "Aurora Bora Palace."

These naming games are indicative of the debt Huxley owes to the utopian tradition, but some critics have suggested that he also owes a great deal to Zamiatin's *We*. Huxley, though, denied having read *We*. There is no evidence, other than perhaps coincidental similarities between the two novels, to indicate Huxley borrowed from Zamiatin. Instead, the central source of inspiration for *Brave New World* was almost certainly Wells and Plato in particular and Huxley's awareness of utopianism in general. Negative echoes of Plato and Wells do reverberate throughout the novel. Other utopists fare little better. Bellamy's naive trust is dealt with harshly in the condemnation of the scientific utopia. The primitivistic utopia suggested by D. H. Lawrence and earlier writers also proves less than ideal. Huxley shows the reader what he believes a modern utopia based upon the classical tradition and science would be like in fact. It is a world of enormous regimentation—loveless, caring not for the individual. Such a world, he insists, deprives man of his creative spirit, his right to live fully, and even his basic humanity.

Brave New World was the first widely-read dystopia in English. Accordingly, its influence has been enormous. The frequency with which it has been translated and reprinted testifies to its continuing popularity. And its picture of the future remains frighteningly believable. The Rand Corporation has produced a study which predicts that genetic manipulation of humans will occur in approximately A.D. 2000, and chemical control of aging in 2020.[15] To be sure, there are earlier works which seek to remind the reader of the dangers of utopia. *The Ecclesiazusae*, by Aristophanes, is at least as old as the *Republic*.[16] Zamiatin's *We*, too, predates Huxley's work and contains a number of parallel ideas. But *Brave New World* has remained one of the most popular and influential symbols of man's right to feel. Each time one encounters the attitude in science fiction that scientific progress will create a society of men like gods, or watches the Six Million Dollar Man flex his bionic arm, one is reminded of Huxley's warning that too soon even man's mind may be controlled by diodes and computer chips. In this event man will be the victim of a science which "takes away with one hand even more than what it so profusely gives with the other."[17]

Fortunately for Huxley and his readers, he did not dwell forever in the nebulous land of negations. After producing a second dystopian work, *Ape and Essence* in 1948, he published a traditionally utopian work, *Island*, in 1962. In fact, when Huxley's home in California burned, he made his way through the flames to rescue from his library one work: the manuscript of *Island*. Apparently he felt that his positive contribution to utopian studies was worth the risk of his life. Sadly, critics have not always shared that opinion. *Island* is much more serious than *Brave New World* and considerably less vibrant. The satire of Western man's emphasis upon science is as pointed as it is in *Brave New World*, but there is a pervasive undertone of didacticism and Vedantic philosophy that makes the work occasionally tedious reading. Still, as an indication of the progression of Huxley's utopian mentality, *Island* is an important addition to the genre.

Some scientific advances from *Brave New World* reappear in a positive form in *Island*. For example, both works made use of a sperm bank. The Palanese people feel, as does Huxley apparently, that "it's more moral to take a shot at having a child of superior quality than to run the risk of slavishly reproducing whatever quirks and defects may happen to run in the husband's family."[18] Artificial insemination is regarded on the island as a viable alternative to conventional conception. Children on Pala, like those in *Brave New World*, are conditioned; but on Pala the conditioning is directed toward "friendliness and trust and compassion."[19] Sex on Pala is nearly as uninhibited as the emotionless unions in *Brave New World*, but on Pala love and tenderness are emphasized instead of repressed. *Soma* is a drug which provides an escape from having to feel, but in *Island* a similar drug is used in religious ceremonies to reveal reality.

Thus the reader sees that Huxley believes the perversion between science and man is reciprocal. Science applied in a limited, judicious manner may actually prove beneficial. But the note of optimism in *Island* is less than compelling. The novel ends with the destruction of Pala by the Essential Horror of the world outside. Even in *Island*, then, Huxley resolves the conflict between sanity and insanity in favor of the forces attacking right thinking and right action. The countless bedlams sheltered in the dark recesses of the human mind, Huxley fears, must overpower man's capacity for intelligence.

Notes

1. *Writers at Work: The "Paris Review" Interviews*, intro. Van Wyck Books, 2d series (New York: Viking, 1963), p. 198.
2. *Brave New World* (1932; rpt. New York: Harper and Row, 1946), p. 5. Textual references to this edition are indicated parenthetically.
3. For a detailed description of the plight of the isolated man, see Colin Wilson's *The Outsider* (New York: Delta, 1967).
4. From a letter to Julian Huxley in *Letters of Aldous Huxley*, ed. Grover Smith (New York: Harper and Row, 1969), p. 483.
5. From a letter to Huxley's father, ibid., p. 351.
6. From a letter to Mrs. Kethevan Roberts, ibid., p. 348.
7. The justification for placing Campanella before Andreae is that while Andreae's work was published first (1619), Campanella's *The City of the Sun* was known in manuscript from 1602 until its publication in 1623.
8. Through Andreae's *Christianopolis* is important as a utopian work, its influence upon English utopian thought is argued against by the fact that it was not translated into English until 1916. It stands, instead, as a cornerstone in the increasing tendency to equate scientific progress with human happiness.
9. Glenn R. Negley and J. Max Patrick, eds., *The Quest for Utopia: An*

Anthology of Imaginary Societies (New York: Henry Schuman, 1952), p. 292.

10. For a discussion of this point see Nell Eurich, *Science in Utopia: A Mighty Design* (Cambridge, Mass.: Harvard Univ. Pr., 1967), pp. 141–44.

11. *A Modern Utopia*, intro. Mark R. Hillegas (1905; rpt. Lincoln: Univ. of Nebraska Pr., 1967), p. 102.

12. See Benjamin Lee Whorf, "Science and Linguistics," in *Language, Thought, and Reality: Selected Writings of Benjamin Lee Whorf*, ed. John B. Carroll (Cambridge, Mass.: MIT Pr., 1956), p. 212.

13. *Aldous Huxley: Satire and Structure* (London: Chatto and Windus, 1969), p. 183.

14. The reference, of course, is to Thomas Malthus (1766–1834), who felt that increases in population must be checked in order to maintain adequate food supplies.

15. As reported in Maxwell H. Norman's *Dimensions of the Future: Alternatives for Tomorrow* (New York: Holt, 1974), p. v.

16. There are at least three commonly held theories that seek to explain the relationship between the *Republic* and the *Ecclesiazusae*. Some critics insist that the *Ecclesiazusae* antedates the *Republic* and thus concerns itself with concepts popular in the oral tradition at the time of its writing. Other critics believe that Aristophanes heard about or possibly even read several books of the *Republic* and therefore had that work in mind. Moses Hadas, in his "Utopian Sources in Herodotus," *Classical Philology* 30 (Apr. 1935): 113–21, feels that both Plato and Aristophanes drew from some source known to Herodotus but no longer extant.

17. Aldous Huxley, *Ape and Essence* (New York: Harper and Brothers, 1948), p. 52.

18. *Island* (New York: Harper and Row, 1962), p. 220.

19. *Island*, p. 222.

7

The Shape of Things to Come:
H. G. Wells and the Rhetoric of Proteus

Ken Davis

Herbert George Wells did not write a utopia; he lived one. His life was fired by an apocalyptic vision of a better world, but this vision was not fully realized in any single work. Rather, Wells's every word and action—literary, political, personal—seems part of a consistent whole. We might say of Wells what Keats said of Shakespeare: that he "led a life of Allegory: his works are the comments on it."

Yet to grasp the central place of Wells in the development of utopian and dystopian fiction, we must narrow our focus, and we can do no better than to narrow it to the 1933 book *The Shape of Things to Come*, and the 1935 "film story," *Things to Come*, based upon it. The former is perhaps the fullest realization, in a single volume, of Wells's utopian vision, while the latter demonstrates the ultimate failure of that vision. Together they embody a rhetorical use of literature as a means for achieving "Protean" change in humanity—a vision which transcends the "Promethean" stance for which Wells is too often condemned.

The Early Wells

To understand this vision, we must begin by taking a time machine to 1866 and the London suburb of Bromley. H. G. was born there to Sarah Wells, an innkeeper's daughter with more than usual schooling, and Joseph, a china-shop proprietor and semi-professional cricketer. The latter enterprise, however, was too often conducted at the expense of the former, and the resulting poverty, combined with the general squalor of the town and the times, drove Sarah to bitterness and religious dogmatism and Joseph to anger, despair, and resignation. For H. G., childhood was thus a time of cruelty and conflict, bringing insecurities and even nightmares. His biographers, Norman and Jean MacKenzie, write that "some of his earliest memories were of terrifying dreams, the raw material from which he later spun his stories. . . . The idea of Nature as a force of mindless cruelty was to appear over and over again in his writings."[1]

When H. G. was fourteen, his mother finally left Joseph, and Bromley, to become housekeeper at Up Park, the country estate where she had worked as a maid before her marriage. When H. G. joined her there soon after, he discovered a whole new world of grace and gentility and order, a world very unlike the world of Bromley. The MacKenzies note that "in later and prosperous years [H. G.] lived as though he were the heir to the Up Park tradition, combining the intellectual interests of the Enlightenment with the morals of the Regency. . . . The great estates, ruled by order and owned by enlightened guardians of scientific intelligence, provided him with the pattern for his utopian societies and the cultivated élites which were to control them" (p. 38).

These conflicting strains in Wells's worldview—his awareness of life's potentials for cruelty and for civility—found an intellectual base four years later when, at eighteen, he was awarded a scholarship at the Normal School of Science. Its dean was T. H. Huxley, the most renowned disciple of Charles Darwin. The one course he took from Huxley made a profound impact on Wells and provided the paradigm for his entire personal, political, and literary life. To Huxley, like Darwin, humanity was the product not of God's will, but of natural law, working through the trial-and-error of genetic variation and selection. Yet while others viewed humanity as the noblest result of this process, Huxley dwelt on our animal origins, from which he saw us not far removed. We are more intelligent than our animal forebears, said Huxley, but not wiser, nor less prone to base instinct and cruelty. For H. G. Wells, Bromley now had an explanation.

But Huxley went beyond nihilism. Humanity, he said, while evolving a mind, had also evolved a conscience, an ethical sense that separates us qualitatively from the other animals. If we can further develop this capacity for good, said Huxley, we may just be able to transcend our animal origins, and replace biological evolution with social evolution. And so the young Wells had found a coherent rationale for both Bromley and Up Park—a scientific gospel that included new versions of both original sin and salvation.

The decade following the encounter with Huxley saw Wells teaching, flirting with politics, marrying, and, most important for us, beginning the series of novels that were to transform popular literature. Starting with *The Time Machine* in 1895, and continuing through *The Island of Dr. Moreau, The Invisible Man, The War of the Worlds, The First Men on the Moon, When the Sleeper Wakes, The Food of the Gods, In the Days of the Comet*, and *The War in the Air*, Wells gives the wildest scientific imaginings "a local habitation and a name," and so sets the tone for all subsequent science fiction. From the first page of *The Time Machine*—when the Traveller explains the operation of his device—Wells makes his speculative premises so easy to accept that we are quickly caught up in their social consequences. As Robert Scholes and Eric S. Rabkin write:

> The great strength of Wells as a writer of science fiction, and his great contribution to the tradition, lay in his ability to combine the fantastic with the plausible, the strange with the familiar, the new with the old. We can see this at every level of his work, from the word and the sentence to the largest structural concepts. If he wishes to show us a fantastic scene, he will present it from the viewpoint of the most matter-of-fact person conceivable. If he wishes to describe an unearthly thing, he will find the most concrete and specific language for it. His Martians will invade an England that is utterly commonplace and believable.[2]

But aside from their remarkable sense of plausibility, what most marks these early "scientific romances" is their pervasive pessimism, much of it straight from Huxley's dismal view of human evolution. The Traveller in *The Time Machine* reaches a future in which first man, then the universe itself, fall victim to inevitable entropy. *The Island of Dr. Moreau* is inhabited by the suffering products of misguided evolution, and *The Invisible Man* embodies the effect of science without conscience. In *The War of the Worlds*, most familiar to Americans through Orson Welles's radio play, Wells gives us a vision of humanity's destruction by a superior species in a clear working-out of Darwinian natural selection. And so it goes. In Wells's early works, his role is, in Jack Williamson's words, a "critic of progress." The cruelty of Bromley has won out over the civilization of Up Park.

The Shape of Things to Come

But H. G. Wells had a second, then a third, career. As he continued his series of "scientific romances," he moved also into a string of almost Dickensian novels of social criticism, including *Kipps* and *Tono-Bungay*. But meanwhile, he had written *Anticipations*, the first of an important series of utopias that was to reach its pinnacle in *The Shape of Things to Come*.

In these later works, Wells did not entirely abandon the evolutionary pessimism that permeated the early novels. But he began more and more to emphasize the other half of Huxley's message: that the conscious, deliberate evolution of humanity's intellectual and moral capacity could come to replace the blind warfare of natural selection. And he came more and more to see a vital role for literature, and for himself, in that mission—a rhetorical role of providing both warnings of what *might* be and promises of what *could* be. The MacKenzies summarize: "Men can learn to will the good life, Wells was saying, but this can happen only if inspiring examples of the shape of things to come . . . are set before them to emulate. Each generation in its turn will produce new dreams, 'until at last from dreams Utopias will have come to be working drawings'" (p. 189).

The introduction to *The Shape of Things to Come* presents a Dr. Philip Raven, diplomat, political theorist, and official in the League of Nations Secretariat. Before his death in 1930, Wells reports, Raven had approached Wells with an incredible story: over the past several years he had been reading a book in his dreams, always the same book, an account of world history into the twenty-second century. On waking each morning, Raven would record in shorthand his night's "reading," and it was these notes that he proposed to give to Wells, for possible anonymous publication. Now with Raven's death, Wells tells us, he sees no need for anonymity or further delay. This conceit aside, we move into the first of five books that comprise *The Shape of Things to Come*, a history of the world written from the perspective of A.D. 2106.

Book the First covers the period from 1914 to 1933 (the book's publication date); these years mark the beginning of "The Age of Frustration" (see chronology). Wells reviews the desolation of the Great War, the breakdown of the world economic system, and the emergence, chiefly in the League of Nations, of the idea of a world state. Wells's view of these phenomena is chiefly Socialist, though the most vivid episode in this first book is a rather sympathetic and poignant account of Henry Ford's "peace ship" mission. Book the First closes with a view of 1933 as a time of futility, economic stagnation, and impending war.

As we read Book the Second from our present vantage point, we encounter not an alternative future but an alternative past, a marvelously reconstructed version of recent history like those in Michael Moorcock's *Warlord of the Air* and Kingsley Amis's *The Alteration*. In this section, Wells recounts the years from 1933 to 1960, beginning with an abortive 1933 World Economic Conference in London; the chief American delegate to this conference was "Roosevelt II." "He leaves a less vivid impression than his predecessor," the account states, "because he did not impend for so long on the European scene."[3]

In the years following the London Conference, totalitarian governments continue to grow in Germany, Italy, and Russia; public education and established religion break down worldwide; and organized crime achieves a stranglehold on the United States. An arms race to produce ever more effective lethal gasses increases international tension until finally, in 1935, Japan invades China. The war is long and devastating, and in 1937 the United States enters it, going against the Japanese navy in the Pacific.

Chronology of *The Shape of Things to Come*

(334 B.C.–ca. A.D. 636	Helleno-Latin Era.)
(Ca. 636–1571	Era of Asiatic Predominance.)
(1571–1914	Era of European Predominance, or Era of National Sovereignty.)
1914–?	Era of the Modern State.
1914	The Great War; Age of Frustration begins.
1933	"'Progress' comes to a halt."
1935	Sino-Japanese war begins; U.S. enters in 1937.
1940	European war begins; lasts until 1950.
1955	Epidemic kills half of world's population.
1965	First Conference at Basra; Air and Sea Control established.
1978	Second Conference at Basra; World-State established; First World Council elected.
CA. 2000	Emergence of Second World Council, also known as Air Dictatorship and Puritan Tyranny; resistance to World-State grows.
2059	Declaration of Mégève; Age of Frustration ends; World-State declared obsolete.
2106	*The Shape of Things to Come* "written."

Meanwhile Hitler's power and ambitions are growing and some thirty-thousand people are killed or injured in Germany between 1932 and 1936. By 1940 Europe finds itself in full-scale war, arising out of a ludicrous incident between a Polish Jew and a young Nazi in Danzig. By 1949, Europe is in ruins, and Britain and America, while managing to remain noncombatants, are bankrupt and strife-torn. But the final blow (in true Huxleyan, and Wellsian, fashion) is Nature's: in 1955 and 1956 a previously unknown disease sweeps the world, leaving its victims wandering mindlessly, like zombies, until they die or are shot by their terrified neighbors. By 1960, half the population of the world has been destroyed, and the survivors have sunk into a new Dark Age, with little organization above the tribal level.

Book the Third continues, for us, the "alternative past," as it moves from 1960 through 1978. Titled "The World Renascence: The Birth of the Modern State," this section focuses on an emerging elite of "men of the vigorous practical type," mostly scientists, engineers, aviators, and businessmen. These "technical revolutionaries" gather at Basra (in Iraq) to establish the Air and Sea Control, a worldwide police and communications network. The tone of this conference, as Wells paints it, is jaunty and hopeful; its delegates share the sense of having, in Tom Wolfe's words, "the right stuff." In one of the few bits of dialogue in the entire work, Wells shows us a confrontation involving a Russian commissar, Peshkoff, a delegate to the Basra Conference. Peshkoff had just denounced the proposed Air and Sea Control as " 'an insidious attempt to restore a capitalist trust in the world.' "

"And how will Moscow prevent it?" asked Ivan Englehart, a Russian aviator and aeroplane builder, rising as Peshkoff sat down. . . .
    By way of reply Peshkoff leant towards him and spat out in Russian, "Wait until you return to Moscow."
    "I may have to wait a little time," said Englehart. "I am a citizen of the world, and I shall go back to Russia in my own time and in my own fashion."
    "This is treason. Wait until Moscow hears of this!"
    "And how and when will Moscow hear of this?"
    "Very soon."
    Englehart was standing a few yards from Peshkoff. He shook his head with a sceptical smile. He spoke gently, like a man who had long prepared himself for such an occasion.
    "You flew here, Tavarish Peshkoff, in my squadron. How do you propose to return?"
    Peshkoff rose to his feet, realized the blank want of sympathy in the gathering, spluttered and sat down again in unconcealed dismay. (P. 280)

The passage of course, looks back to Wells's early novels in its human touch and forward to the screenplay in its portrayal of the visually dramatic moment.

The 1965 Basra Conference also establishes, at least in principle, a new economic system for the world. The system retains the use of money as a convenient medium for distribution of goods, but bases this money not on precious metals or government credit, but on air freight, with a dollar defined as "good for so many kilograms in so much space, for so many kilometres at such a pace." But except for money and immediate personal belongings, individually owned property is abolished; all land, natural resources, and means of production are considered to "belong inalienably to the world commonweal" (p. 281).

Throughout the next decade, the Air and Sea Control expands its influence and achieves a virtual monopoly over all commerce, and much production, in the world. But it begins to encounter predictable opposition, partly from the earth's remaining capitalists and partly from those who see the Control as a threat to individual freedom; to meet this opposition, the Control employs its Modern State Faculty of Social Psychology, a cadre of social engineers who remind us of their *Walden Two* successors.

In 1978, a second Conference is held at Basra, but its participants are generally older, more parochial, and less imbued with "the right stuff" than their 1965 counterparts. As a result, the Air and Sea Control loses some of its *ad hoc* quality, and becomes rigidified into a global government, headed by a World Council. This Council begins to establish a far-flung bureaucracy, and soon khaki uniforms with winged-disc insignia are ubiquitous.

Book the Fourth carries the history forward from 1978 to 2059. As the account opens, the World Council, as part of its Life Time Plan of re-education, is closing religious centers throughout the world: "An Act of Uniformity came into operation everywhere. There was now to be one faith only in the world, the moral expression of the one world community" (pp. 332–33).

Resistance to this Uniformity grows, and with it grows repression. Around 2000, a new Council, also called the Air Dictatorship and, later, the Puritan Tyranny, assumes control of the World-State. Bureaucratic rigidity increases, and popular taste becomes simpler and more austere. At the same time, technology flourishes: old diseases vanish, and the Sahara blooms.

In the midst of this account, one individual personality emerges: the artist Ariston Theotocopulos. Through excerpts from his notebooks, we learn of his resistance to the ordered World-State and his presence at the Mégève Conference of 2059. Wells is indistinct on the details of this Conference, but apparently those who attend it come to the almost mystical realization that the need for the Puritan Tyranny—indeed for any government at all—is over. Like the mythical Marxist State, the World Council simply withers away.

Book the Fifth presents, at last, Wells's version of utopia. In the years after 2059, humanity lives peacefully and happily, in harmony with the earth and with each other. Much of the planet is returned to the animals and plants, and the atmosphere is cleansed. Technology continues to develop, but with great voluntary restraint. Social and sexual prohibitions and inhibitions are removed. Population growth is moderated—again, voluntarily. In language, the Puritan Tyranny's trend toward stripped-down Basic English is reversed, and literature flourishes. Wells's historian summarizes: "Man becomes more curious, more excited, more daring, skilful, and pleasantly occupied every year. The more we learn of the possibilities of our world and the possibilities of ourselves, the richer, we learn, is our inheritance. This planet, which seemed so stern a mother to mankind, is discovered to be inexhaustible in its bounty" (p. 425).

The Shape of Things to Come has thus far exemplified what Patricia Garlan and Maryjane Dunstan label "Promethean" forecasting.[4] Promethean futurists, they say, are "characterized by a faith in science, technology, logic, prediction, and control. People who hold this world view believe that by controlling the environment in which we live, one can direct the way persons behave" (p. 29). For Garlan and Dunstan, Six Prometheans include, as we might expect, B. F. Skinner and Buckminster Fuller, and the work of Wells's World Council anticipates the visions of both these later prophets. But Prometheans can also give their visions a much more human scale, and Wells's world, after the Declaration of Mégève, seems much more in accord with the "appropriate" technology of E. F. Schumacher's *Small is Beautiful* and *The Whole Earth Catalog*.

In the closing pages of *The Shape of Things to Come*, however, Wells transcends even this softer Prometheanism to achieve what Garlan and Dunstan call a "Protean" view of the world. "The Protean futurists," they write, "are those who believe in the changeability of all life forms, including the human. They tend to deny the 'real' existence of the separate enduring self, affirming rather a continual transformation through a merging with the environment. The emphasis is on personal transformation and on personal freedom from the dictates of past experience—whether of history, tradition, culture, or even biology" (p. 33).

Wells's remarkable conclusion to his book clearly reflects this worldview. He sees the post-Mégève years of his history as the beginning of a true biological transformation of our species into something beyond. That something is still unknown even to Wells's historian, but its emerging features can be discerned: humanity is becoming a "single organism" and each individual member of that organism is "an exploring tentacle thrust out to test and learn, to savor life in its fullness and bring in new experiences for the common stock." Wells continues:

> We are all members of one body. Only in the dimmest analogy has anything of this sort happened in the universe as we know it before. . . . As the slower processes of heredity seize upon and confirm these social adaptations, as the confluence of wills supersedes individual motives and loses its present factors of artificiality, the history of life will pass into a new phase, a phase with a common consciousness and a common will. We in our time are still rising towards the crest of that transition. And when that crest is attained what grandeur of life may not open out to Man! (Pp. 429–30)

This conclusion reminds us of the endings of such other Protean works as *Childhood's End* and *2001: A Space Odyssey*. But it resembles more clearly the mystical evolutionary visions of Sir Julian Huxley and Pierre Teilhard de Chardin, with Wells's New Man as Teilhard's "Omega." We should not be surprised, of course, by the resemblance to Julian Huxley; Wells played an almost fatherly role in Huxley's early development, serving as an important link between T. H. Huxley and his grandson. Julian was later to describe humanity as "evolution become aware of itself"; Wells, like Julian, carries T. H. Huxley's pessimistic view of evolution to a next glorious step.

Things to Come

In 1934, the Hungarian producer Alexander Korda approached Wells with the idea of turning *The Shape of Things to Come* into a film. Wells found the prospect appealing: for a number of years, as we have seen, Wells had regarded his role as rhetorical—persuading humanity to reform itself—and motion pictures offered the promise of reaching a far wider audience. This promise must have been especially welcome since Wells's utopian novels had never become as popular as his early "scientific romances."

So Wells began work on a screenplay and Korda began mustering the financial and human resources to produce the film. Both processes were impeded by conflicts; John Baxter, in *Science Fiction in the Cinema*,[5] and the MacKenzies, in their biography, provide the details. But two years and several drafts later, the film, titled *Things to Come*, was released. A late draft of the screenplay—although not a final one—was published in 1935; it has been reprinted, with new apparatus, in the Gregg Press Science Fiction Series (Boston, 1975).

In converting *The Shape of Things to Come* into a screenplay, Wells was faced with two main problems. The first was the almost complete absence of *characters* in the book; except for a few pages of "close-ups" (like the dialogue between the two Russian delegates at Basra, quoted above) the book takes an exceedingly wide view of its subject, characterizing classes, nations, and philosophies rather than individuals. Wells, therefore, created over twenty totally new characters for the film, retaining only one (the artist Theotocopulos) from the book.

Wells's second problem was the great time period covered by the novel; its events cover nearly two centuries. Wells, like other playwrights from the Greeks onward, solved this problem of "unity of time" by focusing on a small number of short time periods and covering the intervening years with exposition and flashback. Specifically, the screenplay is set in two time periods, each with its own generation of characters; the second-generation characters are either actual or symbolic great-grandchildren of the first. (In the film, the same actors play both first-generation characters and their descendents.) The first period includes the years from 1936 through 1970, with most of its action occupying a few weeks in the latter year; the second part of the published screenplay is set in 2054, although in the filmed version the year is changed to 2036, the centennial of the picture's release.

The central character of the first part of *Things to Come* is John Cabal, an aeronautical engineer and pilot. During the course of a pair of Christmas scenes set at Cabal's home in "Everytown," we see the coming and outbreak of the "Second World War" and meet Cabal and his friend, but philosophical adversary, "Pippa" Passworthy. Passworthy, as his name rather clumsily suggests, is the naive idealist, first denying the possibility of war, then embracing it with jingoistic fervor. Cabal (played in the film by Raymond Massey) is the practical realist, dreading war for its destruction but stoically accepting his duty. In one of the screenplay's best scenes, we see a dogfight between Cabal and a young enemy pilot, and their subsequent poignant conversation beside the wreckage of the dying boy's plane.

In newsreel-style transition scenes, we see the war continue for thirty years. We then return to a devastated Everytown for a look at the "wandering sickness," the 1955 epidemic from the book, here moved a decade later and presented not as a natural disaster but as an application of biological warfare. Finally we settle in 1970 for the remainder of the film's first part. Everytown is in ruins, a feudal city-state under the control of a gangster-warlord known only as Boss Rudolf.

After several scenes establishing the character of the Boss and several other Everytown residents, we hear the approach of an aircraft, apparently the first one seen in many years. It lands and we discover that its pilot is an older John Cabal, a participant in the Basra Conference and now a kind of roving ambassador for the Air and Sea Directorate, here called "Wings over the World." When the Boss rejects Cabal's offer of peaceful aid and imprisons him, Cabal escapes, returns to Basra, and orders in an airstrike on Everytown, using not bombs but the "Gas of Peace", a nonlethal general anesthetic. Everytown is taken; Wings over the World has brought yet another part of the globe under its benevolent control.

The following sequence of vignettes links the two major parts of the film. Edited to synchronize with a specially composed musical interlude by Sir Arthur Bliss, these scenes show the rebuilding and eventual transformation of technological society. Wells orders a "monstrous changeover" to accompany scenes of "giant cranes" and "the clearing up of old buildings and ruins." Then the music assumes "a smoother rhythm as efficiency prevails over stress." "The lines of the new subterranean city of Everytown begin to appear, bold and colossal."[6] A quick scene introduces the rebel artist Theotocopulos, who proclaims "'I don't like these mechanial triumphs'"; then a second transition device, an old man giving his great-granddaughter a history lesson, provides exposition and introduces the world of A.D. 2054.

The central character of this second part of the screenplay is Oswald Cabal, John's great-grandson and president of the World Council. He, too, has a friend and nemesis: Raymond Passworthy, great-grandson of "Pippa." Their present confrontation concerns their children, Cabal's daughter Catherine and Passworthy's son Maurice, who have fallen in love and have volunteered to be the first passengers on a projectile fired to the moon from the newly developed Space Gun.

The proposed mission creates conflict between the two men, Cabal fearful for his daughter's safety but proud of her spirit of adventure, and Passworthy arguing that the enterprise is unnecessary and foolhardy. Meanwhile, Theotocopulos goes on worldwide television with an impassioned plea against technological progress in general and the Space Gun in particular:

> "These people who are so kind as to manage our world for us declare that they leave us free to do as we please, . . . that never has there been such freedom as we have to-day. And as the price of this limited freedom we enjoy, they ask us to ignore the hard and dreadful persistence of their own inhuman researches. But is our freedom really the freedom they pretend it is? . . . We want the freedom to arrest. We want the freedom to prevent. Have they the right to use the resources of this world to torment us by the spectacle of their cruel and mad adventures? Have they the right to mar the very peace of our starry heavens by human sacrifices?" (P. 121)

We see next a number of examples of public reaction to the speech, mostly negative. Three old men praise modern medicine for giving them a healthy old age. A pair of nursery-school teachers laud the decline in infant mortality. A group of scientists belittle Theotocopulos and his followers: "'What *is* the natural life of man? . . . Lice and fleas. Endless infections. Croup to begin with and cancer to finish. Rotten teeth by forty. Anger and spite. . . . And yet these fools listen to Theotocopulos. They want Romance! They want flags back. War and all the nice *human* things. They think we are Robots—and that drilled soldiers in the old days weren't. They want the Dear Old World of the Past—and an end to all this wicked Science!'" (p. 126).

Yet Theotocopulos does attract a considerable following and leads an attack on the Space Gun site. To save the Gun from the mob, Cabal arranges to move up the firing date. The Gun is fired, with Catherine and Maurice aboard the projectile. The film ends as Cabal and Passworthy watch their children arc toward the moon.

Critical response to the screenplay has been largely negative. Baxter concludes that "the film's ideas often exhibit a . . . paucity of imagination, especially in the future sequences," and, again, "politically and sociologically *Things to Come* is specious" (pp. 63, 64). W. Warren Wagar, one of Wells's most perceptive critics, writes that "*Things to Come* was Wells' worst, most lopsided Utopia, conceived in haste to hammer home one simple message to a mass audience incapable of digesting more than one idea at a time."[7]

To be sure, *Things to Come* is lopsided. In its central conflict—the striving, technology-centered impulse versus the stable, human-centered impulse—surely the former prevails. And the film, set as it is at the peak of what the book labels the Puritan Tyranny, never allows us to see Wells's real utopia, the stateless, humane, individualistic world that lies beyond the Declaration of Mégève. Thus the film never transcends a solidly Promethean worldview to reach the Protean view at the end of *The Shape of Things to Come*.

And yet the screenplay is not as one-sided as has been charged. The critics of *Things to Come* seem to have taken Cabal as Wells's spokesman in the film, and Cabal certainly is presented sympathetically, as a reasonable yet feeling character. Yet Cabal's opponents—Theotocopulos, Passworthy, Cabal's ex-wife (prominent in the screenplay, yet cut from the final print of the film), even the old man who introduces us to the future state—are also portrayed sympathetically, and can easily be taken as spokesmen for Wells in his "critic of progress" role. The old man, perhaps the most sympathetic character in the film, praises the technology of his age, but muses, "'I suppose I'm an old man, my dear, but some of it seems almost like going too far. This Space Gun of theirs that they keep on shooting'" (p. 96). Wells, in first describing the Space Gun, says "It crouches monstrously" (p. 111), and later shows us Cabal himself, in a private moment, soliloquizing, "'Have we been making the pace too hard for Humanity? Humanity! What *is* Humanity? Is it Theotocopulos? Is it dear old Passworthy? Is it Rowena? Is it I?'" (p. 131).

It seems clear that Wells envisioned the screenplay, at least in its early forms, as an open-ended rhetorical document, intended to ask a crucial question without answering it. The very time period he selects from his book in which to set the bulk of the film is a strong clue to this intention; A.D. 2054 puts us just before the Mégève conference, when feelings for and against the World-State are at their highest pitch. Wells chooses to dramatize this debate by creating a cast of reasonable, sympathetic characters on both sides.

Perhaps the evenhandedness of this approach was lost in the acclaimed portrayal of Cabal by Raymond Massey; more likely it fell victim to cinematic demands for a strong protagonist on which to focus. But, at any event, what could have been a major effort at creating wide public discussion of an important social issue becomes a polemic for a lopsided future.

The closing lines of the screenplay are like the closing lines of "The Lady or the Tiger?" and John Brunner's *The Shockwave Rider* in turning the central question of the work back on the audience. But this effort at rhetoric, in the best sense of the word, becomes *mere* rhetoric, in the worst sense. Cabal, looking toward the moon-bound spacecraft, asks:

> "If we are no more than animals—we must snatch at our little scraps of happiness and live and suffer and pass, mattering no more—than all the other animals do—or have done." (He points out at the stars). "Is it that—or this? All the universe—or nothingness. . . . Which shall it be, Passworthy?"
>
> The two men fade out against the starry background until only the stars remain.
>
> The musical finale becomes dominant.
>
> Cabal's voice is heard repeating through the music: "Which shall it be, Passworthy? Which shall it be?"
>
> A louder, stronger voice reverberates through the auditorium: "WHICH SHALL IT BE?" (P. 142)

After Wells

The central place of H. G. Wells in the development of utopian and dystopian fiction is best treated in *The Future as Nightmare: H. G. Wells and the Anti-Utopians* by Mark R. Hillegas.[8] Hillegas's argument is twofold. First, he points out, Wells, particularly in his "scientific romances," provided all later utopian and dystopian writers with their most powerful tool: the trick of making the speculative seem absolutely plausible, of showing us completely unfamiliar societies peopled by completely familiar characters.

But in addition, Hillegas writes, Wells, particularly in his later "utopian" works, virtually created the twentiety-century dystopian movement by providing the chief models which such writers as Eugene Zamiatin, Aldous Huxley, and George Orwell reacted so strongly against.

Yet Wells gives us something else besides. With his view that humanity and its societies are radically alterable, that evolution has not stopped, Wells sets the predominant tone for much of twentieth-century speculative fiction. And with this view that fiction can be used rhetorically, to influence humanity's evolution by providing models of alternative worlds, he establishes a context in which speculative fiction can be seen as valuable, even vital, to a culture. Michael Rossman, whose book *On Learning and Social Change*[9] is perhaps the most perceptive analysis of student unrest in the 1960s, writes that "science fiction—the speculative extension of technological man—has been crucial to the present rise of visions with new force among the young. Its impact hasn't really been recognized yet. But many of my generation found it a precious, funky medium for opening our imaginations—not least, about social reconstruction. It taught us to play with our minds about what man might become and how, in all the Ways of his being" (pp. 199–200).

Wells funky? Hardly. But Rossman's last sentence certainly captures the rhetorical, Protean vision of H. G. Wells, in his lifelong quest to see, and change, the shape of things to come.

Notes

1. *H. G. Wells* (New York: Simon and Schuster, 1973), p. 24.
2. *Science Fiction: History, Science, Vision* (London: Oxford Univ. Pr., 1977), p. 23.
3. *The Shape of Things to Come* (New York: Macmillan, 1983), p. 115.
4. *Star Sight: Visions of the Future* (Englewood Cliffs, N.J.: Prentice-Hall, 1977), pp. 28 ff.
5. New York: A. S. Barnes, 1970.
6. London: Cresset, 1935.
7. *H. G. Wells and the World State* (New Haven, Conn.: Yale Univ. Pr., 1961), p. 238.
8. New York: Oxford Univ. Pr., 1967.
9. New York: Vintage Books, 1972.

8

Mixing Behaviorism and Utopia: The Transformations of *Walden Two*

Kenneth M. Roemer

I

Such an innocent little tale: no bloody revolutions or class wars; no test-tube babies; no Big Brothers; no drawn-out economic, political, or religious polemics; no overwhelming mazes of technological hardware, no bureaucratic redtape, or megalopolitan sprawl; no improbable space flights, hundred-year sleeps, or time warps through black holes. Instead B. F. Skinner's *Walden Two* (1948) offers the reader a simple narrative about a brief visit (Wednesday morning through Monday afternoon during the spring of 1945) by two professors and two couples to a pleasant, rural community.[1] Even the origins of *Walden Two* seem tame. In 1945 Skinner was bothered by domestic questions: the way wives winced when they "printed 'housewife' in those blanks asking for occupation," the shortcomings of Julie Skinner's first grade school experience, and the fact that he would soon have to leave a talented group of Minneapolis string players when he moved to Indiana in the fall (p. v, W). Skinner's immediate inspiration came at a dinner party. One of the guests, Hilda Butler, asked Skinner how the soldiers returning from World War II could maintain their "crusading spirit." He suggested that they should "explore new ways of living," perhaps set up experimental communities as some reformers had done during the nineteenth century. Hilda wanted details, details that eventually grew into *Walden Two*.[2]

A narrative about a pleasant retreat inspired by domestic queries and dinner-party chat—no wonder one student of utopian literature has described *Walden Two* as the paradigm for the modern shrunken utopia.[3] And yet, *Walden Two* may well be the most controversial utopia ever written.

The controversy didn't start overnight.[4] But when it did, both the supporters and the critics of *Walden Two* voiced strong opinions. One of Skinner's ardent supporters was Fred S. Keller, a behavioral psychologist who met Skinner in graduate school. After seeing a copy of the typed manuscript of *Walden Two*,[5] he told Skinner that it was "tremendously exciting" and predicted that it would be "the most talked about book in the country" (p. 329, SB). During the 1960s, psychologists and academics in other disciplines assigned *Walden Two* in their classes.[6] But the success of *Walden Two* has not been limited to classrooms or to behavioral modification applications in mental institutions and hospitals. Before its publication Keller speculated about setting up a Walden Two community. This type of speculation became reality during the late 1960s and the 1970s. Twin Oaks, the subject of a recent PBS documentary, was the first commune inspired by *Walden Two*.[7] Now there are several Skinner-inspired communities; five of them have formed an organization called the Federation of Egalitarian Communities.[8] Larger applications of the Walden Two model have been advocated by academics and government officials: for example, one social scientist has argued that "the architects of the Welfare Society" should consider, with care, possible uses of behavioral engineering,[9] and a State Department official has called Skinner to tell him that the United States "ought to stop trying to export the American way of life and export Walden Twos instead" (p. xv, W).

Skinner's critics often wanted to exorcise rather than export *Walden Two*. Admittedly, some of the criticism was mild, some very specific (as when John Kenneth Galbraith chided Skinner for having his communal dairymen milk Herefords[10]), and some constructive, especially the debates among Skinner's colleagues about the scientific validity of behaviorial psychology and the relationships between behavioral science and values.[11] But much of the criticism came in the form of broadside attacks: derogatory comparisons to *1984* and *Animal Farm*; name-calling that linked Skinner to Machiavellians, Communists, and Fascists; and exclamations of disgust that proclaimed the "shocking horror" and ignobility of *Walden Two*.[12] Two critics even wished that they could burn "every copy" of the book.[13] The most extreme expression of censure, however, appeared in an anonymous *Life* review, which Skinner's wife has called "one of the most vicious reviews I've ever seen."[14] The reviewer, John K. Jessup, asserted that the only freedom in Skinner's utopia was the freedom of "Pavlovian dogs" and that *Walden Two* was a "menace," a "slur upon a name [Walden]," and "a corruption of an impulse [utopian idealism]" (pp. 247–48, SB).

Skinner often responds to such hostility by feigning ignorance: "What's eating these people?"[15] Of course, he has a pretty good idea of what's eating them; in *Walden Two* he created a character, Augustine Castle, who anticipated most of the criticisms, and the early sections of *Science and Human Behavior* (1953) and much of *Beyond Freedom and Dignity* (1971) directly or indirectly analyze the objections to behavioral psychology and *Walden Two*. The critics are responding to Skinner's controversial theories about human nature, which, stated in a drastically simplified form, are: that the correct way to study humans is to consider only directly observable data and to adhere rigorously to experimental approaches; that humans are analogous to machines controlled by external environments; that by carefully manipulating environments, especially by creating situations that will positively reinforce desired behavior, it is possible to shape human behavior to predetermined specifications; that we should attempt to do such experiments; and that the primary criterion for behavior is its survival value.[16] Skinner and others have reasoned that such theories about human nature not only challenge established schools of psychology, they also raise fears associated with "planned" societies and "control"; dispute "cherished" humanistic values related to concepts of free will, responsibility, guilt, innocence, good, and evil; eliminate the mysterious, spontaneous, and unique from the human experience; and threaten to take away or at least to define out of existence what often appears to be the last vestige of privacy and control left in modern society—the individual "mind." The undeniable successes of behavioral modification techniques over the past two decades and the fact that—unlike economics, politics, religion, and other utopian means—the science of behavior seems so *close* to everyday experience, add intensity, even frenzy, to the discussions of these real and supposed threats posed by Skinner's utopian behaviorism.

Hence "what's eating" the critics, encouraging the advocates, and spurring Skinner on to continue his defense of a thirty-year-old book (despite his recent pessimism about the ability of humans to solve their problems[17]) is a debate that goes to the marrow of the human condition by raising questions about what humans are and what they can and should be. But as is the case with many profound debates inspired by provocative books, the original document is often forgotten or misrepresented: a superstructure of assertions, charges, and countercharges grows above the point of provocation, and eventually the superstructure takes on a life of its own apart from its source, though the debaters often delude themselves into thinking that they are still discussing the original issue. To be more specific, many of the arguments about *Walden Two*, including some of Skinner's defenses, are founded upon two misleading assumptions: that all or at least most of *Walden Two* is "about" behavioral engineering, and that *Walden Two* can, indeed should, be treated as a nonfictional work. Actually very little of *Walden Two* involves explicit expositions of the theories of behaviorism, and both the form and the content of the book are dictated by long-established conventions of the literary utopia, particularly the conventions of the guided tour, the Platonic dialogue, and the conversion narrative.

The remainder of this essay represents an attempt to correct these misconceptions by examining how Skinner used the conventions of utopian literature—especially the idyllic rural setting, the prosaic details of daily life, the familiar utopian characters, and the carefully paced presentation of Americanized versions of controversial ideas— to reveal his views of human nature and utopia to an American reading audience. I trust that the intent behind this approach will not be misunderstood. If Augustine Castle were undertaking such a study, he might use the results to prove how evil Skinner was: after all, if Castle thought that the founder of Walden Two, T. E. Frazier, represented the "most diabolical" ruler, "the silent despot" (pp. 236, 237, W), then he might use such a study to prove that the even more silent dictator—the author behind the characters—was more diabolical than Frazier. That is not my goal. Nor do I intend to persuade anyone that *Walden Two* is an undiscovered literary masterpiece. Skinner did have quite a bit of literary training before he wrote *Walden Two*: he began writing poems and stories as a child, went through Hamilton College as an "aspiring writer" who briefly attracted the attention of Robert Frost, and spent the first year after college attempting, unsuccessfully, to write fiction.[18] By the end of this "Dark Year," he had concluded that he "had no reason to write anything" (p. 264, P). He changed fields and enrolled in Harvard's psychology department. Later in life he found "reason" to write a work of fiction, *Walden Two*. But the book was written very quickly (in seven weeks during the summer of 1945), and Skinner did not pretend to offer a great work of literature. He even interjects a bit of self-satire when Frazier describes his own writing: "You can hear my mind creak in the pompous cadences of my prose" (p. 271, W).

Neither an attempt to expose the hidden devil behind *Walden Two* nor to unveil a literary genius, the following examination instead reveals how important it is to consider the literary contexts of influential utopias and seeks to illuminate the transformation of controversial and specialized knowledge into appeals that are communicable to wide reading audiences.

II

Rogers and Jamnik, the two veterans created in response to Hilda Butler's dinner-party challenge, visit Rogers's former teacher, Professor Burris, who occasionally discussed utopian communities in his rambling lectures. The veterans are excited about an essay describing an experimental community. Burris knew the founder as a "queer duck" of a graduate student. Eventually Burris makes arrangements to visit the community, and on a Wednesday morning during a spring, pre-examination break, the three of them, accompanied by a philosopher (Castle) who has taught a course in utopian thought, and two young women, Barbara Macklin and Mary Grove, set out to visit Walden Two.

By the standards of utopian literature, the setting they discover is remarkably accessible and old-fashioned. All it takes to get to utopia is the price of bus and train tickets and a few bumps endured while traversing a rural road in a station wagon. There are no trips to a dazzling future or a past Golden Age, and Walden Two is much nearer than Anarres, Utopia, Erewhon, Altruria, or even Rasselas's Happy Valley. And most of the physical characteristics of the area would not have surprised W. D. Howells's Altrurian Mr. Homos, who visited a New England summer resort. Walden Two is set in a "pleasant countryside"—a "prosperous farmland . . . about thirty miles from the largest city in the state" (possibly in the Midwest). The population of the community is small (1,000). The landscape is completed by the living quarters, which remind Burris of a "big summer hotel," some old and some new buildings, a "grove of pines," a stream, a pond, and a "wooded hill" (pp. 12–13, 17, 18, 197, W). Probably the only physical aspects of Walden Two that would have startled Thoreau are the rammed earth building materials, the modern labor-saving devices in many of the buildings, and the fact that the pond was man-made.

The primary sources of this setting suggest nineteenth-century or even earlier attitudes. One of Skinner's colleagues at the University of Minnesota, Alice F. Tyler, sent him a copy of her book *Freedom's Ferment*, published in 1944 (p. vi. W);[19] part two of this book surveys most of the well-known eighteenth- and nineteenth-century American communes. In 1939 Skinner and philosopher Alburey Castell (the model for Castle) visited St. John's Abbey, a Benedictine community in Collegeville, Minnesota.[20] During graduate school, Skinner read and reread *Walden* and visited Walden Pond (p. 296, SB), and his undergraduate college, Hamilton, was located near the site of John Humphrey Noyes's Oneida Community (p. 292, SB). One specific childhood source was a book in his grandparents' (Burrhus) library that ridiculed communes (p. 17, P). But the most important childhood influence on the setting of Walden Two was the town of Susquehanna, Pennsylvania, where Skinner was raised. The Pennsylvania country-side, the amateur "musical and theatrical performances," and the nearness of the place where Joseph Smith dictated the Book of Mormon and the Harmony settlement, all foreshadow the community discovered by Burris and his friends (pp.3, 19, 75–76, P).[21]

There are at least three advantages to using such an old-fashioned, rural community as the setting for a utopia advocating a science as controversial as behaviorism. First, the small-town setting makes the utopian model seem believable. No new technologies are needed, and Skinner argues that positive reinforcement works better in small, stable communities than in large urban areas where personal contacts are often transitory: "Why should anyone be affected by the praise or blame of someone he will never see again?"[22] It also seems logical to expect that experiments in behavioral engineering would be easier to initiate, monitor, and evaluate in a small, isolated community than in a large city. A second type of advantage might be expressed in the following syllogism (which begs more than a few questions): Small is beautiful; behavioral engineering works best in small environments; therefore behavioral engineering is beautiful. In his introduction to the new (1976) edition of *Walden Two* Skinner uses a similar type of logic to capitalize on current stereotypes of the wasteful and frenzied life in cities (pp. ix–xi, W). A third, and possibly the most important, advantage is that the small, rural community setting offers the reader a familiar and reassuring introduction to a potentially disturbing concept of utopia. The significance of this type of introduction can be seen when the opening chapters of *Walden Two* are compared to the initial sections of Skinner's introductory text, *Science and Human Behavior*, which according to Skinner provides scientific support for *Walden Two*.[23] There is really very little that would "scare readers off" in the beginning of the novel, whereas section one of *Science and Human Behavior* immediately plunges the reader into concepts of human nature that may be strange and threatening.

But in spite of the several advantages of the setting of *Walden Two*, Skinner's use of this traditional utopian landscape poses a difficult problem. Should his rural community be read as a speculative construct primarily intended to encourage a reevaluation of the "real" world, or should it be read as a blueprint intended as a practical guide for action? In other words, should we read Skinner as we read Plato and More or as we read Edward Bellamy and Theodore Herzl? The narrative itself gives no absolute answer to this question. The Skinner of the 1940s did not force the burden of blueprint realism on his imaginary countryside. But the Skinner of the 1970s does force the issue. In his 1976 introduction he looks toward the future and presents a "network of small towns or Walden Twos" as a practical solution to many contemporary problems. In spite of the many benefits of small community life, such a proposal seems almost as impractical as King Camp Gillette's late nineteenth-century plan (outlined in *The Human Drift*, 1894) to relocate the entire population of the United States in one city. Thus the added suggestion that the setting be taken as a practical proposal may, ironically, undermine the credibility of Skinner's utopia.

Fortunately, in the descriptions of the setting during the tour of Walden Two, Skinner used another convention of utopian literature—detailed discussions of everyday objects and events—to sustain the reader's "willing suspension of disbelief." Admittedly, not all of Skinner's descriptions of life in Walden Two intrigue the reader with captivating details.[24] Furthermore, concrete descriptions are sometimes interrupted for general discussions of labor and economics (a labor credit system somewhat like Bellamy's), government (Board of Planners appointed for maximum terms of ten years; Managers appointed to oversee various aspects of production, distribution, and everyday life), and social structure (planners, managers, scientists, workers—all levels must do some manual labor; all receive similar housing and food). Such discussions are expected in literary utopias.[25] But in *Walden Two* these topics are handled very briefly; chapter 8 covers most of the material on labor, economics, government, and social structure. Instead of dwelling on such issues, Burris's guide, T. E. Frazier, prefers to concentrate on visits to and descriptions of the nursery, dairy, health/science center, dining rooms, kitchen, and covered walkways. In the large efficient kitchen Frazier draws the guests' attention to the ingenious transparent trays, "which saved two operations . . . because the tray could be seen to be clean on both sides at once" (p. 42, W). In one of the sheltered walkways (Jacob's Ladder) between the children's quarters and the main rooms Frazier points out the inviting alcoves, the views from the many windows, the art work on the walls, and the tea service: "tall glasses, set in braided grass jackets, to which loops of string were attached so that the glasses could be carried like pails" (pp. 25–26, W). Frazier's defense of the tea service, which was carefully designed by domestic engineers, is almost as long and is more enthusiastic than his defense of Walden Two's economic system.

Frazier's fascination with ingenious devices is undoubtedly a reflection of Skinner's talent for design, expressed in childhood inventions as well as complex laboratory equipment, notably the Skinner Box. The time pressure upon Skinner (he had to wedge the book in between a June first deadline and his departure for Indiana) may have also forced him to concentrate on "touches of prosaic detail," to borrow H. G. Wells's phrase, rather than on complex economic, political, and sociological theories. Whatever the cause of the focus, there are several significant consequences of Frazier's and Burris's detailed descriptions: Frazier's enthusiasm about various devices and techniques helps to make him more human than many of the bloodless guides of utopian fiction; the details offer an "easy start," as Frazier puts it (p. 25, W), into an unusual utopia; the emphasis on mundane details reinforces Skinner's intent to examine everyday existence; the focus helps the reader to experience vicariously several days in utopia; and the attention paid to practical applications of experimental theories gives Frazier's brand of behaviorism an air of pragmatism that would appeal to many American readers. Because Skinner presented his technology in the "here and now" and kept his labor-saving devices, medical equipment, and nursery air-cribs on a domestic scale, he also avoided the fate of so many utopists and science-fiction writers who make grand speculations about the communication and transportation systems of the distant future only to see their predictions made obsolete by NASA, Japanese engineers, and Ma Bell in less than a decade.

Even the most ardent admirers of *Walden Two* would have to admit that Skinner lavishes more attention on Frazier's beloved trays and tea glasses than on some of his characters. Skinner may have avoided the obsolete-technological-prediction flaw of utopian fiction, but he did not escape the temptation of creating utopian characters that are disembodied voices or gestures representing identifiable viewpoints or fulfilling very limited narrative or ideological functions.[26]

This type of characterization is particularly noticeable in Skinner's minor characters (many of these were based on acquaintances and relatives).[27] Two examples should suffice. The female architect introduced in chapter 27 demonstrates the sexual equality of Walden Two and also indicates that Frazier is not a dictator: she completely ignores his request to speak to the guests. Similarly an old woman, Mrs. Olson, encountered by Burris in chapter 26 is not in awe of Frazier. All she can recall about him is that he " 'has a little goatee. A thin man. He thinks too much' " (p. 204, W). Mrs. Olson exemplifies the contentment of the members at Walden Two and also suggests the age diversity of the community. She is, moreover, a convenient excuse for a discussion of the advantages of a small community and of the real democracy of Walden Two (as contrasted to the sham democracy on the outside). The planners and managers are not elected by the citizens; they rise to their positions according to their talents and industry. But "about once a year" Mrs. Olson and the rest of the members are contacted personally and asked if they are "satisfied with everything" (p. 205). The planners and managers pay close attention to the response to these surveys.[28]

The two couples accompanying Burris and Castle are a bit more complex than the typical citizens of Walden Two; they are plywood rather than cardboard characters. Steve Jamnik and Mary Grove are wholesome and diligent representatives of America's working classes. Their decision to remain at Walden Two allows Skinner to make clear-cut contrasts between what the working classes can expect to experience inside and outside Walden Two during the post-war era (pp. 168–69, W). As a member of the upper classes, Barbara Macklin's prospects outside are not as bleak as Steve's and Mary's. Barbara is a snobbish, hypocritical dilettante who pretends to enjoy her visit but actually despises Frazier and his utopia, especially because she perceives Walden Two as a threat to her planned marriage with Rogers. Rogers is a fairly common type of utopian character. He is forced to choose between a personal commitment made before his encounter with utopia and his enthusiasm for utopia. He finally opts for Barbara and leaves with her. Because she is the most despicable character in the book, the reader is left with the distinct impression that Rogers (and by implication all the ambivalent Rogerses in the world) has made the wrong decision.

The three major characters—Augustine Castle, T. E. Frazier, and Professor Burris—represent combinations of familiar utopian types: the foil/devil's advocate, the founder-guide, and the narrator-convert. Each plays an important role in Skinner's attempts to make his science of human behavior accessible to a wide reading audience.

Augustine Castle was loosely modeled on Alburey Castell, the philosopher who accompanied Skinner on his visit to the Benedictine community in 1939. The dialogues between Frazier and Castle were based on various viewpoints, including Castell's, expressed in a discussion group at the University of Minnesota composed of philosophers, literary critics—including Robert Penn Warren—and Skinner (pp. 235, 296–97, SB).[29] As the readers for Appleton-Century (who rejected *Walden Two*) and the readers for Macmillan (who accepted it) remarked, the Castle-Frazier dialogues on labor, economics, government, family structure, freedom, and behaviorism make for a "talky" book (p. 329, SB). But Castle is not the incompetent straw man found in so many utopian works (recall, for instance, the Voice of Nature in Wells's *A Modern Utopia* or even several of Socrates's opponents in *The Republic*). He "conversed extremely well" (p. 9. W); directly or indirectly he anticipates almost all the criticisms of *Walden Two* summarized at the beginning of this essay; and his arguments are persuasive enough to have convinced some early reviewers and Skinner's father (p. 347, SB). Castle's attacks also help to humanize Frazier by uncovering "the ragged edges of [his] personality."[30] Furthermore, Castle's criticism inspires Frazier to present arguments that are often more vivid and appealing than the dry and rather rigid "answers" Skinner offers to hypothetical "objections" in the opening pages of *Science and Human Behavior*. But Skinner fixed the dialogues. Castle is no match for Frazier. From his first to his last appearance he is a caricature of an ivory tower (or castle) academic and an unkempt philosopher (he is fat; his mustache is sloppy; he is awkward and sweats and grunts, and is last seen heading for a men's room). More important, he can only tolerate intellectual honesty for so long; then his mind clamps shut on a simplistic answer and all serious thought stops. Castle is impressed by Jacob's Ladder and other details presented early in the tour, and for a while he tries to evaluate constructively Frazier's utopia. But his frustrations build as Frazier constantly outmaneuvers him. Finally he decides that Frazier is a Fascist—a "silent dictator" Fascist—and that relieves him of any further responsibility for careful consideration of Walden Two.

The target of Castle's attacks is one of the most fascinating guides in utopian literature. T. E. Frazier—the primary talker or "phraser" in the novel[31]—combines the mannerisms and viewpoints of two of Skinner's Harvard professors, W. J. Crozier and L. J. Henderson, and Skinner's friend Fred Simmons Keller (pp. 296, 319, SB).[32] Skinner may have also recalled a man named Frazier who donated a colored-glass window to his Presbyterian church in Susquehanna (pp. 60–61, P), and Peter Wolfe has suggested that the initials T. E. may have come from T. E. Lawrence, who combined the roles of intellectual and activist.[33] But the most significant source for Frazier was, of course, B. F. Skinner. Both author and character liked to make use of scraps; both had once been heavy pipe smokers; both were fair pianists; both kept messy offices; and, most important, both shared similar views on society and the science of human behavior.

Undoubtedly the fact that Frazier was modeled on Skinner's professors, a close friend, and B. F. Skinner himself enabled Skinner to create an emotional and intimate portrait of a utopian guide— intimate, that is, as compared to the portraits of the cold and some-times smug guides found in utopian works, such as Bellamy's Dr. Leete. One way that Skinner attempted to make Frazier more than a self-assured authorial mouthpiece was to give him emotions, even what Skinner calls "negative charisma."[34] Frazier can be charming and enthusiastic, but he can also be moody, even downright impolite. On various occasions he responds "dryly" or "gruffly," or with a scowl or a "vicious glance" (pp. 28, 20, 79, 103, W). He also registers annoyance and disgust at Castle and Barbara (pp. 16, 38, W). Frazier sometimes even abandons the role of talkative guide when he strains for answers using "labored phrases," becomes "moodily silent," or admits his ignorance about specific operations at Walden Two (pp. 17, 210, 71, W). These varying moods and role shifts are in part caused by Castle's attacks and by time pressures—Frazier desperately wants to convert the visitors, but he only has a few days before the professors must return to give final exams. But his behavior is also shaped by other less immediate forces, especially his ambivalent role at Walden Two: he is below and above the other members; he is not one of them. His feelings of inferiority are most clearly expressed in an impassioned speech that Skinner typed "in white heat" (p. 298, SB). Frazier knows that Burris thinks that he is "conceited, aggressive, tactless, selfish." Frazier responds by saying, "*'Can't you see? I'm—not—a—prod-uct—of—Walden—Two!'*" He adds, "'Give me credit for what I've done or not, as you please, but don't look for perfection. Isn't it enough that I've made other men likable and happy and productive? Why expect me to resemble them? Must I possess the virtues which I've proved to be best suited to a well-ordered society? . . . Must the doctor share the health of his patient?'" (pp. 233–34, W). His superiority complex takes the form of what Burris refers to as "a sizable God complex" (p. 281, W). Reclining above Walden Two on a high ledge called the Throne, Frazier tells Burris, "'I look upon my work and, behold, it is good.'" Not content to be only one member of the Trinity, he assumes "the position of crucifixion" while continuing to make blunt comparisons between himself and God. Burris is frightened; he thinks Frazier "might be going mad." But suddenly Frazier drops his godly comparisons and poses; his blasphemy is not "literal" (p. 278, W). It is a tense combination of self-aggrandizement and self-satire.

The combinations of self-assurance, quirks, and self-doubts Skinner built into the character charged with articulating his utopian behaviorism fulfill a variety of literary and nonliterary functions: they humanize the utopian guide; they demonstrate that Walden Two was not controlled by or dependent upon saints, geniuses, or heroes; they emphasize that the best products of behaviorism had to be conditioned from birth; and, as Robert Elliott has argued, they establish an "ironic distance" between author and character that prevents Frazier from becoming a shallow authorial mouthpiece.[35] This ironic distance made Frazier an excellent vehicle for the expression of Skinner's first grand applications of his science of human behavior. Fred Keller once noted that Skinner "says a thing in its most extreme form and takes some of it back if he has to" (p. 80, SB). Frazier permitted Skinner to make statements as extreme as "Give me the specifications, and I'll give you the man!" (p. 274, W). But the outrageous nature of some of Frazier's claims combined with his painfully obvious inferiority and superiority complexes qualify the extreme positions with satire. Like Raphael Hythloday in More's *Utopia*, Frazier is a wise fool—an appropriate spokesman for the articulation of theories Skinner wanted to shout from the mountaintops but dared not to because at this point in his life he wasn't certain whether he would be shouting divine wisdom or blasphemous absurdities.

The other main character, Professor Burris, also expresses Skinner's excitement and doubts as he made his bold public leap from rats and pigeons to people.[36] The primary source for the narrator of *Walden Two* is, of course, Burrhus Frederic Skinner.[37] The crisis Burris faces is a choice between a secure but pedestrian existence as a bachelor psychology professor who no longer enjoys teaching and research in a typical university environment and a commitment to an exciting but unfamiliar experiment in living founded by a "queer duck" of a psychologist he knew in graduate school. As Burris fluctuates between these two poles, the reader becomes engaged in his dilemma not only because, as a first person narrator, he can reveal his private thoughts to the reader, but also because his voice is characterized by a combination of open-mindedness and skepticism not unlike the attitudes of the voices of the persona "More" in *Utopia* and The Owner of the Voice in *A Modern Utopia*. Thus the reader can trust Burris and identify with him as he struggles toward a decision.

Peter Wolfe has characterized this struggle as a mixture of "shock, protest, and annoyance in no predictable pattern."[38] This description is valid in that it suggests some of the variety characteristic in Burris's responses to Walden Two. But there is a "predictable pattern"; Thomas Hooker, Edward Taylor, and Jonathan Edwards would have spotted it immediately—the drama of a personal conversion experience. Burris passes through at least eleven stages in preparation for his conversion, and these stages represent the major "plot" in *Walden Two*.

Burris's initial response to Walden Two is mild annoyance mingled with a sense of his own shortcomings. When Rogers and Jamnik appear in his office inquiring about Frazier and his community, Burris categorizes utopian communities as one of those "unimportant details" that his students always remember, while they forget the significant aspects of his courses (p. 2, W). Hence Walden Two is associated with a feeling that something is wrong with him (a common preconversion feeling), and Rogers aggravates this sense of failure by proclaiming that a true psychologist must experiment with his own life, "'not just sit back in an ivory tower somewhere'" (p. 5, W). Burris's reactions to the first few hours at Walden Two are more complex than his initial response to the two veterans: he likes some of the things he sees, but he also perceives this New Way as a threat. He is irritated by Frazier's silences and promises designed to whet his curiosity (pp. 13, 22, W), frightened when he is momentarily left alone with a group of Waldenites (p. 24, W), and "outraged" by the fact that most members work only four hours a day (p. 45, W). This second stage suggests that he is afraid of losing parts of his old "identity." Burris's third stage is brief; it involves his first strong positive feelings about Walden Two, and it is experienced on an emotional and personal level. He feels a "strange affection" for Frazier when he seems "ashamed of his excitement" as he describes the fair distribution of work in Walden Two (p. 51, W). This strange sympathy for Frazier and his ideas grows, and near the end of the next day (Thursday) Burris experiences his first crisis in which he assumes Frazier's role as the questioner of his beliefs.

As he listens to a performance of Bach's B Minor Mass, Frazier's claims and questions echo in his ears. Then suddenly it is Burris's own voice he hears shouting "*Why not? Why not?*" During the *Kyrie eleison*, Burris can only control himself by fiercely gripping his chair, as if he were desperately clinging to the self he knows as he is confronted by the possibilities of a new self (pp. 84–85, W). But he cannot stifle the new possibilities. On Friday in at least two instances Burris finds himself defending Frazier (pp. 103, 161, W). In his sixth stage, late on Friday, his ambivalence is acute. At one point he actually assumes Frazier's role as guide by reassuring Mary and Steve about Walden Two (p. 169, W). After they leave, he even begins to speculate about how he would feel if he were a member. But that tentative and speculative commitment is too risky at this stage. It evokes a violent recoil: "I decided not to be a damn fool and went to sleep" (p. 171, W). On Saturday Burris passes on to another stage—he decides to resolve his "soul-shaking" doubts and damn-fool notions by "desperately" hunting for flaws in Walden Two. He sneaks off alone only to discover Mrs. Olson, who confirms Frazier's glowing descriptions of life in Walden Two. Burris then changes his perspective and wonders whether this delightful lady is part of some satanic plot to capture him (p. 207, W); he is obviously scraping the bottom of his barrel of defenses against his positive feelings about Walden Two. At breakfast on Sunday Burris asserts his identity by refusing to help Frazier recoup from a crude bit of "behavioral engineering"—a hypocritical compliment bestowed upon Barbara (p. 229, W). But later in the day as he argues against Castle, he realizes that on an intellectual level he has been converted; but he still cannot make a total commitment. Jonathan Edwards might say that Burris was at the stage in which he has an intellectual understanding of honey, but still has not tasted honey. On Monday morning, Burris knows that Frazier will make a final play for him, since he is scheduled to leave after lunch. Burris probably expected Frazier's speech about the opportunity to join history's greatest experiment, but he seems totally unprepared for Frazier's ironic assumption of godhood. This stuns him, so that for the rest of the time before his departure (the tenth stage) he seems almost passive. He follows the others to the truck and heads back to the bus stop.

All the preparatory stages experienced just before and during Burris's visit to Walden Two (the exact number of these stages is certainly open to debate) culminate in a final stage—the "dreamer awakes" episode—that is familiar to readers of utopian fiction. In this episode the potential convert leaves utopia and reenters his old world, which he sees with new eyes. In *Walden Two* the setting, actions, and props of this scene are typical of similar scenes in utopian literature. Burris is in a dirty train station waiting to catch a train back to the university. He walks outside and sees a rundown warehouse and some poor, filthy kids. He returns and, like Julian West in Bellamy's *Looking Backward*, picks up a newspaper. His (new) eyes fall on a cliché-ridden oration about education delivered by his college president. Burris is repulsed; the speech is a painful proof of how much he hates his old academic world. He rushes to a telegraph operator. His printed message " . . . YOU MAY TAKE YOUR STUPID UNIVERSITY . . ." (p. 296, W) is never finished or sent, but he has made his decision. He does not know exactly when he made the decision, but he knows he must return to Walden Two.[39] With Burris's conversion two cycles are completed: first, Burris began with a guarded admission of the failure of Professor Burris, the academic, and now he has the courage to break with that identity and begin a new one; second, he began by separating himself from Frazier, and now he will join him. (The coming together of the guide and narrator is cleverly suggested by the fact that, as a graduate student, Frazier sent a letter to his college president and by the similarities between Frazier's and Burris's printing [pp. 6, 10, 295, W].)

The first "act of expiation" for this new convert is his "religious pilgrimage" (his walk) back to Walden Two (p. 294, W). In a back-ward glance at the end of the book the reader discovers that Burris has been quite a productive convert. He has written an account of his conversion (*Walden Two*), which will soon be distributed by the community's Office of Information. Thus unlike the guilt-ridden Julian West, Burris can live in utopia and earn his place in "noplace" by revealing Walden Two to the world.

The rural setting, the prosaic details, the typical minor characters, a foil, an eccentric guide, and an engaging narrator-convert help to transform Skinner's science of behavior into a personal and familiar story. But these elements borrowed from utopian literature do not encompass all the utopian conventions used by Skinner. Like Bellamy, he realized that the presentation of his controversial means of achieving utopia had to be handled very carefully. Skinner's strategy was complex: he carefully paced the introduction of his theories, empha-sized applications and parables rather than general behaviorist theory, associated behaviorism with traditional secular and religious values and goals, and used a utopian concept of history to elevate and justify his means.

The pacing and applications are quite important. Skinner knew that if he presented too much theoretical discussion of behaviorism too soon he might offend or bore his readers. (Being boring was contrary to the Walden Code.) Hence the first eleven chapters—the "easy start"—contain only brief hints about behaviorism: occasional words and phrases, such as "behaviorial engineering" and "control of infant behavior," and a few assertions by Frazier, such as " 'The real problems are psychological' " (pp. 10, 12, 73, W). Even the first extended discussions of the science of human behavior in chapters 12 through 14 are primarily limited to applications and several sample experiments, which are closer to parables than to descriptions of laboratory procedures. In the nursery (chaps. 12–13) one of the professional staff members, Mrs. Nash, focuses the visitors' attention on the health advantages of the baby-cubicles (Skinner's air-cribs), especially the ability of the staff to use the personal environments to gradually increase the infants' tolerance to conditions in the outside world, thus simultaneously insuring protection for the babies' systems and the development of resistances. In chapter 14 Frazier introduces some of Skinner's theories. But he articulates these theories by describing two series of experiments designed to develop self-control. In the first series the children are given lollipops coated with powdered sugar ("so that a single touch of the tongue can be detected" [p. 98, W]). They are not allowed to eat them until a specific time. In the second series hungry children are given delicious hot soup, but they are not allowed to eat until certain conditions are fulfilled. The lollipop and soup drills are calculated to help children gradually develop tolerances for increasingly difficult real-life situations (instead of allowing them to learn such tolerances in haphazard and potentially dangerous ways). In *Science and Human Behavior* such experiments usually involve rats or pigeons, though analogies to humans are used frequently. These experiments are more complex, and the language used to describe them much more technical ("operant behavior," "aversive stimuli," "manipulation of the environment," "satiation and deprivation"). In *Walden Two* the experiments are humanized and simple; they seem closer to the Stage Coach and Water Tank parables in Bellamy's *Looking Backward* and *Equality* than to descriptions of scientific experiments.

Another quality of the descriptions of the applications of and experiments in behaviorism that makes them familiar to the reader is that they are linked to traditional secular goals: happiness, health, elimination of drudgery, opportunity to develop talents, close personal relationships, rest, and relaxation (pp. 148, 195). But more significant than these general associations are the connections Frazier makes between behaviorism and Christianity, which of course complement the religious overtones of Burris's conversion experience. Each important speech about behaviorism—including the brief theoretical discussions in chapter 29—is either prefaced or followed by comparisons to Christian beliefs. The control of jealousy and aggressive competitiveness in children is linked to the "simple pacifism of Christianity" (p. 93, W); techniques designed to encourage self-control are related to Jesus's achievement of "peace of mind" and his command, "Get thee behind me Satan" (pp. 97, 98, W); and Frazier's theoretical discussion of the ineffectiveness of punishment and the effectiveness of positive reinforcement is associated with Jesus, who discovered the "power of refusing to punish" by preaching "Love your enemies" (p. 246, W). Near the end of *Walden Two* Burris even concludes that "Frazier's program was essentially a religious movement" (p. 289, W). Comparisons to Christian beliefs were common in nineteenth-century American socialistic utopias; these utopists, like Skinner, used the comparisons to make their "foreign" ideas seem familiar, to lend spiritual authority to secular reforms, and to make the adoption of controversial programs seem like the return to and the reestablishment of a Golden Age.[40] But the effectiveness of Skinner's use of this utopian convention is debatable. Some of the parallels are convincing. Nevertheless, Frazier's Christian comparisons are often such blatant attempts to make his arguments seem acceptable that the reader may become annoyed. Furthermore, Frazier's "blasphemous" comparisons to God and Jesus pronounced from the Throne near the conclusion of the novel might, in retrospect, make even good Christian readers suspect the earlier, very different types of comparisons to Christian beliefs.

The effectiveness of Skinner's use of a utopian concept of history is also debatable. Eighteenth-, nineteenth-, and early twentieth-century American utopists frequently appropriated early American and even earlier millennial hopes that the New World represented the opportunity to break away from the past.[41] Skinner did not stress the nationalistic chauvinism of this concept of history, and despite his use of Christian comparisons, he did not use millennial eschatology. But he did use the "break from history." Rogers and Jamnik come to Walden Two looking for a "fresh start" (p. 4, W), and the rural setting echoes both the eighteenth- and nineteenth-century communal attempts to escape history in the backwoods and the desire for new beginnings expressed by the first European settlers and later by the pioneers lighting out for the virgin land of the West. In spite of these apparent historical parallels, Frazier repeatedly emphasizes that Walden Two represents a new departure—an ahistorical experiment with no exact parallels in past communal settlements or in large-scale experiments such as Russia (pp. 144, 258–59, W).

Frazier's view of history certainly elevates Walden Two above the realm of transparent trays and tea glasses. It gives him a sense of mission, which in turn helps to convert Burris. But Frazier's ahistorical view forces contradictions: the comparisons to past Christian figures clash with the denial of historical precedents; in his desire to portray Walden Two as unique, Frazier sometimes gives his utopia a static quality ("'This *is* the Good Life. We know it'" [p. 149, W]), which contradicts his constant emphasis on experimentation; and his disillusioned attitude about our ability to "know" the past because of our lack of information about former events, is contrary to his naive view that the myriad of concurrent phenomena—that fiction called the present—is knowable. Such contradictions do not add to the humanization of Frazier the way his idiosyncrasies do. Instead they tend to undermine the reader's confidence in Frazier's (and by implication, Skinner's) ability to handle complex questions.

Skinner achieved mixed results when he mixed behaviorism and conventions of utopian literature. His avoidance of technical jargon and long theoretical discussions, his prosaic details, and his characterizations of Frazier and Burris are praiseworthy; the minor characters and Castle are familiar but often too predictable; the rural setting is an appealing and reassuring introduction to a controversial utopia, but Skinner may overburden this setting by trying to sell it as a plan of action; and for some readers, several of the Christian comparisons and the ahistorical perspective may undermine Skinner's efforts to present behaviorism as an understandable and convincing way to perceive the nature and potential of humanity. How mixed the results are will depend upon what each reader brings to *Walden Two*. But one thing should be clear: any arguments about *Walden Two* that ignore the importance of Skinner's reliance on the conventions of utopian literature will probably misinterpret Skinner's arguments and distort his intentions.

III

B. F. Skinner's decision to use utopian fiction to reach a wide audience transformed his life. Writing *Walden Two* allowed him to pretend that a science of human behavior existed. In his previous influential study, *Behavior of Organisms* (1938) he "had refused to apply [his] results outside the laboratory" (pp. v–vi, W). But the guise of utopian fiction permitted him to "say things that I myself was not yet ready to say to anyone" (p. 298, SB). Hence Skinner was following the advice of America's most famous utopist, Edward Bellamy, who once justified his use of utopian fiction by arguing that "in adventuring in any new and difficult field of speculation I believe that the student cannot do better than to use the literary form of fiction."[42]

Of course there are dangers inherent in this use of fiction; for instance, such a writing experience could transform a scientist into a "scientian" who extrapolates "the currently known data of his field— and, if necessary, the data of other branches of science—in order to discourse on the *whole* of man."[43] Some critics feel that Skinner has undergone such a change and that he has become a "moral philosopher" whose "beliefs have overtaken his theory."[44]

There may be truth in this charge, though Skinner's recently expressed pessimism about world leaders ever utilizing behavioral sciences to solve world problems blunts some of this criticism.[45] Nevertheless, Skinner's decision to pretend that he knew the "answers" resulted in one of the most provocative books of the twentieth century—provocative and healthy, since Frazier's gospel and Burris's conversion are qualified with goodly doses of self-satire. Furthermore, Skinner's willingness to risk the transformation of his scientific knowledge into speculative fiction manifests his commitment to a principle articulated in *Science and Human Behavior*: "By distributing scientific knowledge as widely as possible, we gain some assurance that it will not be impounded by any one agency for its own aggrandizement."[46] The existence of *Walden Two* does not insure that behavioral engineering will always be used wisely. But Skinner's innocent little tale and the furor it caused have helped millions of people to be aware of the utopian and dystopian possibilities of Frazier's declaration: "Give me the specifications, and I'll give you the man!"[47]

Notes

1. Various forms of the word "pleasant" appear at least forty-four times in the lastest edition of Skinner's *Walden Two* (New York: Macmillan, 1976). Hereafter all page references to this edition will be made in parenthesis in the text. The page number will be followed by "W."

2. B. F. Skinner, *The Shaping of a Behaviorist: Part Two of an Autobiography* (New York: Knopf, 1979), pp. 292–93. Hereafter all page references to this book will appear in parenthesis in the text. The page number will be followed by "SB."

3. Robert Plank, "The Modern Shrunken Utopia," in *America as Utopia*, ed. Kenneth M. Roemer (New York: Burt Franklin, 1981), pp. 206–30.

4. It wasn't until about 1960 that the sales of *Walden Two* rose sharply. Skinner speculates that the successes of behavioral modification during the late 1950s and the turmoil of the 1960s attracted attention to the novel (pp. vi–vii, W). But the controversy among the book reviewers did begin soon after publication of *Walden Two* (pp. 346–49, SB).

5. At this stage the book was actually entitled *The Sun Is But a Morning Star.*

6. Admittedly, all teachers who assign *Walden Two* do not agree with Skinner. A newsletter, *Human Perspectives on Technology*, published at Lehigh University often contains descriptions of courses relating to *Walden Two*. See also Robert L. Stilwell, "Literature and Utopia: B. F. Skinner's *Walden Two*," *Western Humanities Review* 18 (Autumn 1964):335–36.

7. See "A World of Difference: B. F. Skinner and the Good Life," a script for this NOVA program, copyrighted by WGBH Education Foundation in Boston (n.d.).

8. See "Federation of Egalitarian Communities," a pamphlet distributed from Box FB2, Tecumseh, Miss., 65760.

9. Dennis Saleeby, "Pigeons, People, and Paradise: Skinnerian Technology and the Coming of the Welfare State," *Social Service Review* 50 (Sept. 1976):390.

10. "World of Difference," p. 7.

11. For example, see the discussion of criticism by Calvin S. Hall and Gardner Lindzey in Peter Wolfe, "*Walden Two* Twenty-Five Years Later: A Retrospective Look," *Studies in the Literary Imagination* 6 (Fall 1973):22; Morris S. Viteles, "The New Utopia," *Science*, 16 Dec. 1955, pp. 1167–71; and Carl R. Rogers and B. F. Skinner, "Some Issues Concerning the Control of Human Behavior," *Science*, 30 Nov. 1956, pp. 1057–66.

12. Rogers and Skinner, p. 1062; review of *Beyond Freedom and Dignity*, by Richard Sennett, *New York Times Book Review*, 24 Oct. 1971, p. 1; B. F. Skinner, "An Autobiography," in *Festschrift for B. F. Skinner*, ed. P. B. Davis, as quoted in Wolfe, p. 24; *The Quest for Utopia; An Anthology of Imaginary Societies*, ed. Glenn Negley and J. Max Patrick (New York:

Henry Schuman, 1952), p. 580; and Joseph Wood Krutch, *The Measure of Man*, as quoted in B. F. Skinner, "Utopia as an Experimental Culture," in *Contingencies of Reinforcement; A Theoretical Analysis* (New York: Appleton-Century-Crofts, 1969), p. 30.

13. "World of Difference," p. 6; and p. 348, SB.

14. "World of Difference," p. 6.

15. "B. F. Skinner: Interview," *Omni*, Sept. 1979, p. 78.

16. Even though it is more than thirty years old, one of the best introductions to Skinner's views is B. F. Skinner, *Science and Human Behavior* (New York: Macmillan, 1953).

17. See Joel Greenberg, "B. F. Skinner Now Sees Little Hope for the World's Salvation," *New York Times*, 15 Sept. 1981, pp. C1, C3.

18. B. F. Skinner, *Particulars of My Life* (New York: McGraw-Hill, 1976), pp. 93, 163, 248, 264. Hereafter all page references to this book will appear in parenthesis in the text. The page number will be followed by "P."

19. Skinner's wife also encouraged him to read Louis Bromfield's *The Strange Case of Miss Annie Sprague*, which is about the daughter of the leader of a religious community (p. 292, SB).

20. Some specific parallels between the fictional and actual visits include staying in a "spartan" guest room, eating delicious homemade bread, and being asked by the philosopher if he were ready to "sign on the dotted line" (p. 235, SB).

21. One other possible indirect source is the "pleasant flower world" of Julie Skinner's fantasies (p. 278, SB).

22. *Beyond Freedom and Dignity*, (New York: Knopf, 1971) as quoted in Sennett, p. 14.

23. Letter to Kenneth M. Roemer, 8 August 1979.

24. For example, on page 24 Burris's description of the conversation of a group in Jacob's Ladder is quite vague.

25. Skinner included these topics in his original outline for the book. He originally planned a "chapter or two" on "religion and politics." These were never written (p. 296, SB).

26. For an interesting discussion of characterization in utopian fiction see Jean Pfaelzer, "The Impact of Political Theory on Narrative Structure," in *America as Utopia*, pp. 117–32.

27. The conductor, Fergy was based on Donald Ferguson, who conducted the B Minor Mass at Minnesota; the architects were based on Winton Close and Lisl Scheu; the college president, Mittlebach, was based on Middlebrook, the Minnesota comptroller; Mrs. Olson was based on Skinner's Aunt Alt; and for Deborah's birthday party Skinner used the name of his youngest daughter and the memory of her sister Julie's third birthday party (pp. 297, 303, SB).

28. Except for the architect and a dentist, the women introduced to the

visitors have jobs associated with traditional female roles: Olson (cook), Nash (nursery), Meyerson (female clothing). But they are all professionals and Mrs. Meyerson is a manager.

29. Other possible sources for Castle include a professor at Harvard named Castle, two philosophers who lived at the Faculty Club at Minnesota, and a poem entitled "That Pessimistic Fellow," written by Skinner when he was ten (pp. 171, 190, SB; p. 93, P).

30. Wolfe, p. 14.

31. Wolfe "discovered" this pun, p. 18.

32. A character named Simmons helped Frazier found Walden Two (p. 96, W). Skinner wrote a chapter about the founding of the community, but that chapter and another on the race "problem" were cut from the final draft and "inadvertently thrown away" (p. 330, SB).

33. Wolfe, 18.

34. "Utopia as Experiment," p. 44.

35. Robert Elliott, *The Shape of Utopia; Studies in a Literary Genre* (Chicago: Univ. of Chicago Pr., 1970), p. 135.

36. Skinner had already applied behavioristic approaches to the study of humans, especially human verbal behavior. But *Walden Two* represented a much broader application.

37. As a college student, Skinner had already made literary use of his mother's maiden name: he occasionally used "Sir Burrhus" as a pseudonym (p. 267, P).

38. Wolfe, p. 13. A brief and rather superficial treatment of Burris's conversion is presented in James P. Farrelly, "Compromise, Commitment, or Capitulation: Conversion as a Central Theme in *1984, Walden II[sic], The Dispossessed* and *Ecotopia*," a paper delivered at the Fourth Annual Utopian Studies Conference in Denver, 13 Oct. 1979.

39. The nature of this decision again parallels religious conversions.

40. See Kenneth M. Roemer, *The Obsolete Necessity: America in Utopian Writings, 1888–1900* (Kent, Ohio: Kent State Univ. Pr., 1976), pp. 95–101.

41. Ibid., pp. 15–34; and see part 4 of *America as Utopia*, especially Joel Nydahl's essay, "From Millennium to Utopia Americana," pp. 237–53.

42. Edward Bellamy, "How I Wrote 'Looking Backward,'" *Ladies Home Journal*, Apr. 1894, p. 2.

43. Malachi Martin, "The Scientist as Shaman," as quoted in Saleebey, p. 398.

44. Sennett, p. 14.

45. See Greenberg, "Skinner Sees Little Hope."

46. *Science and Human Behavior*, p. 442.

47. I would like to thank Mr. Skinner for reading the manuscript of this essay and for correcting several factual errors.

9
Utopia Reconsidered: Comments on *1984*
William Steinhoff

George Orwell resembled Samuel Johnson in the many ways that Jeffrey Meyers has suggested but not in his attitude toward government. Living in an age when the balance of power between ruler and ruled was less disproportionate than it is now, Johnson was optimistic enough to believe that arbitrary and overweening power was bound to fail in the end: "I consider that in no government power can be abused long. Mankind will not bear it. If a sovereign oppresses his people to a great degree, they will rise and cut off his head. There is a remedy in human nature against tyranny that will keep us safe under every form of government."[1]

Orwell did not share this opinion; long before *1984* was written, events in Europe had shown him that no "remedy in human nature" could prevail against the organized assaults of fascism and communism, bolstered as they were by armies and massive armament as well as by control of the press. But, though he paradoxically called himself a socialist, Orwell went farther than most in believing that the state had come to weigh so heavily on individuals that even the act of love could turn into a political gesture of submission or rebellion, and questions about the sum of two plus two could lead to the epistemological certainty, guaranteed and enforced by the power of the state, that the answer was five.

This belief did not, of course, emerge full blown in *Burmese Days*, his first novel. In it individual weakness is opposed to power in the relatively narrow context of imperialism; but as Orwell's experience and theoretical understanding widened, his conception of this struggle became less parochial. With *1984* the British empire becomes a super-state called Oceania, and the central issue is not so much the exploitation of the masses for profit as it is the nature and use of power as these have developed in the twentieth century. Pervading every aspect of this clearly defined subject is the bewildered feeling, so poignantly expressed in *Animal Farm* and *1984*, that something in modern life has gone wrong, that human beings were not meant to be so ill at ease in the world, and that the explanation of the puzzle is somewhere to be found in politics.

Orwell conceived *1984* as a utopia with a difference. He wrote to F. J. Warburg, his publisher, "I don't like talking about books before they are written, but I will tell you now that this is a novel about the future—that is, it is in a sense a fantasy, but in the form of a naturalistic novel. That is what makes it a difficult job—of course as a book of anticipations it would be comparatively simple to write."[2]

One does not have to be displaced in space or time—to New Zealand or the year 4000—to be shocked into awareness of Orwell's satirical warning about the perversions to which a centralized economy is liable and "the totalitarian ideas that have taken root in the minds of intellectuals everywhere."[3] Orwell's naturalistic novel is grounded in the world as he observed it, and it merely transposes into the near future characters, situations, and themes familiar to us in his work from *Burmese Days* to *Animal Farm*.

In these earlier works the individuals at the center of the story are constrained to the point of rebellion by the peculiar atmosphere of their daily lives. Whether the story hinges on a search for love or spiritual health, a longing to recapture the past, a desire to make the best of perceived talents, or a bid for freedom, the struggle is set in a political context in such a way that motives and conduct are shown to be inseparable from political assumptions. Each of the major characters is an underdog, a lonely human being pitted against an oppressive, seemingly invulnerable society. The conflict invariably ends in defeat for the individual, but the drama of opposition is substantiated with such intensity that the predictability of the outcome is more than balanced by the sense one has of reading the truth about a principal fact of modern life.

To make this truth comprehensible and convincing in *1984*, Orwell wanted Winston Smith and Julia to be no less believable as human beings than the lovers in *Keep the Aspidistra Flying*, despite the outrageous conditions under which they live and the outrageous things that are done to them. The pervasive and corrupting influence of the Party becomes clear when Winston listens to the thrush and asks, "What made it sit at the edge of the lonely wood and pour its music into nothingness? He wondered whether after all there was a microphone hidden somewhere near." Yet the landscape of the Golden Country, which Smith sees in his dream and almost finds again with Julia, is what any country walk in England might uncover: "an old, rabbit-bitten pasture, with a foot track wandering across it and a molehill here and there. In the ragged hedge on the opposite side of the field the boughs of the elm trees were swaying very faintly in the breeze."[4]

The conditions that make life in Oceania so disagreeable had their counterparts in wartime Engand, and it was reasonable that Orwell should think that tyranny would inflict the same blighting effect as the war had done, creating shortages, disorganizing transport and services, oppressing the spirit, and destroying the solaces that nature had once afforded. In 1944 he had described the British scene in a passage that foreshadows life under Big Brother: "Everything grows shabbier and more rickety. Sixteen people in a railway carriage designed for ten is quite common. The countryside has quite changed its face, . . . and in the remotest places one cannot get away from the roar of aeroplanes, which has become the normal background noise, drowning the larks."[5] *Homage to Catalonia* records the same discomfort and dreariness, with the addition of what Orwell called a "nightmare atmosphere," and since he frequently remarked during World War II that no permanent return to peace seemed probable, any novel he wrote about the future was bound to depict the actual conditions he had known so well in Spain and England.

Critics have complained that too much effort has been spent dissecting *1984*, when any intelligent reader can see what Orwell's intention was and how he carried it out. The actions which carry Winston Smith from resentment against the regime to secret defiance and finally to hopeless capitulation are presented straightforwardly enough. In fact, however, most of the important writings about *1984* have not been concerned with novelistic treatment but with the statement the book makes about the threat of totalitarianism. Winston Smith is not an especially engaging hero. He is fearful, intellectually undistinguished, and an awkward lover. Because he can only assert his views inwardly in an "interminable, restless monologue that had been running inside his head for years,"[6] he has no influence on his fellows. He appeals chiefly to our sense of pathos. His noteworthiness comes, not from any singularity, but from the grotesque disparity between his feebly rebellious acts and the calculated total destruction of his humanity by the Party.

The progress of his education, tellingly delineated through changes in his inner life, shows ironically that the ideal of totalitarianism is to make men perfect, and in the outcome this means making them inhuman. If Winston Smith is to be "reintegrated," his illusions about objective reality have to be dispelled and a satisfactory answer provided for the question, Why does the Party seek power? The process of interrogation, abuse, torture, instruction, and "love" to which O'Brien subjects him is the means by which he is perfected; he learns, understands, and at last transforms O'Brien's teaching into love of Big Brother.

The Party has to control objective reality because it seeks control over the individual. Smith's error is to suppose (as nearly all of us do) that somewhere a state of things exists which is not amenable to human wishes or acts—a reality that power cannot alter. But O'Brien at last persuades him that he is wrong. Doublethink and Newspeak are but two of the means by which the Inner Party enforces its will. It controls the past and future by creating a continuous present, thus destroying history and hope. It isolates citizens from outsiders by warfare and from insiders by espionage and suspicion, depriving them of the knowledge and confidence essential to making comparisons and contrasts, which in turn could lead to rebellion.

Orwell came to think that "when one is making out one's weekly budget, two and two invariably make four. Politics, on the other hand, is a sort of sub-atomic or non-Euclidean world where it is quite easy for the part to be greater than the whole or for two objects to be in the same place at the same time."[7] In such a contradictory and unstable environment freedom is in danger because the essence of freedom (and implicitly therefore the success of the democratic socialism Orwell valued so highly) is some apparently unshakable guarantee— like $2 + 2 = 4$—which the individual resisting authority could use as a last resort in affirming his independence. Every external assurance Smith thinks of is subverted by O'Brien: "human nature," natural law (e.g., gravity), history, or the demonstrable existence of some foreign regime.

The possibility of being free "inside one's head" is also removed. In other books, notably *A Clergyman's Daughter* and *Down and Out in Paris and London*, Orwell had considered whether or not one could be free in the mind even if condemned to the prison of exhausting drudgery and poverty, and he had concluded that no one (especially not an intellectual) could be free who was also isolated and lonely. So dependent are we on others for stimulation and encouragement that "it is almost impossible to think without talking."[8] Isolated and disoriented, Smith is transformed into a model citizen. As Hannah Arendt says, "The ideal subject of totalitarian rule is not the convinced Nazi or the convinced Communist, but people for whom the distinction between fact and fiction (*i.e.*, the reality of experience) and the distinction between true and false (*i.e.*, the standards of thought) no longer exist."⁹

Orwell also dramatized two other features of totalitarianism in *1984*—its unceasing drive to expand and its passion for internal consistency. Hermann Rauschning was one of the first to identify the totalitarian ideal of ever-expanding power. Most obviously, of course, it expands geographically: the old joke has Hitler saying, "All I want is the land next to my own," another version of the slogan, "Today, Germany; tomorrow, the world." Power also turns inward as it seeks ever-increasing control over the individual. Orwell's representation of this process is corroborated by what Arendt called "the preparation of the victim," the three-step process by which human beings are destroyed—that is, converted into model citizens in the totalitarian style.

First, the "juridical person," whose identity is guaranteed by the existence of law, is eliminated by the arbitrary exercise of power under the guise of love in such a way that even the possibility of freely consenting to arrest and imprisonment is denied. An essential part of an individual is destroyed when his civil rights are taken away without regard to the law. Smith, it is true, is a thought-criminal, but Ampleforth, Syme, and Parsons are guilty only of being, not doing. Second, Arendt specifies the "murder of the moral person in man." Because martyrdom is made impossible, the victim can have no place in history; indeed history itself is abolished. O'Brien makes Smith understand that posterity will not vindicate him: " 'Nothing will remain of you: not a name in a register, not a memory in a living brain. You will be annihilated in the past as well as in the future. You will never have existed.' "¹⁰

Smith struggles nevertheless to preserve what the autobiographical persona of "Such, Such Were the Joys" calls the "incorruptible inner self." History (i.e., posterity) may not know him or his righteousness, but in his own soul he will cherish the devotion to principle he has withheld from O'Brien. Even this last refuge is removed when he repudiates Julia, a betrayal implicit in his earlier concession that the end justifies the means.

Arendt distinguishes a third stage in this exercise of control—the degradation of human beings by reducing them to the status of sick animals. When, near the end of his strength, Smith asserts his "moral superiority," O'Brien compels him to look at himself in a mirror. He sees a "bowed, gray-colored, skeleton-like thing," the pitiful image familiar to us in photographs of concentration camp victims. O'Brien calls him " 'a bag of filth. . . . Do you see that thing facing you? That is the last man. If you are human, that is humanity,' ' "[11] a passage which explains why Orwell once thought of calling his book *The Last Man in Europe*.[12] What Orwell dramatized and what Arendt stressed is the inner logic of totalitarianism driving toward power over men. Logic even at the expense of reason is the test. " 'You are a flaw in the pattern, Winston. You are a stain that must be wiped out.' "[13] In a word, the inhumane ideal of the rulers of *1984* is perfection, the perfection of consistency.

The utopian ideal, like the ideal of equality, has haunted the human mind for centuries despite the perversions it has succumbed to in practice. The literary mode of the ideal, uncontaminated by actuality, has been especially successful and inspiring. Certainly Orwell had a lifelong interest in this genre and its typical themes; he was absorbed by the relation of rulers to ruled, the satirical portrayal of utopias, the consequences of technological developments, and what the actual future was going to be like.

The man who most fully explored these matters in his books was of course H. G. Wells, one of the favorite writers of Orwell's boyhood. The world in *The Shape of Things to Come* exemplifies the vision of the future that Emmanuel Goldstein described as the dream of twentieth-century intellectuals, "a glittering antiseptic world of glass and steel and snow-white concrete."[14] The rulers Wells portrayed, austere and fanatical, relying on "mental reconstruction" and "psychic surgery" to accomplish their subjection of the less gifted, strongly suggest a kinship with O'Brien. *The New Machiavelli*, in which Sidney and Beatrice Webb are caricatured, pictures the way in which these aristocrats of understanding, helped by expert technicians, hope to create a new society; and their logic is the logic O'Brien uses in explaining to Smith why he must submit to his own destruction.

Despite these likenesses and Orwell's admiration for Wells's inventiveness, Orwell did not adopt the older writer's outlook. The physical surroundings in *1984* spring, as we have seen, from actual conditions in time of war, but they are also clearly intended to deny Wells's confident belief that the triumph of the "scientific man" over the "romantic man" would improve the lot of mankind. Contradicting this theory, Orwell had written in 1941: "Modern Germany is far more scientific than England and far more barbarous. Much of what Wells has imagined and worked for is physically there in Nazi Germany. The order, the planning, the State encouragement of science, the steel, the concrete, the aeroplanes, are all there, but in the service of ideas appropriate to the Stone Age."[15] As Irving Howe has noted, "Orwell had not been taken in by the legend that totalitarianism is at least efficient." He was painting Oceania, according to Howe, in the likeness not only of wartime England but of the "modern Russian cities with their Victorian ostentation and rotting slums."[16]

Though still acknowledging Wells's great influence and the lasting impression Wells had made on his own mind, Orwell rejected Wells's later, more pessimistic, view that is foreshadowed in *When the Sleeper Wakes*, where "the privileged live a life of shallow gutless hedonism," while the workers become utter slaves.[17] Orwell thought that Wells was "too sane to understand the modern world. . . . He was, and still is, quite incapable of understanding that nationalism, religious bigotry and feudal loyalty are far more powerful forces than what he himself would describe as sanity."[18] These are precisely the forces that Big Brother most tellingly exploits through the appeals broadcast to the masses of Oceania.

If Wells lacked the strain of irrationality that Orwell felt to be so marked in modern life, it is amply present in Jack London's *The Iron Heel*. Commenting on the Oligarchy, the fanatical, brutal, power-hungry tyrants in London's novel of the future, Orwell said, "It's one of the best statements of the outlook of a ruling class—of the outlook a ruling class must have if it's to survive—that has ever been written."[19] The consistent, ruthless, and self-conscious exercise of power is an important feature of *The Iron Heel*, as it is of *1984*. Certain details are also echoed: the proles, the three-class hierarchy, even the metaphor of the iron heel itself.

Orwell's regard for London's book may have been a matter of temperament rather than intellect, but his criticism of Aldous Huxley's *Brave New World* was based on rational disagreement. He praised Huxley for portraying cleverly the kind of a world our so-called progress could lead to, but felt it had no relation to the actual future.[20] He also believed that Huxley showed a lack of political awareness and that he did not sufficiently understand what the outlook of the ruling class must be if it is to continue to hold power. Comparing Huxley's ruling class with that portrayed by London, Orwell said the leaders in *Brave New World* lacked one of the essential qualities of a successful ruling class: "a strict morality, a quasi-religious belief . . . , a mystique."[21]

When he came to write his own novel about the future, Orwell departed in important ways from Huxley's model. Shoddiness and scarcity replace the cleanliness, novelty, comfort, and efficiency of *Brave New World*. Victory Gin's violent nastiness is what Oceania offers in place of soma. In *1984* everyone's life is dominated by war and politics. Sexual frenzy expresses itself in the public rallies against the enemies of Oceania, in contrast to the meaningless copulating and easy pacifism of Huxley's people. O'Brien as the invulnerable logician-priest, combining in one person unlimited power and fanatical dedication, comes from a world far different from that of Huxley's benevolent despots.

Gulliver's Travels seems an unlikely ancestor of *1984*, but Orwell saw in it three important features of totalitarianism. The first appears in Book III. Swift had, said Orwell, "an extraordinarily clear prevision of the spy-haunted 'police state,' with its endless heresy hunts and treason trials, all really designed to neutralize popular discontent by changing it into war hysteria."[22] The Kingdom of Tribnia with its informers, plots, and suspected persons made Orwell feel "positively in the midst of the Russian purges."[23] Elsewhere in Book III he found simplified languages, books written by machinery, brain surgery—all exemplifying, he thought, Swift's "perception that one of the aims of totalitarianism is not merely to make sure that people will think the right thoughts, but actually to make them less conscious,"[24] exactly the view that Arendt was to suggest from her own first-hand knowledge.

Book IV of *Gulliver's Travels* exhibits another, even more important, aspect of totalitarianism, which Orwell incorporated in the Ministry of Love. The Houyhnhnms, he observes, are governed by reason, whose imperatives are transmitted by advice or exhortation, not by overt constraint, and least of all by force. This permissiveness, what Herbert Marcuse called "repressive tolerance," molds conduct. The Houyhnhnms in fact surpass the Inner Party because they have established a society where dissident opinions cannot exist, not because the citizens fear punishment but because they have lost the ability to resist public opinion, which they equate with love or reason. A rule of law establishes guidelines within which individuals have at least some sense of freedom; under a rule of love the pressure to conform pervades every act and blocks all development. O'Brien tells Smith: "'The command of the old despotisms was "Thou shalt not." The command of the totalitarians was "Thou shalt." Our command is *"Thou art."* No one whom we bring to this place ever stands out against us. Everyone is washed clean. Even those three miserable traitors. . . . There was nothing left in them but sorrow for what they had done, and love of Big Brother.'"[25] Orwell said of *Gulliver's Travels*, "Its fascination seems inexhaustible." Considering the intellectual riches which were transmuted from it to *1984*, this judgment is not surprising.

G. K. Chesterton also interested Orwell, though we may not make much of the fact that *The Napoleon of Notting Hill* is set in 1984 (as is Asgard, one of Jack London's "wonder cities") and that it features a world-wide truce "or deadlock which had made foreign wars impossible" and therefore permits a local war to occur.[26] More significant is Orwell's opinion that "Chesterton, in a less methodical way [than Hilaire Belloc] predicted the disappearance of democracy and private property, and the rise of a slave society which might be called either capitalist or Communist."[27]

Orwell found in *The Man Who Was Thursday* a conspiracy of the intelligentsia (artists, philosophers, scientists), who aim to seize power and establish themselves as a new ruling class. The conspiracy is organized into an inner and outer circle; those in the outer ring look forward to "the paradise of the future," but the sinister inner ring aims first to destroy humanity and then itself. Its motive resembles that of the Eastasian philosophy of Death-worship (corresponding to Oceania's Ingsoc and Eurasian Neo-Bolshevism), "better perhaps rendered as Obliteration of the Self."[28]

One of Orwell's major themes, his belief that the concept of objective reality was being eroded, also appears in this thriller. Chesterton's hero, Gabriel Syme (a poet, not a philologist), encourages what he calls "the starry pinnacle of the commonplace," from which he observes the decencies of "common and kindly people in the street." This vantage point is also symbolized by the equation $2 + 2 = 4$ and contrasted with, in Chesterton's language, "the thing which the modern people call Impressionism, which is another name for that final skepticism which can find no floor in the universe."[29]

Eugene Zamyatin's *We* is important for students of Orwell and the idea of utopia if only because so eminent a historian as Isaac Deutscher asserted that Orwell borrowed the idea of *1984* and most of its other features from Zamyatin and that "it is perhaps only the thoroughness of Orwell's English approach that gives to his work the originality it possesses."[30] *We* and *1984* are indeed both anti-utopian novels, but Deutscher's claim will not stand inspection. Orwell thought *We* important enough to review at length and to recommend to his friends and help its sale, but the two books are radically different. *We* belongs to the same class of hedonistic anti-utopias as *Brave New World*, which Orwell believed to be partly derived from it;[31] and its atmosphere, like that of Huxley's work, contrasts markedly with the shabbiness, discomfort, violence, and induced hysteria of *1984*. As George Woodcock says, "what distinguishes it [*1984*] even more strikingly from previous Utopias and even anti-Utopias is that the pretense of providing happiness as a compensation for the loss of freedom is not maintained. Even the synthetic pleasures and comforts promised by Zamyatin and Huxley no longer exist."[32]

Secondly, as Orwell said in his review, although *We* has political implications, "it is not about Russia and has no direct connection with contemporary politics." *We* is a criticism of industrial civilization; Zamyatin had "a strong leaning toward primitivism," and his book "is in effect a study of the machine."[33] Orwell, of course, though he had no great love for the machine age, realized that the socialism he advocated depended on a strong industrial base and that a reversion to some sort of agrarian society was a chimera. When Deutscher asserted the importance of *We* for Orwell he apparently knew nothing of Orwell's considerable knowledge of utopian literature, nor did he show an awareness of how many situations and themes from Orwell's earlier writing reappear in *1984*.

In any survey of the fiction which has a bearing on *1984* an account must be given of Arthur Koestler's *Darkness at Noon*. We know from reading *Homage to Catalonia* that Orwell acquired first hand some rather dangerous experience with communism in action; this knowledge was amplified by his reading of Boris Souvarine and Franz Borkenau. From Souvarine's *Cauchemar en U.R.S.S.* he learned, for example, about the enormous lies being propagated by the purge trials, and about Trotsky's being forever the accused, "the eternal offender." He found too that physical cruelty had been supplemented by spiritual torture, to the point where Leon Blum, the French Socialist leader, could speak of "how the Stalinist terror adds a sort of mental decomposition to the spiritual perversion."[34]

Darkness at Noon confirms these insights and adds others, among them the disappearance of law and the deliberate isolation of Soviet citizens from the outside world and from the past. Gletkin is one of a "new race of monsters" having no tie to tradition, no memories of an older world with its "vain competitions of honour" and its "hypocritical decencies." Rubashov, the Party oldtimer, had forfeited his right of protest, corrupting himself by his steadfast devotion to the principle that the end justifies the means; "We were neo-Machiavellians in the name of universal reason—that was our greatness."[35] In Koestler's novel Orwell found a parallel drawn between the Communist party and the Roman Catholic church; he found also significant intimations of "thought-crime" and "doublethink," and examples of the inexorable logic of the totalitarian mentality which led accused Party members to confess enormous crimes they had not committed, thus maintaining the belief that the Party was infallible.

Two works of nonfiction that interested Orwell and shaped his thoughts about the future were James Burnham's *The Managerial Revolution* and Hilaire Belloc's *The Servile State*. When Orwell reviewed the latter in 1940 he called it "a very prescient book" because it "foretold with astonishing accuracy the things that are happening now."[36] The first point that impressed him was the possibility that a hierarchical version of socialism might easily develop instead of one that was democratic; and the second was an idea that haunted his mind for years, namely that civilization might revert to a long period of slavery. This conception is at the center of Belloc's analysis; he foresaw, that is, a kind of socialism in which people would make a legal sacrifice of liberty in exchange for economic security, a system of freely chosen slavery.

Burnham's theory about the way Western society is going to develop out of a declining capitalism is expressed in *The Managerial Revolution* and his more general views about politics in *The Machiavellians* and *The Struggle for the World*. These books, about which Orwell wrote on at least five occasions, offered him an analysis of contemporary political and social developments as well as an account of their underlying causes. The motive Burnham stresses is the continuing struggle for power among men, seen by Machiavelli and his followers as the dynamo of politics—the source of change and political instability.

Orwell derived from Burnham a vision of the future which he incorporated in *1984*: three superpowers dividing the world between them, engaged in permanent warfare, each knowing that it cannot conquer the others; a hierarchical social system with an oligarchy at the top ruling by force and fraud; "scientific" managers free of illusions about democracy, equality, and justice, and immune to the myths they invent in order to govern; the "exploitation of backward areas," that is, those portions of the globe not directly controlled by one of the superstates; a steady decline in the power of ordinary citizens and a corresponding increase in the power of the state.

Orwell emphatically did not accept the future that Burnham envisioned. In 1946 he wrote that "as an interpretation of what *is happening*, Burnham's theory is extremely plausible, to put it at the

lowest. The events of, at any rate, the last fifteen years in the USSR
can be far more easily explained by this theory than by any other," and
he adds, " . . . if one considers the world movement as a whole, his
conclusions are difficult to resist."[37] Nevertheless Orwell resisted.
Burnham, he said, like other pessimistic political thinkers, mistakenly
supposes that what is happening is going to continue to happen; he
overestimates the power of Communist fanaticism and discounts the
significance of the rapid turnover in Communist party membership; his
acceptance of selfishness as the primary human motive is falsified by
the pragmatic test of history; there are good motives in politics, and
power worship is not supreme; his apocalyptic view of history distorts
the illogical, slow way things actually happen. In sum, although Orwell
used Burnham's theory in *1984*, he did not believe in it.

In the years immediately after Orwell's death, and despite the
phenomenal success of *Animal Farm* and *1984*, either the quality of his
work was underestimated or the image of what was thought to be the
man was regarded more highly than what he had done. A surprised
and rather grudging admiration seemed to set the tone of comment, as
if a writer whom one was accustomed to call a journalist could not
really have produced books of lasting value. Recently, however, his
achievement has been evaluated more justly. One can now say with
some assurance that an impressive body of work—some of the essays,
The Road to Wigan Pier, Homage to Catalonia, Coming Up for Air—is
likely to survive in addition to the classic *Animal Farm* and *1984*, one
of the few novels written in English in the twentieth century to be both
a critical and a popular triumph. Its metaphors—Doublethink, Orwell-
lian, "War is Peace," Big Brother, and 1984 itself—live in the public
mind because the conditions they so vividly epitomize are among the
most important matters people now think and write about.

The year 1984 will soon be memoralized by books and articles
about the ever-increasing power of the state, speculation about the
powerful "new class" emerging in Western Europe and the United
States, and the continuing threat posed by unstable totalitarian regimes throughout the world. In 1954 Deutscher called *1984* an "ideological superweapon in the cold war,"[38] and it has had that effect
because so many features of its superstates bring into focus the conflict
between the Soviet Union and the NATO countries.

Orwell's warning, however, was not aimed just at Communist or
fascist regimes but at tendencies evident in the democracies of Western Europe and America, and his message reached a large, responsive
audience. Thirty years later people are even more sensitive to the

intrusion of politics and state control into daily life, and some at least acknowledge how common the tendency is to expect that the state should accomplish ends once considered incompatible with political solutions. Issues formerly settled more or less amicably and naturally between individuals or between individuals and social institutions like the church, business, school, or the family are now increasingly subject to intervention by the state through the apparatus of the courts, regulatory agencies, and administrative decrees. The state supplants the private conscience; and even when judgments are presumably free they are manipulated by media forces scarcely less powerful than the state. Warfare and other forms of violence are only the most dramatic means by which state power is extended; in the democracies at least, inflation and taxes have been equally potent. In sum, as a warning *1984* continues to be relevant to contemporary life.

Considered from a different angle, *1984* marks a new stage in the concept of the materialistic utopia. Belief that human perfectibility might be attained through changes in the environment has been one of the principal themes of life and literature, to say nothing of "Utopia books," ever since the beginning of the Romantic movement. Reforms of all sorts, revolution if they fail, liquidation of class enemies, wars to end war or to make the world safe for democracy, Fabian and apocalyptic visions—all have in common a feeling that human existence on this earth can be made perfect or something close to it. Side by side with this optimistic bent in thought and conduct, powerful feelings of nihilism have also found expression in literature and life.

1984 represents both these lines of development. Orwell's values, sometimes called old-fashioned, were derived from his admiration of virtues he associated with the working class: the wholesomeness of family life, loyalty to friends and country, honesty, and a decent regard for others. The positive side of *1984* is its assertion that these virtues are worth preserving. Furthermore, Orwell implies that not only are most people richly capable of love and generosity and patriotism, but that their feelings naturally tend in those directions. Left in comparative freedom, the proles in *1984* may be vulgar and ignorant, but they are admirably human in their affections and outlook.

1984 also shows that a materialist utopia does little to foster the virtues Orwell cherished; indeed technology, by robbing men of opportunities to do manifestly useful work, makes it hard for them to keep their self-respect. Morally the intellectuals suffer most of all from this lack of a clear need for their talents. More important, the ideal of a material utopia is inwardly corrupt; it turns into its opposite because individuals are inherently imperfect, and a perfect state demands that they be forced into patterns alien to their natures. In his review of Viscount Samuel's *An Unknown Land* Orwell, after observing that technologically "ideal" conditions "are always profoundly unappetizing to read about," added, "It is noticeable that a 'perfect' society only becomes thinkable if the human mind and even human physiology are somehow got rid of."[39]

Although physical torture, death, and wholesale massacre are obvious means of destroying dissidents like Winston Smith, in *1984* these are supplemented by education or conversion carried on by an intellectual elite for whom the inner world is more real than external actuality. The ideology of the ruling class intellectuals in *1984* compels them to regard human beings as material to be molded or discarded as the system demands; in the actual world their counterparts, led by Hitler and Stalin, committed unbelievable crimes of ideological fanaticism with a like end in view. From Butler to Zamyatin thinkers had recognized the possibility that if an all-powerful state were in control, material progress might end in the subjugation of humanity. In *1984* Orwell carried the idea to its limit, arguing that if such a ruling class were allowed to develop the end would not be merely the subjection but the destruction of humanity.

Notes

The abbreviation CEJL is used here for *The Collected Essays, Journalism and Letters of George Orwell*, ed. Sonia Orwell and Ian Angus, 4 vols. (London: Secker and Warburg, 1968). The original sources of the essays and journal articles are also given because critical judgments can hinge on the date when a piece first appeared or the audience to whom it was addressed. Unless otherwise noted, the writings cited below are by Orwell.

1. James Boswell, *Life of Johnson*, 2 vols. (London: Oxford Univ. Pr., 1922), 1:452.
2. Letter to F. J. Warburg, 31 May 1947, *CEJL*, 4:329–30.
3. Letter to Roger Senhouse, 26 Dec. 1948, *CEJL*, 4:460.
4. *1984* (New York: Harcourt, Brace and World, 1949), pp. 124–25.
5. "London Letter," *Partisan Review*, 24 July 1944, *CEJL*, 3:195.
6. *1984*, p. 9.
7. "In Front of Your Nose," *Tribune*, 22 Mar. 1946, *CEJL*, 4:125.
8. "As I Please," *Tribune*, 28 Apr. 1944, *CEJL*, 3:133.
9. Hannah Arendt, *The Origins of Totalitarianism*, 2d enlarged ed. (Cleveland: World Publishing Co., 1958), p. 474.
10. *1984*, pp. 257–58.

11. Ibid., p. 275.
12. Letter to F. J. Warburg, 22 Oct. 1948, *CEJL*, 4:448.
13. *1984*, p. 258.
14. Ibid., p. 189.
15. "Wells, Hitler and the World State," *Horizon*, Aug. 1941, *CEJL*, 2:143.
16. Irving Howe, "*1984*: History as Nightmare," in *Politics and the Novel* (Greenwich, Conn.: Fawcett, 1967), p. 247.
17. *The Road to Wigan Pier* (New York: Harcourt, Brace and World, 1958), p. 234.
18. "Wells, Hitler and the World State," *CEJL*, 2:145.
19. "Jack London," BBC broadcast, 8 Oct. 1945, script no. 37 in Orwell Archive, University College, London.
20. "Notes on the Way," *Time and Tide*, 6 Apr. 1940, *CEJL*, 2:17.
21. "Prophecies of Fascism," *Tribune*, 12 June 1940, *CEJL*, 2:31.
22. "Politics vs. Literature: An Examination of *Gulliver's Travels*," *Polemic*, no. 5, Sept.–Oct. 1946, *CEJL*, 4:213.
23. Ibid.
24. Ibid., 214.
25. *1984*, pp. 258–59.
26. G. K. Chesterton, *The Napoleon of Notting Hill* (London: John Lane, Bodley Head, 1904), p. 15.
27. "James Burnham and the Managerial Revolution," in *Polemic*, no. 3, May 1946, under the title "Second Thoughts on James Burnham." Printed as a pamphlet with the present title by the Socialist Book Centre, Summer 1946. *CEJL*, 4:163.
28. *1984*, p. 197.
29. *The Man Who Was Thursday* (New York: Modern Library, n.d.), pp. 188–89.
30. Isaac Deutscher, "'*1984*'—The Mysticism of Cruelty," in *Russia in Transition*, rev. ed. (New York: Grove Pr., 1960), p. 252.
31. Review of *We* by E. I. Zamyatin, *Tribune*, 4 Jan. 1946, *CEJL*, 4:72.
32. *The Crystal Spirit: A Study of George Orwell* (Boston: Little, Brown, 1966), pp. 215–16.
33. Review of *We*, *CEJL*, 4:75.
34. " . . . à la perversion morale la terreur Stalinienne ajoute une sorte de décomposition mentale." Quoted in Boris Souvarine, "Cauchemar en U.R.S.S.," *Revue de Paris*, 1 July 1937, p. 167.
35. Arthur Koestler, *Darkness at Noon* (New York: Macmillan, 1941), pp. 97–98.
36. "Notes on the Way," *Time and Tide*, 6 Apr. 1940, *CEJL*, 2:16.
37. "James Burnham and the Managerial Revolution," *CEJL*, 4:165.
38. Deutscher, p. 250.
39. Review of *An Unknown Land* by Herbert Lewis Samuel, *The Listener*, 24 Dec. 1942, p. 826.

10

Vonnegut's *Player Piano:* An Ambiguous Technological Dystopia

Howard P. Segal

Kurt Vonnegut's *Player Piano* (1954) takes place at an unspecified future date in the town of Ilium, New York. At this time the United States is the dominant world power, and there are no apparent rivals for international hegemony. The United States achieved this position through victory in a third world war some years earlier.

That international conflict, however, had a second, no less important result: the domination of technology over mankind, at least in the United States. In order both to meet wartime production needs and to compensate for the drainage of manpower into the armed forces, automated machinery replaced most manual laborers and computers replaced most supervisors of those laborers. These changes remained in effect after the war, despite the return to America of millions of former or future workers and supervisors. The inevitable consequence of their return was so-called "technological unemployment."

At the time of the story, however, the United States is hardly an economically depressed society. Quite the opposite: its technology has made the country more prosperous than ever and has in fact made possible both cradle-to-grave medical care and a guaranteed annual wage for all citizens. The changes technology has brought about are so profound as to be termed the Second Industrial Revolution.

By "technology," it should be emphasized, Vonnegut implicitly means more than tools and machines alone—that is, more than "hardware." He means as well the use of that hardware in the organization and administration of society and the technical knowledge and skills necessary to operate whatever hardware is not automatic and to make whatever decisions and policies are not made by computer. Such a comprehensive conception of technology is at once sophisticated and accurate.

The United States of *Player Piano* is, in a sense, itself a giant automated machine, with millions of parts. Not only is life for all citizens overwhelmingly automated, but every citizen has an assigned part in the social mechanism. Moreover, one huge computer, named EPICAC XIV (i.e., thirteenth addition to the original model), makes the major decisions about national policy and so largely determines the fate of all citizens. To be sure, technically trained human beings control EPICAC insofar as they built and continue to operate it in its Carlsbad Caverns home. But they always defer to its answers to their questions—as do, they make certain, all other citizens.

To the managerial and engineering elite who, if only in theory, nevertheless run the United States, the nation is a veritable "technological utopia." Although American society will develop further—unlike many other, wholly static utopias—its fundamental form is permanently established.

To most of Vonnegut's Americans, however, contemporary society is far from utopian. They appreciate the material benefits of technology but resent their loss of meaningful labor and in turn of personal identity and social purpose. Many adults, it must be stressed, do "work." But their work is menial and unsatisfying and contributes practically nothing to American society. It is restricted to three areas: (1) the army, which requires enlistments of twenty-five years but which is unarmed save for its occasional overseas duty—for fear of possible rebellion against the ruling elite and sabotage against its tools and machines; (2) the Reconstruction and Reclamation Corps (derisively called the "Reeks and Wrecks"), which apparently has shorter enlistment requirements but no more significant duties, being restricted to the infrequent road repairs for which automated tools and machines would be too expensive; and (3) various self-employment positions, running from bartender to barber to pool shark. The elite positions are restricted to those whose IQ's and vocational aptitudes—as measured in nationwide tests scored by computers—grant them opportunities for advanced education and then managerial and engineering positions. Not only are the overwhelming majority of citizens excluded from childhood on from significant jobs, but even most of those who manage to obtain Ph.D.'s—nearly all of them in technical areas—are excluded too, so small is the ruling elite.

These nationwide divisions between the elite and the masses are, in the case of Ilium and presumably other communities, exacerbated by the separation of their places of residence. In Ilium, the elite live in a plush suburban-like setting near the Ilium Works, the area's principal production unit. The Ilium Works manufactures "parts for baby carriages and bottle caps, motorcycles and refrigerators, television sets and tricycles,"[1] all by automated assembly lines. So few are the number of persons needed for the production process that the night shift at least can commute to and from work in a single station wagon. The masses live across the Iroquois River in a township of prefabricated dwellings called Homestead. Few of them have any association with the Works and most of them work, if at all, at the menial tasks already described. Once again, however, the masses do not suffer economic deprivation. Rather, they enjoy glass and steel houses whose amenities include microwave ovens, ultrasonic dishwashers and clothes washers and dryers, automatic ironers, and twenty-seven-inch color television sets. Yet their living conditions do not compensate for their working conditions and thus do not eliminate their gnawing resentment and discontent. Homestead is therefore somewhat closer to the site after which it is named—the huge steel plant outside Pittsburgh operated by Andrew Carnegie and the scene of a violent clash in 1892 between labor and management—than is Ilium to the site after which it is named: Troy, home of the Trojans, captured by the Greeks through use of the wooden horse and completely destroyed. For the banality of the modern Ilium contrasts unfavorably with the grandeur of the original.[2]

The central plot of *Player Piano* revolves around Dr. Paul Proteus, the thirty-five-year-old manager of the Ilium Works. His job is the most important and most prestigious in the entire community, but he is being seriously considered for a similar position at the larger and more important Pittsburgh Works. He in fact is the favorite for the post, partly because of his own achievements to date but partly too because of the achievements of his late father. His father was "the nation's first National Industrial, Commercial, Communications, Foodstuffs, and Resources Director, a position approached in importance only by the presidency of the United States."[3] Indeed, the National Industrial Planning Board which grew out of his father's position has since become far more powerful than the presidency. Paul's prospects for the post are further enhanced by his friendship with Dr. Anthony Kroner, of America's Eastern Division (which includes both Ilium and Pittsburgh), the supreme manager, who will make the decision, and by Kroner's admiration for Paul's father. Paul's prospects are still further enhanced by the aggressive efforts of his wife, Anita, to make her husband as socially appealing as possible, through endless parties, gossip, prep talks, and other means of social climbing.

From the outset of the story, however, Paul appears vaguely discontented with life in general and, in the eyes of first Kroner and then Anita, insufficiently eager for the promotion to Pittsburgh. Paul's prospects are undermined more directly by the gossiping of Dr. Lawson Shepherd, a former college classmate but presently envious subordinate at the Ilium Works, that Paul is losing his nerves and so his competency. Even before learning of these rumors, Paul rightly calls Shepherd "Dog-Eat-Dog."

Whatever his reservations about his present or future position, Paul remains passive until prodded by others and by unforeseen events. The prodding begins at a dinner party given by the Ilium Works for Kroner, a party affording Paul an ideal opportunity to secure his promotion. To the party comes Ed Finnerty, an eccentric old friend of Paul who left the Works for a major managerial post in Washington, D.C., still the nation's capital. Finnerty, however, has recently resigned from his post and has returned to denounce the entire "system"—much to the disgust of all at the party, save Paul. Though Paul does not endorse Finnerty's critique, he is aroused by it and accompanies Finnerty on a drinking spree to Homestead. There they meet an equally outspoken critic of society, James Lasher, a sometime anthropologist, barfly, and chaplain. Paul is shaken by Lasher's comments but returns home.

By contrast, Finnerty remains with Lasher and forms the Ghost Shirt Society, an underground organization named after a nineteenth-century American Indian band which fought white settlers. Just as the Indians sought to restore their domination over the remaining parts of the American frontier, so the Society seeks to restore Americans' domination over technology. It even looks to the Indian civilization as an example of a healthier and happier social order. Finnerty and Lasher secretly recruit like-minded members of the ruling elite—several of them Paul's associates—and plan a nationwide uprising. Soon, however, the Society's existence becomes known to the authorities, and its members are forced to go into hiding to escape capture. That the original Ghost Shirt Society failed in its task seems not to daunt its successor; if anything, it strengthens the members' resolve.

Paul does not betray his fellow dissidents but likewise refuses to join the Society. Rather, he seeks temporary escape from his problems through acquisition of an old, dilapidated, and, most important, virtually unmechanized farm. There he plans to live with Anita. Anita is unaware of Paul's ulterior motives and approves of the purchase under the assumption that the farm will be thoroughly mechanized and modernized. Yet eventually Paul finds himself too far removed from nature to become a traditional farmer and abandons this scheme.

The turning point of the story, however, comes during the ruling elite's annual summer retreat on the Meadows, an island in the St. Lawrence River. The retreat is designed to bring together the members of the elite in order for them to celebrate the society they lead. The retreat is restricted to men—even in utopia women, as epitomized by Anita, remain subordinates—and its participants are divided into four teams. Paul is designated a team leader but accepts the honor reluctantly, given his decreasing enthusiasm for the "system." He is much more reluctant to accept an assignment as a double agent, a supposed convert to the Ghost Shirt Society but actually a spy and so subverter of it. The assignment, however, is made a test of his loyalty to that system and a precondition for his promotion, and he finally agrees to it.

Ironically, this act of loyalty to the system ends Paul's already shaky marriage. For Anita, like most other members of the elite, is deliberately kept ignorant of her husband's "true" intentions and instead sees him publicly branded a "saboteur," the most loathsome designation in society. She then leaves him in disgust for Shepherd. Paul still loves Anita, indeed loves no one else, and is deeply saddened but not altogether surprised by her actions.

Ironically, too, Paul refuses to spy on the Society, much less turn its members over to the authorities. Instead, he becomes their nominal leader and is arrested for treason. As his trial proceeds the predicted rebellion begins, the courtroom is invaded, and Paul is liberated. As a result of these developments Paul finally becomes conscious of the hitherto only semi-conscious dissatisfactions with his life: namely, its increasing monotony and shallowness. Gradually, too, he becomes aware of the outright desperation of the less fortunate masses, whose lives are far duller and less fulfilling than his.

On the eve of the uprising Paul agrees to sign a letter composed for him by one of the other rebel leaders, Professor von Neumann. The letter is then widely distributed as Paul's own. In it the Ghost Shirt Society declares its intention to make tools and machines subordinate to mankind; to put the well-being and desires of mankind above the ideal of efficiency; to recognize mankind as an imperfect species created by God to improve but never to perfect itself; and to accept mankind's imperfection as a virtue, not a vice.

The Ghost Shirt Society uprising nevertheless fails. Although successful in Ilium and a handful of other communities, it never becomes a nationwide upheaval. Ilium and the other rebellious sites are soon surrounded by armed government troops and are informed, via messages from robot helicopters, that they face fatal besiegement if the Society leaders do not promptly surrender. Paul is already disillusioned not only with the outcome of the uprising but also with the now apparent selfish motivations of his fellow leaders, the indiscriminate destruction of tools and machines they have allowed, and the paradoxical obsession of many rebels with repairing the most useless tools and machines they have just smashed. Paul therefore joins the other leaders in surrender. Like the nineteenth-century Indians who thought their ghost shirts could stop the white men's bullets, the rebels must pay the supreme price for their act of folly: their rebellion against technological progress.

Player Piano has a secondary plot only indirectly related to the central plot. This other plot—or series of subplots—revolves around the official visit to the United States of the Shah of Bratpuhr, the spiritual leader of six million members of the Kolhouri sect. The Shah comes to the United States in order to compare his admittedly "primitive" society to this avowedly "advanced" one. Almost from the outset of his visit, however, he raises embarrassing questions—sometimes innocently, sometimes deliberately—about the actual differences between the two societies. In particular, he wonders openly about first, the degree to which Americans are slaves to technology in the manner in which many of his subjects are slaves to him or others, and second, the fact that Americans, despite their material bounty, are no happier than most of his infinitely poorer subjects.

In the course of his visit the Shah meets a soldier who dreams of retirement in twenty-three years and of the opportunity only then of telling off his superiors for making army duty so monotonous; a barber who yearns for his retirement in two years before machines replace all barbers; a housewife who alleviates boredom by doing the family laundry by hand in the bathtub instead of in the ultrasonic washer, and whose husband, a member of the Reelds and Wrecks, alleviates his by having an affair with a neighbor; the wife of an aspiring writer who offers herself as a prostitute to earn money for her husband, who stubbornly refuses to write works of officially approved length, depth, and outlook, the only works ever published; and the EPICAC computer, which cannot answer an ancient riddle the Shah puts to it. The Shah is accompanied by a State Department official, Ewing J. Halyard, who later loses all three of his university degrees—B.A., M.A., and Ph.D.—and so his position and identity because a computer discovers he had never completed an undergraduate physical education requirement. Having steadily defended the United States against the Shah's criticisms, this official nevertheless becomes a non-person, one of the masses. Through these and other experiences the Shah soon reaches conclusions about the nature of American society remarkably similar to those reached more slowly by none other than Paul. Where Paul is too much a part of the "system" to recognize its problems until forced to confront them, the Shah is the acute outside observer characteristic of both science fiction and utopian fiction (and, specifically as an Oriental observes, of the Western literary genres as well).

Primarily because of these two plots and the alternation between them throughout the book, *Player Piano* is a fragmented work. Ironically, a meeting between Paul and the Shah not only would have lessened this fragmentation but also might have clarified Paul's anxieties regarding his life and his society. But such a meeting never occurs.

The considerable number of major and minor characters who appear, disappear, and reappear as a result of these alternating plots adds to this incohesiveness. Moreover, none of the characters, including Paul, is as fully developed as one might wish, and most are two-dimensional characters if not outright stereotypes. "Proteus" is an ironic name, for unlike the classical sea god after whom he is presumably named, Paul fails to change either rapidly or completely. Rather, as indicated, he changes gradually, even falteringly, and only after being provoked from several quarters. None of the other major characters, save perhaps Finnerty and Lasher, changes as much as Paul, and Finnerty and Lasher themselves seem rebellious by nature, where Paul seems complacent. Indeed, *their* names, like those of other major characters, are more literally true: Finnerty the irreverent, hard-drinking, emotional Irishman, and Lasher the cynical critic "lashing out" at society. Similarly, Kroner the supreme manager and Baer, the Eastern Division's chief engineer, are both cold, efficient, unemotional Germans.

Whether Vonnegut intended his characters to be as limited in personal development, as machinelike in nature, as the "technological society" in which they live cannot be determined. Certainly he meant to picture Anita as a machinelike wife and social climber, Shepherd as a machinelike organization man, Kroner as a machinelike manager, and many of the technocrats and rebels alike as machinelike worshippers of technology. Yet all his characters, including Paul, are sufficiently complex as to be neither altogether good nor altogether evil. Just as none of the rebels, again including Paul, is without some vices, so none of the ruling elite, including Kroner, is without some virtues. None of the elite is as machinelike as the supermen Alphas of Aldous Huxley's *Brave New World* (1932), a book to which, as will be seen, *Player Piano* is closely akin.

If anything, Vonnegut appears sympathetic to virtually everyone in the novel insofar as everyone is ultimately a victim of technological domination. Like Charles Dickens's *Hard Times* (1854) and Emile Zola's *Germinal* (1885), two pioneering novels of the social consequences of industrialization, *Player Piano* portrays the "winners" of the industrial revolution, or the Second Industrial Revolution, as no happier than the "losers." For the material comforts of the ruling elite do not compensate for their emotional and spiritual deprivations—the same deprivations, to be sure, affecting many of the masses as well. Thus despite failing to describe and develop them fully, Vonnegut treats his characters with at least some depth.

Player Piano was Vonnegut's first novel, and the style of writing he used for it is one he used for later works as well: short sentences, paragraphs, and chapters; a fast pace; and a language which is sometimes journalistic and contrived and is rarely eloquent. Like most of the book's characters, the book's style is mechanical. Whether Vonnegut intended the style to mesh with, much less to symbolize, the book's principal theme of mechanization in society cannot be determined. The relationship between style and content may simply have been coincidental. Given the relative primitivism of television in the early 1950s, when *Player Piano* was written, it is, contrary to the assertions of some literary critics, unlikely that he consciously modeled its style upon stories on television. The similarity in mechanical style between the book and television is almost certainly coincidental.

Player Piano is not as deadly serious in either tone or content as George Orwell's *1984* (1949), a work with which it is frequently compared. Rather, it is more closely akin to Huxley's *Brave New World*, a work with which it is also frequently compared. Both books mix humor and satire with solemn social criticism. No less important, they share a fear of technological domination in the form of rule over the masses by a relative handful of technocrats and a myriad of sophisticated tools and machines—in the very name of universal happiness and progress. The overlapping of theme is hardly surprising, for Vonnegut has confessed that he "cheerfully ripped off the plot of *Brave New World*, whose plot had been cheerfully ripped off from Eugene Zamyatin's *We*."[4] Moreover, *We* (1920) and *1984* are both comparable in many respects with *Player Piano* as well as with *Brave New World*. Each work, however, is sufficiently distinctive as to be more than a mere imitation of another. And each work is sufficiently important to deserve separate treatment.

Indeed, one of the flaws in literary criticism of *Player Piano* is the assumption that the book is nothing more than an imitation of earlier and perhaps subtler works. Thus Mark Hillegas, in a generally fine study of H. G. Wells and a tradition of anti-utopian or dystopian writings which he largely inspired, claims that *Player Piano* not only is within that tradition but also is as nightmarish as *1984* and other works within it.[5] I cannot entirely agree. I suggest that the humor of *Player Piano* and the mixture of good and evil in all its characters make it a less overtly nightmarish book than *1984* and the other works Hillegas examines, save perhaps *Brave New World*. So too does its distinctive Americanness, which I will discuss shortly.

To be sure, *Player Piano* is an avowedly dystopian work which, like most of those Hillegas studies, views technology as the principal problem. Hillegas is on stronger ground in stating, if too casually, that "The only difference between Vonnegut's nightmare and its ancestors is that Vonnegut's seems closer to coming reality as we may come to know it." It is precisely here that, as Hillegas continues, "*Player Piano* makes its most profound comment."[6] And it is precisely in this respect that *Player Piano* is a nightmarish work and an even more terrifying work than its more overtly terrifying predecessors.

The uniqueness of *Player Piano* can nevertheless best be appreciated through further consideration of the traditions of which it is paradoxically a part. The first of these traditions, the one Hillegas treats, is that of "technological dystopianism." The tradition dates back at least as far as Mary Shelley's *Frankenstein* of 1818 but does not mature until the appearance of Wells's *When the Sleeper Wakes* in 1899. Other prominent technological dystopias include Wells's *The First Men in the Moon* (1901), E. M. Foster's "The Machine Stops" (1912), Karel Čapek's *R.U.R.* (1921), *We, Brave New World*, and *1984*.

If technology—more precisely, unadulterated technological advance—is the immediate problem in all of these works, human nature, it must be emphasized, is the underlying problem. For all of these works recognize that technology's eventual omnipotence reflects mankind's initial desire to dominate the entire world through technology and to have technology solve all of mankind's problems. If technology somehow comes to dominate mankind, it is still a human creation, and ultimate responsibility for technology's domination and possible destructiveness rests with its creators.

Player Piano treats technology and human nature similarly. Much of the ambivalence toward mankind's future at the conclusion of the novel stems exactly from Vonnegut's view of human nature as permanently, inherently flawed. As indicated, this is a belief propounded by the Ghost Shirt Society in its widely circulated letter bearing Paul's signature. The failure of the Society's uprising itself reflects imperfections in the character of its members as well as in that of its opponents—most notably, the obsession of many of the rebels with repairing the most useless tools and machines they have just destroyed. Consequently, even if the uprising had been successful, there would have been no guarantee either that its replacement society would be qualitatively better or that another technological dystopia would not arise someday. Hence the basis for Vonnegut's ambivalence about the future.

Player Piano must also be seen as part of a reaction against a second and older tradition: that of "technological utopianism." Like technological dystopianism, technological utopianism originated in Europe. It can be traced back as far as Johann Andreae's *Christianopolis* (1619), Tommaso Campanella's *The City of the Sun* (1623), and Francis Bacon's *The New Atlantis* (1627). It includes as well Marquis de Condorcet's *Sketch for a Historical Picture of the Progress of the Human Mind* (1795) and the nineteenth-century writings of Henri de Saint-Simon and Auguste Comte. A number of late nineteenth- and early twentieth-century Americans, I have found, also wrote technological utopias, but Edward Bellamy's *Looking Backward* (1888) is the only prominent work among them.[7] Despite the growing questioning of unadulterated technological advance, technological utopianism persists today in many quarters. Buckminster Fuller is probably the most popular of these contemporary visionaries.

Without technological utopias, it can be safely assumed, technological dystopias like *Player Piano* either would not exist at all or else would lack power and influence. This is because the same technological developments in the "real world" which in the nineteenth and twentieth centuries spurred the composition of the one set of works gradually spurred the composition of the other. In both cases the issue is not simply the actual or potential impact of technological change upon society. It is also the unprecedented ability to bring about revolutionary social changes hitherto deemed "utopian" exactly because hitherto deemed "impossible." As Frank Manuel and other scholars of utopianism have observed, the conception of utopia moves from the "impossible" to the "possible" and even the "probable."[8] But as political theorist George Kateb, himself a defender of utopianism, has aptly put it about dystopian critiques of technological change, "There is not, for the most part, skepticism about the capacity of modern technology and natural science to execute the most vaulting ambitions of utopianism; on the contrary, there is a dread it will."[9]

In addition to being part of these general Western traditions of technological utopianism and dystopianism, *Player Piano* is part of distinct American strains within both. What makes these American strains distinct is not just the greater prospect for realizing utopias or dystopias in the United States as compared with Europe; the notion of the United States as a potential paradise or hell to be brought about through technological change has been endlessly examined and need not be detailed here.[10] Rather, the distinction is also due to what I would characterize as the lesser creativity of American writings as compared with European ones. American utopias and dystopias alike are generally less imaginative—less enticing and less chilling—than their European counterparts, and not least in regard to technology. Most American technological utopias and dystopias are banal and even dull, and one is tempted to describe them as exemplars of what, paraphrasing Hannah Arendt, might be termed the banality of good or of evil.

To be sure, Americans have usually been enthusiastic for technology, and more enthusiastic than Europeans. Although the absence of accurate polls of public opinion until the mid-twentieth century makes dogmatic pronouncements about earlier periods questionable, it is evident that the anxiety about technological advance which Leo Marx ascribes to America's foremost writers has generally failed to pervade other segments of the American population.[11] Not surprisingly, there have been far fewer American technological dystopias than utopias, but there have been some: for example, Mark Twain's *A Connecticut Yankee in King Arthur's Court* (1889), Ignatius Donnelly's *Caesar's Column* (1890), Jack London's *The Iron Heel* (1906), Bernard Wolfe's *Limbo* (1952), Ira Levin's *This Perfect Day* (1970), and portions of Henry Adams's *The Education of Henry Adams* (1907) and *The Deg-*

radation of the Democratic Dogma (1919); and, for that matter, *Player Piano* itself. These dystopias have, to repeat, been less frightening than their European counterparts (though certainly disturbing in themselves).

Although more numerous than the technological dystopias, the American technological utopias have likewise suffered by comparison with their European counterparts. The principal criticism which has been invariably leveled against even so well-written and so well-planned a work as *Looking Backward* is that life in that technological utopia would probably be less nightmarish than plain boring. And painfully few American utopian works of any stripe measure up to the style and content of that classic.

The banality of these American technological utopias and dystopias is nevertheless significant, and is not necessarily a liability. Their very banality makes many of them, including *Player Piano*, more believable and so more realistic than their more imaginative European counterparts. If, like *Player Piano*, they suffer from inadequate character and plot development, they do make the prospect of utopia or dystopia more probable than in those European counterparts by providing a narrower gap between pre-utopia and utopia or dystopia. Moreover, the road to utopia or dystopia is often smoother in the American works than in the European ones.

These distinct American strains of technological utopianism and dystopianism clarify Hillegas's casual comment about the greater realism of *Player Piano* as compared with the other dystopian writings he studied. For nearly all of the latter were written by Europeans and were more creative but less realistic than *Player Piano*. Being more realistic in these respects, *Player Piano* might, despite its humor, indeed be a more nightmarish work than its European predecessors.

Player Piano has not had substantial influence as a work of social criticism. Vonnegut did not become a popular novelist until roughly fifteen years after the book appeared. To be sure, the extraordinary popularity of his later works has generated renewed, perhaps unprecedented, interest in his earlier ones. But as the discussion below of principal sources for *Player Piano* indicates, the book more reflected than shaped attitudes about the early 1950s and has not, in any case, greatly affected historical judgments about that period.

Insofar, however, as there has recently been a clear decline in Americans' faith in unadulterated technological advance, *Player Piano* may be praised for being prophetic even if not influential.[12]

Equally important, insofar as concerns for the fate of "technological society" have broadened—or narrowed—from totalitarianism and warfare to everyday life, the book may again be praised for being prophetic. The more sophisticated later critiques of the role of technological domination in everyday life by Jacques Ellul (*The Technological Society*), Herbert Marcuse (*One-Dimensional Man*), and Langdon Winner (*Autonomous Technology*), among others, confirm the foresight of Vonnegut in the early 1950s.

Vonnegut's refusal to propose escapism from technology and its problems is also commendable. There is considerable nostalgia in *Player Piano*, but it is nostalgia for a less technological society rather than for a non-technological society. Not the barely mechanized farm, which Paul abandons, but a building once used by Edison within the Works complex, the Building 58 which he lovingly restores and periodically visits, represents Paul's—and presumably Vonnegut's—degree of nostalgia. Every society has had some forms of technology, and American society, Vonnegut understands, has historically been highly receptive to new forms. For Vonnegut it is as much an illusion that utopia—or, for that matter, any good society—can come about without technology as it is that technology is a panacea and the means to utopia. The problem, as noted, is more human nature than technology. Hence the reduction of technology and of technological domination would not themselves bring about utopia—any utopia.

The principal symbol of the book, the player piano in the Homestead bar, reflects Vonnegut's grasp of these issues. The player piano is a comparatively old machine, dating back to the nineteenth century, and so a symbol of a supposedly happier and more innocent time. Yet it *is* a machine and it *did* replace human finger and foot movements with holes punched on paper. Similarly, Rudy Hertz, the retired master machinist whose unexpected encounter in the bar with Paul stirs fond memories for both men, is himself a symbol of meaningful labor in a technological society. Yet he recalls the past by putting a nickel in the piano and letting it play by itself. Moreover, young Hertz's wonderful—and, to Paul, quite musical—hand movements on the lathe were themselves taped by Paul on another machine. Finally, Hertz himself was replaced by still another machine, one operated by computer tape, and has become an idle worker and, as Hertz and Paul themselves admit, a living ghost. The question raised by the player piano incident is not, to repeat, whether to live in a technological society but rather in what kind of technological society to live. That is an exceedingly difficult question to answer, but it is the proper question to raise if *Player Piano* is not to become a real-life dystopia.

There are several probable sources for *Player Piano* and a few possible ones. This list is not, however, to discount other possible sources.

1. Vonnegut grew up in Indianapolis and has often compared the strong sense of community, of family, and of culture which he felt there with its apparent absence from American society today—thanks in part to the pervasive social fragmentation brought about by technological change. Surely the unhappiness permeating Homestead, if not Ilium, reflects a similar sense of lost roots. Yet in this instance, as in others already noted, Vonnegut's is a qualified nostalgia, even regarding technology. According to James Lundquist, "Vonnegut not only believes that people should spend their lives in one place, he would restore the old emphasis on family relationships by having the government create an artificial extended family. Computers would assign, say, twenty thousand people in the United States a middle name like Daffodil; and no matter where someone went, there would be a member of his 'family' he could call up or see."[13] This is certainly an ironic but not necessarily paradoxical resort to one form of technology to repair damage inflicted on American society by other forms.

2. Vonnegut resented his father's simultaneous obsession with work—he was an architect—and insistence that Vonnegut pursue practical rather than literary studies at college. Proteus several times confesses to a similar rebelliousness and even hostility toward his late father. Indeed, his rebellion against American society is, quite literally, a rebellion against his father as well, for his father, as noted, helped create that very society.

3. Between 1947 and 1950 Vonnegut worked for General Electric in Schenectady, New York, as a public relations specialist in a research laboratory. He has indicated his dislike of that job and, for that matter, of most jobs in modern large corporations. Although the Ilium Works employs only a handful of workers, its impersonality is probably modeled after that of General Electric, as is probably the impersonality of industrial work as a whole in *Player Piano*. Ilium itself is almost certainly modeled after Schenectady. Vonnegut quit his job at G.E. in order to write a novel in which machines "frequently got the best of it, as machines will."[14] *Player Piano*, he continues, "was my response to the implications of having everything run by little boxes. . . . To have a

little clicking box make all the decisions wasn't a vicious thing to do. But it was too bad for human beings who got their dignity from their jobs."[15]

4. Charles *Proteus* Steinmetz (1865–1923) was a misshapen German immigrant of socialist views who was nevertheless hired by General Electric in 1892 when that then-new company sought promising scientists and engineers. Steinmetz perfected electric motors and was eventually rewarded with his own laboratory in Schenectady. In turn he gradually altered his socialist views and instead looked to the modern corporation as both the means and the model of social reform in twentieth-century America. Paul Proteus is hardly the inventive genius Steinmetz was, but like Steinmetz he is a talented industrial manager who can at once fit into the organization and stand out as one of its leaders. Where, however, Steinmetz accommodated himself to large-scale industrialism, Paul obviously does not.[16]

5. From about 1910 to 1955 General Electric operated an annual summer retreat similar to that described in *Player Piano*. The company used its own island (Association Island), as does the ruling elite of the novel, and had its junior and senior executives indulge in the same activities depicted in the book. Vonnegut himself states that the G.E. retreat closed in embarrassment after *Player Piano* appeared.[17] However, a larger and more important summer retreat, the Bohemian Grove, has persisted since the early twentieth century and continues to flourish. North of San Francisco, the retreat welcomes corporate and political leaders from across America and for the same purposes as the Meadows: to get better acquainted and to celebrate the "system," here corporate capitalism more than, as in *Player Piano*, technological progress. Two recent studies of the Bohemian Grove have emphasized its significance for "real world" America's ruling elite. In addition, the Bohemian Grove, like the Meadows, seeks to restore close relationships with nature but like its fictional counterpart never achieves more than a superficial return to nature.[18]

6. The conformity which thus characterizes both the work and the play of the ruling elite in *Player Piano* was a concern in the "real world" at the time the book appeared. Throughout the late 1940s and 1950s there were studies of the willingness of Americans to conform in order to achieve status and success in a variety of areas. In the area of business the most famous and influential such study, and probably the most critical one, was William H. Whyte's *The Organization Man* (1956). By the time the book appeared, Vonnegut was presumably

already quite familiar with the "organization man" mentality. Yet the book provides useful historical references for understanding *Player Piano*.[19]

7. An equally useful work is *The Human Use of Human Beings: Cybernetics and Society* (1950) by Norbert Wiener. Professor of Mathematics at M.I.T., Wiener was a pioneer in the development of computers and coined the term "cybernetics." *The Human Use of Human Beings* was a revised, layman's version of his landmark monograph, *Cybernetics*, which had appeared two years earlier. Vonnegut certainly used the later book, if not the earlier ones, for *Player Piano* incorporates several terms and concepts popularized by *The Human Use of Human Beings* most notably, the "Second Industrial Revolution" to be brought about by cybernetics and cites Wiener himself as the source. Far from advocating the wholesale adoption of computers, however, Wiener raised questions about their possible misuse. He warned against allowing computers to make decisions which might eventually lead to their domination over human beings—precisely what occurs in *Player Piano*.

8. A related source for *Player Piano* is the original "real" computer itself, called ENIAC (Electronic Numerical Integrator and Computer), a name obviously similar to that of the computer of the novel, EPICAC. Completed in 1946, the machine took up the entire fifteen thousand square feet of the basement of the Moore School of Electrical Engineering at the University of Pennsylvania. Its principal inventors were Dr. John W. Mauchly and Dr. J. Presper Eckert, Jr., who went on to invent far smaller and more powerful computers.

These are the likeliest biographical and historical sources for *Player Piano*. One otherwise probable source, utopian and science fiction before 1952, has been discounted by Vonnegut himself as an influence on his thinking and writing—save *Brave New World*. There are several other possible sources for the novel which can merely be listed here:

1. The American fascination, even obsession, with tools and machines, as caricatured by cartoonist Rube Goldberg early in the twentieth century. Whether Goldberg's drawings and designs profoundly influenced Vonnegut, they surely form a backdrop to the tools and machines of *Player Piano*, which not only put millions out of work and create untold misery but also do not always operate efficiently. This obsession with tools and machines manifests itself as well in the successful efforts of Bud Calhoun, Paul's subordinate, to invent a

machine to take his own place and of Calhoun and other Ghost Shirt Society members to repair, as noted, the most useless tools and machines they themselves earlier smashed during their uprising. Not surprisingly, Vonnegut's only mention of Goldberg's name is in connection with Bud.

2. The partly successful attempts during the New Deal to engage in national and regional planning. Large-scale planning is taken for granted in *Player Piano*, but it has never been applied in real-world America to the extent that its foremost advocates would like. Such early federal government experiments as the Works Progress Administration and the Civilian Conservation Corps—both possible models for the novel's Reconstruction and Reclamation Corps—were frequently ridiculed as wasteful or condemned as socialist. The Technocracy movement of the same period, a private crusade taking to logical if extreme ends the same assumptions regarding the value of planning, was largely dismissed as fanatical and fascist. Yet planning, as well as tools and machines, makes possible the technological utopia of *Player Piano*.[20]

3. The sense of American hegemony in the late 1940s and early 1950s, the beginning of *Time* editor Henry Luce's envisioned "American Century." The supreme power of the United States as described at the beginning of *Player Piano* parallels the state of affairs Luce predicted.

4. The "end of ideology" ideology of the 1950s and early 1960s, as expressed most prominently in Daniel Bell's *The End of Ideology: On the Exhaustion of Political Ideas in the Fifties* (1960). The absence of widespread ideological disagreements within the United States of *Player Piano*, save for the Ghost Shirt Society, likely reflects the alleged absence of such disagreements in the "real world" of the same period—a condition celebrated by Bell and others. More generally, the comparative absence of serious ideological differences throughout American history as compared with European history probably accounts in part for the lesser creativity and boldness of the utopian and dystopian writings of the United States as compared with Europe. This is not, however, to characterize the United States at any period as non-ideological.[21]

5. The Luddite "machine breakers" of early nineteenth-century England, the epitome of opposition to the first industrial revolution. The indiscriminate machine-breaking of *Player Piano* parallels the popular image of the Luddites, whose heyday was 1811–1816. Yet

recent studies of the Luddites have shown them to have been opposed not to technology per se but only to those forms which put them out of work. In this respect they are likewise akin to the rebels of the novel, who, as noted, hardly oppose technology as a whole. Unlike those fictional rebels, however, the Luddites did not repair the machines they destroyed.[22]

Like the prophecies of numerous other technological utopias and dystopias, those of *Player Piano* have in many respects been borne out by subsequent events—and, as with those other works, frequently earlier than the author expected. To be sure, Vonnegut, unlike most other such visionaries, provides no specific or even approximate date for the achievement of, in his case, technological dystopia. Moreover, he might not have had a date in mind but might instead have hoped that the publication of *Player Piano* would prevent at least some of the problems he describes. Yet rooting much of the story as he clearly does in the early 1950s would suggest a genuine concern on Vonnegut's part for the likelihood of *Player Piano* becoming a real-life dystopia in the then-near future. Needless to detail here, this concern, if actual on Vonnegut's part, has been amply justified by the evolution of American society since *Player Piano* appeared. In this regard the comments of Huxley upon the republication of *Brave New World* in 1946 offer an interesting comparison: "All things considered it looks as though Utopia were far closer to us than anyone, only fifteen years ago, could have imagined. Then, I projected it six hundred years into the future. Today it seems quite possible that the horror may be upon us within a single century. That is, if we refrain from blowing ourselves to smithereens in the interval."[23]

For Vonnegut as for Huxley and certain other prophets of technological dystopia, there is sadness as well as anxiety about the future. The sadness arises from their recognition that, contrary to the beliefs of prophets of technological utopia, technological progress has not meant and probably will never mean equivalent social progress. Rather, the relationship between the two may be partially antithetical. That technological achievements merely dreamed about for so many generations have not, when finally realized, brought about the expected widespread happiness and fulfillment is an irony richly appreciated by both Vonnegut and Huxley, among others. As the well-publicized letter bearing Paul Proteus's signature puts it, "'Man has survived Armageddon in order to enter the Eden of eternal peace, only to discover that everything he had looked forward to enjoying there, pride, dignity, self-respect, work worth doing, has been condemned as unfit for human consumption.' "[24]

For Vonnegut and Huxley alike, technology itself is not, to repeat, the principal problem, which is instead human nature. Yet technology for both is nevertheless a very real and very complex problem, one which can hardly be wished away in the manner of some of technology's most avowedly "humanistic" critics. Apart from altering human nature, the solution, at least for Vonnegut, is somehow to live happily and humanely in a "technological society." *Player Piano* provides no blueprint for achieving this kind of good society. But in formulating the issue as such it contributes notably to the possible design of that society.

Notes

1. *Player Piano* (1954; rpt. New York: Dell, 1974), p. 11.
2. As several literary critics have noted, the opening paragraph of *Player Piano* parodies the opening paragraph of Julius Caesar's *Commentary on the Gallic War*.
3. Vonnegut, *Player Piano*, p. 10.
4. The quotation comes from Vonnegut's interview with David Standish in *Playboy*, July 1973, p. 68.
5. *The Future as Nightmare: H. G. Wells and the Anti-Utopians* (1967; rpt. Carbondale and Edwardsville: Southern Illinois Univ. Pr., 1974), pp. 159–62.
6. Ibid., p. 161.
7. See Howard P. Segal, "American Visions of Technological Utopia, 1883–1933," *The Markham Review* 7 (July 1978):65–76.
8. See Frank E. Manuel, "Toward a Psychological History of Utopias," in *Utopias and Utopian Thought*, ed. Manuel (Boston: Beacon Pr., 1967), pp. 69–98.
9. *Utopia and Its Enemies* (New York: Free Pr., 1963), pp. 14–15.
10. But see these recent and revisionist studies of the "American Dream": Zane L. Miller, "Scarcity, Abundance, and American Urban History," *Journal of Urban History* 4 (Feb. 1978):131–55; and Kenneth E. Boulding, Michael Kammen, and Seymour Martin Lipset, *From Abundance to Scarcity: Implications for the American Tradition* (Columbus: Ohio State Univ. Pr., 1978).
11. See Leo Marx, *The Machine in the Garden: Technology and the Pastoral Ideal in America* (New York: Oxford Univ. Pr., 1964); *Readings in Technology and American Life*, ed. Carroll W. Pursell, Jr. (New York: Oxford Univ. Pr., 1969); *Changing Attitudes Toward American Technol-*

ogy, ed. Thomas Parke Hughes (New York: Harper and Row, 1975); and Segal, "Leo Marx's 'Middle Landscape': A Critique, A Revision, and An Appreciation," *Reviews in American History* 5 (Mar. 1977):137–50.

12. On this declining faith see Pursell, part 14, and Hughes, part 1.

13. *Kurt Vonnegut* (New York: Ungar, 1977), p. 13. Lundquist's study contains illuminating details about Vonnegut's life, as does Stanley Schatt's study, *Kurt Vonnegut, Jr.* (Boston: Twayne, 1976). I have used both these works in relating Vonnegut's life to his work.

14. Vonnegut, "Science Fiction," *New York Times Book Review*, 5 Sept. 1965, p. 2. On Vonnegut's experiences at General Electric see Robert Scholes, "A Talk with Kurt Vonnegut, Jr.," in *The Vonnegut Statement*, eds. Jerome Klinkowitz and John Somer (New York: Delta, 1973), pp. 91–94.

15. Vonnegut, *Playboy* interview, p. 68.

16. On Steinmetz's life and thought see James Gilbert, *Designing the Industrial State: The Intellectual Pursuit of Collectivism in America, 1880–1940* (Chicago: Quadrangle Books, 1972), chap. 7.

17. See Scholes, pp. 93–94.

18. See John Van der Zee, *The Greatest Men's Party on Earth: Inside the Bohemian Grove* (New York: Harcourt Brace Jovanovich, 1974); and G. William Domhoff, *The Bohemian Grove and Other Retreats: A Study in Ruling-Class Cohesiveness* (New York: Harper and Row, 1974).

19. Of historical interest in this regard are Bellamy's *Looking Backward*, with its highly conformist civilian "industrial army," and Sinclair Lewis's *Babbitt* (1922), with its obsessive concern for conformity. On the latter's many parallels with *Player Piano*, see Mary S. Schniber, "You've Come a Long Way, Babbitt! From Zenith to Ilium," *Twentieth Century Literature* 17 (Apr. 1971):101–06.

20. On planning in modern America see Otis L. Graham, Jr., *Toward a Planned Society: From Roosevelt to Nixon* (New York: Oxford Univ. Pr., 1976).

21. For a useful summary of the issues raised by Bell and his supporters and critics alike see *The End of Ideology Debate*, ed. Chaim I. Waxman (New York: Simon and Schuster, 1969).

22. For revisionist interpretations of the Luddites see Eric J. Hobsbawm, "The Machine Breakers," in his *Labouring Men: Studies in the History of Labour* (Garden City, N.Y.: Doubleday, 1967), chap. 2; and Malcolm I. Thomas, *The Luddites: Machine-Breaking in Regency England* (New York: Schocken, 1972).

23. Aldous Huxley, *Brave New World* (New York: Harper and Row, 1969), pp. xiii–xiv.

24. Vonnegut, *Player Piano*, p. 284.

II

Mass Degradation of Humanity and Massive Contradictions in Bradbury's Vision of America in *Fahrenheit 451*

Jack Zipes

Perhaps it is endemic to academic criticism of science fiction to talk in abstractions and haggle over definitions of utopia, dystopia, fantasy, science, and technology. Questions of rhetoric, semiotic codes, structure, motifs, and types take precedence over the historical context of the narrative and its sociopolitical implications. If substantive philosophical comments are made, they tend to be universal statements about humanity, art, and the destiny of the world. Such is the case with Ray Bradbury's *Fahrenheit 451*. As a result, we hear that the novel contains a criticism of "too rapid and pervasive technological change" within a tradition of "humanistic conservatism."[1] Or, it is actually "the story of Bradbury, disguised as Montag and his lifelong affair with books" and contains his major themes: "the freedom of the mind, the evocation of the past; the desire for Eden; the integrity of the individual; the allurements and traps of the future."[2] One critic has interpreted the novel as portraying a "conformist hell."[3] Another regards it as a social commentary about the present which levels a critique at "the emptiness of modern mass culture and its horrifying effects."[4]

All these interpretations are valid because they are so general and apparent, but they could also pertain to anyone or anything that lived in a "little how town." Their difficulty is that they form abstractions about figures already extrapolated from a particular moment in American history, and these abstractions are not applied to the particular moment as it informs the text, but to the universe at large. Thus, *Fahrenheit 451* is discussed in terms of the world's problems at large when it is essentially bound to the reality of the early 1950s in America, and it is the specificity of the crises endangering the fabric of American society which stamp the narrative concern. The McCarthy witch hunts, the Cold War, the Korean War, the rapid rise of television as a determinant in the culture industry, the spread of advertisement, the abuse of technology within the military-industrial complex, the frustration and violence of the younger generation, the degradation of the masses[5]—these are the factors which went into the making of *Fahrenheit 451* as an American novel, and they form the parameters of any discussion of the dystopian and utopian dimensions of this work.

Bradbury is an eminently careful and conscious writer, and he always has specific occurences and conditions in mind when he projects into the future. In *Fahrenheit 451*, he was obviously reacting to the political and intellectual climate of his times and intended to play the sci-fi game of the possible with his readers of 1953. Obviously this game is still playable in 1983 and may continue to appeal to readers in the future. It depends on the author's rhetorical ability to create a mode of discourse which allows him to exaggerate, intensify, and extend scientific, technological, and social conditions from a current real situation to their most extreme point while convincing the reader that everything which occurs in the fantasy world is feasible in the distant future. Belief in reality is at no time expected to be suspended. On the contrary, the reader is expected to bear in mind the reality of his/her situation to be able to draw comparisons and appropriate correspondences with the fictional correlates which are projections not only of the author's imagination but of the probabilities emanating from the social tendencies of the author's environment. Thus, in *Fahrenheit 451* specific American problems of the early 1950s are omnipresent and are constantly projected into the future, estranged, negated, and finally exploded in the hope that more positive values might be reborn from the ashes in phoenix-like manner. *Fahrenheit 451* is structured around fire and death as though it were necessary to conceive new rituals and customs from the ashes of an America bent on destroying itself and possibly the world. Bradbury's vision of America and Americans assumes the form of the sci-fi game of the possible because he wants it to be played out in reality. That is, the ethical utopian rigor of the book imbues the metaphorical images with a political gesture aimed at influencing the reader's conscience and subsequent behavior in society. While Bradbury obviously takes a position against the mass degradation of humanity, there are curious massive contradictions in his illumination of social tendencies which make his own position questionable. Let us try to recast the discursive mode of the narrative in light of the sociopolitical context of Bradbury's day to see what he perceived in the social tendencies of the

1950s and what alternative paths he illuminated in anticipation of possible catastrophes.

First, a word about Montag and his situation at the beginning of the novel. As a law-enforcer, Montag symbolizes those forces of repression which were executing the orders of McCarthy supporters and the conservative United States government led by General Dwight D. Eisenhower, John Foster Dulles, and J. Edgar Hoover. He is not a simple law officer but belongs to the special agency of liquidation and espionage, similar to the FBI and CIA. Moreover, he is an insider, who at thirty years of age has reached full manhood and is perhaps at his most virile stage. This is exactly why he was created and chosen by Bradbury. At thirty, as we know from real life and from numerous other novels of the twentieth century,[6] Montag is also entering a critical stage and is most susceptible to outside influences. Therefore, he is perfect for initiating the game of the possible. Montag likes his job. He gets pleasure out of burning, and his virility is closely linked to "the brass nozzle in his fists, with this great python spitting its venomous kerosene upon the world."[7] We first encounter Montag in a fit of orgasm, idealistically fulfilling his mission of purging the world of evil books. The image of book-burning, the symbolic helmet, the uniform with a salamander on the arm and a phoenix disc on his chest suggest a situation of the past, namely the Nazis, swastikas, and book-burning of the 1930s. But it is not far from the realm of possibility in the early 1950s of America that Montag as an American fireman might be pouring kerosene over books and burning them. The censorship of books which dealt with socialism, eroticism, and sexuality in the early 1950s made the extension of Montag's actions conceivable for Bradbury and his readers. Indeed, *Fahrenheit 451* begins with an acceptable statement for the silent 1950s in America which demanded a silence to all dissent: "It was a pleasure to burn" (p. 11). Here male identity is immediately associated with liquidation and destruction, with dictatorial power. Bradbury plays with the unconscious desires of the American male and extends them into the future as reality while at the same time he immediately questions that reality and machoism through Montag's misgivings.

The narrative thread of the American male vision of 1950 hangs on Montag's piecing together what has made him into the man he is at age thirty so that he can pursue a more substantial and gratifying life. This means that he must undo social entanglements, expose his understanding to the world, and burn in a different way than he does at the beginning of the narrative. His sight is our sight. His possibilities are our possibilities. His discourse with the world is ours. What he does in the future corresponds to the tasks set for us in the 1950s which may still be with us now. Though not exactly a *Bildungsroman, Fahrenheit 451* is a novel of development in that Montag undergoes a learning experience which lends the book its utopian impetus. Let us consider the main stages of Montag's learning experiences because they constitute Bradbury's angry critique of America—and here we must remember that Bradbury was writing about the same time as the Angry Young Generation in England and the Beat Generation in America, groups of writers who rejected the affluence and vacuousness of technological innovation in capitalist societies.

The first phase of Montag's learning experience is initiated by Clarisse McClellan, who makes him wonder why people talk and why he does not pay attention to small things. The name Clarisse suggests light, clarity, and illumination, and Montag must be enlightened. His own ability to discuss, see, feel, and hear has been muted. He is unconscious of his own history and the forces acting on him. Clarisse infers that his consciousness has been stunted by the two-hundred-foot-long billboards, the parlour walls, races, and fun parks, all of which she avoids because they prevent her from being alone with her own thoughts. Thus, she illuminates the way Montag must take not only for his own self-questioning but for the reader's own questioning of the consciousness industry in America. Bradbury wants to get at the roots of American conformity and immediately points a finger at the complicity of state and industry for using technology to produce television programs, gambling sports games, amusement parks, and advertising to block self-reflection and blank out the potential for alternative ways of living which do not conform to fixed national standards. As Bradbury's mouthpiece, Clarisse wonders whether Montag is actually happy leading a death-in-life, and Montag quickly realizes that he is not happy when he enters his sterile and fully automatic house. He proceeds to the room where his wife Mildred is ostensibly sleeping and senses that "the room was cold but nonetheless he felt he could not breathe. He did not wish to open the curtains and open the french windows, for he did not want the moon to come into the room. So, with the feeling of a man who will die in the next hour for lack of air, he felt his way toward his open, separate, and therefore cold bed" (p. 19). The image of death is fully impressed upon him when he becomes aware that his wife has attempted suicide. This is startling, but what is even more startling for Montag is the mechanical, indifferent way the operators treat his wife with a machine that revives her by pumping new blood into her system. Moreover, he becomes highly disturbed when the pill given to his wife by the operators makes her unaware the next morning that she had tried to take her own life. Montag witnesses—because Clarisse has made him more sensitive—the manner in which technology is being used even in the field of medicine to deaden the senses while keeping people alive as machines. He is part of the deadening process. In fact, dead himself he now begins to rise from the ashes like the phoenix. He is testing wings which he never thought he had.

Clarisse is his first teacher, the one who teaches him how to fly. For one intensive week he meets with Clarisse, who instructs him through her own insight and experience why and how the alleged antisocial and disturbed people may have a higher regard for society and be more sane than those who declare themselves normal and uphold the American way of life. Bradbury attacks the American educational system through Clarisse's description of classes in school which are centered on mass media and sports and prevent critical discussion. Schooling is meant to exhaust the young so that they are tame, but the frustration felt by the young is then expressed in their "fun" outside the school, which always turns to violence. Communication gives way to games of beating up people, destroying things, and playing games like chicken. Clarisse admits that she is " 'afraid of children my own age. They kill each other. Did it always used to be that way? My uncle says no. Six of my friends have been shot in the last year alone. Ten of them died in car wrecks. I'm afraid of them and they don't like me because I'm afraid' " (pp. 35–36). But it is not simply fear that cannot be shown in public but all kinds of feelings. Form has subsumed emotions and substance, dissipated humanity, so that the medium has become the message. Art has become abstract, and people are identified with the things they own. They themselves are to be purchased, used, and disposed of in an automatic way.

Montag's life was in the process of becoming a permanent fixture in a system of degradation, but it was fortunately upset by Clarisse for a week. And she upsets it again by disappearing. Despite her disappearance, she has already served an important purpose because Montag is now somewhat more capable of learning from his own experiences, and he moves into his second phase. Significantly it begins with his entering the firehouse where he will start doubting his profession. The mood is set by the firemen playing cards in the tidy, polished firehouse, idling away the time until they can destroy, and the "radio hummed somewhere.[6] . . . war may be declared any hour. This country stands ready to defend its—' " (p. 38). Throughout the novel, war lurks in the background until it finally erupts. The obvious reference here is to the Cold War and the Korean War which might lead to such an atomic explosion as that which occurs at the end of the book. Again the media spread one-sided news about the nation's cause, driving the people hysterically to war instead of convincing them to seek means for communication and co-existence.

Montag gradually learns how the government manipulates the masses through the media, shows of force, and legal measures to pursue its own ends. His first lesson is quick and simple when he discusses a man who was obviously sane but was taken to an insane asylum because he had been reading books and had built his own library. Captain Beatty remarks: " 'Any man's insane who thinks he can fool the Government and us' " (p. 39). Montag's next lesson comes from his direct experience of witnessing a woman destroy herself because her books are burned by the firemen. This incident causes Montag to bring a book back to his own house and to question what it is in books that would make a woman want to stay in a burning house. For the first time in his life he realizes that human effort and feelings go into the making of a book, and he resolves, despite a warning visit from Beatty, to pursue an experiment with his wife so that they can understand why their lives are in such a mess. Beatty had already attempted to give a false historical explanation of how firemen had been organized by Benjamin Franklin to burn English-influenced books. This time he tries a different ploy by placing the responsibility on the people and arguing that the different ethnic minority and interest groups did not want controversial subjects aired in books. This led to vapid and insipid publications. " 'But the public, knowing what it wanted, spinning happily, let the comic-books survive. And the three-dimensional sex-magazines, of course. There you have it, Montag. It didn't come from the Government down. There was no dictum, no declaration, no censorship, to start with, no! Technology, mass exploitation, and minority pressure carried the trick, thank God. Today, thanks to them, you can stay happy all the time, you are allowed to read comics, the good old confessions, or trade-journals' " (p. 61).

Thus, in Beatty's view—one which, incidentally is never contradicted by Bradbury—the firemen are keepers of peace. He cynically argues that the profession of firemen had to expand to keep the people happy and satisfy their complaints. This is why it conducts espionage and has a computerized system to keep track of each and every citizen in the United States. Yet, despite Beatty's explanation, Montag is firm in his resolution, for he suspects that there is more to Beatty's analysis than meets the eye. Intuitively he recalls Clarisse's discussion about her uncle and the front porches which were eliminated from people's homes because the architects (i.e., the government) did not want people to be active, talking, and communicating with one another. This is why it has become so important for him to talk to his wife and share the experiment in reading with her. However, she has been too conditioned by the television parlour games and by the seashell in her ear—the electronic waves which broadcast music and programs to prevent her thinking. Therefore, Montag is now forced to seek help from Faber, a retired English professor, who had been dismissed from the last liberal arts college because the humanities had in effect been dismissed from the educational system.

By establishing contact with Faber, whose name connotes maker or builder, Montag enters into his third stage of learning experience and begins to assume command of his own destiny. Faber teaches him that the alienation and conformity in society have not been caused by machines but by human beings who have stopped reading of their own accord, and that too few resisted the trend toward standardization and degradation of humanity—including himself. However, Montag gives him hope and courage. So he decides to begin subversive activities with a printer and to set up a communication system with Montag which will depend on the fireman's initiative. He gives Montag a green bullet through which they can communicate and plan their activities without being observed. Here technology is employed to further emancipatory and humanistic interests. The green bullet will also allow Faber to share his knowledge with Montag so that the latter will begin to think for himself. After a violent outburst at home which he knows will end his relationship with Mildred for good, Montag knows that he has made a complete rupture with his former life and recognizes the significance of his relationship with Faber. "On the way downtown he was so completely alone with his terrible error that he felt the necessity for the strange warmness and goodness that came from a familiar and gentle voice speaking in the night. Already, in a few short hours, it seemed that he had known Faber a lifetime. Now he knew that he was two people, that he was above all Montag, who knew nothing, who did not even know himself a fool, but only suspected it. And he knew also that he was the old man who talked to him and talked to him as the train was sucked from one end of the night city to the other one on a long sickening gasp of motion" (pp. 101–2). From this point on Montag moves toward regaining touch with his innermost needs and desires, and he will not be sucked into anything. He avoids the trap set for him by Beatty and burns his real enemies for the first time. His flight from the claws of the mechanical hound, which represents all the imaginative technological skills of American society transformed into a ruthless monster and used to obliterate dissenting humanity, is like the flight of the phoenix born again. Not only is Montag a new person, but he also invigorates Faber, who feels alive for the first time in years. It is a period of war on all fronts, a period of destruction and negation which is reflective of the Cold War, the Korean War, and the oppressive political climate of the 1950s. Yet, there are signs that a new, more humane world might develop after the turmoil ends.

Montag's last phase of learning is a spiritual coming into his own. He escapes to the outside world and follows the abandoned railroad track which leads him to a man whose name, Granger, indicates that he is a shepherd. Granger takes him to the collective of rebels, who are largely intellectuals. Here Bradbury suggests—as he does in many of his works—that the anti-intellectual strain in America forces most intellectuals to take an outsider position from which it is difficult to influence people. The tendency in America is to drive forward without a humanistic intellectual core.[8] Still, Montag learns that certain intellectuals have not abandoned the struggle to assert themselves and still want to assume a responsible role *within* society. Granger informs him:

> "All we want to do is keep the knowledge we think we will need, intact and safe. We're not out to incite or anger anyone yet. For if we are destroyed, the knowledge is dead, perhaps for good. We are model citizens, in our own special way; we walk the old tracks, we lie in the hills at night, and the city people let us be. We're stopped and searched occasionally, but there's nothing on our persons to incriminate us. The organization is flexible, very loose, and fragmentary. Some of us have had plastic surgery on our faces and fingerprints. Right now we have a horrible job; we're waiting for the war to begin and, as quickly, end. It's not pleasant, but then we're not in control, we're the odd minority crying in the wilderness. When the war's over, perhaps we can be of some use in the world." (P. 146)

By the end of his adventures, there is very little that Montag can learn from his mentors anymore. That is, he will undoubtedly continue to share their knowledge, but he, too, has become an imparter of knowledge. He takes the world into himself and becomes at one with it. The notions of the Book of Ecclesiastes are carried by him, and he will spread its humanistic message to help heal the rifts in the world. There is a suggestion at the end of the novel that the American society is largely responsible for the wars and destruction brought upon itself. A time has come, a season, Montag envisions, for building up. He is no longer a fireman but a prophet of humanity. The dystopian critique gives way to a utopian vision.

In their book on science fiction, Robert Scholes and Eric Rabkin state that "dystopian fiction always reduces the world to a 'State,' and presents us with the struggles of an individual or a small group against that State."[9] Later they amplify this statement by maintaining that "most twentieth-century writers have seen no way to get beyond the enslavement of technology, and we thus find a series of distinguished dystopias (like Huxley's *Brave New World*, 1932) that predict a dismal future for humanity. Some writers, however, have tried to get beyond this doom by postulating psychic growth or an evolutionary breakthrough to a race of superpeople. These tactics, of course, presume the possibility of a basic change in human nature; they do not so much see a way beyond technology as around it."[10] In *Fahrenheit 451*, Bradbury depicts the struggle of the individual against the state, or individualism versus conformity. In the process, despite the overwhelming powers of state control through mass media and technology, he has his hero Montag undergo a process of re-humanization. That is, Montag must shed the influences of the state's monopoly of the consciousness industry and regain touch with his humanistic impulse. In this regard, Bradbury follows the postulates of dystopian fiction as outlined by Scholes and Rabkin. However, there is a curious twist to the "humanistic" impulse of Bradbury which accounts for great contradictions and quasi-elitist notions of culture in *Fahrenheit 451*.

Bradbury does not locate the source of destruction in the state, class society, or technology, but in humankind himself. He has remarked that "machines themselves are empty gloves. And the hand that fills them can be good or evil. Today we stand on the rim of space, and man, in his immense tidal motion, is about to flow out toward far new worlds . . . but he must conquer the seed of his own selfdestruction. Man is half-idealist, half-destroyer, and the real and terrible fear is that he can still destroy himself before reaching for the stars. I see man's self-destructive half, the blind spider fiddling in the venomous dark, dreaming mushroom-cloud dreams. Death solves all, it whispers, shaking a handful of atoms like a necklace of dark beads."[11] This is all rather poetic and virtuous, but it is also naive and simplistic because Bradbury, while recognizing the awesome power and tentacles of the state in *Fahrenheit 451*, shifts the blame for the rise of totalitarianism and technological determination onto man's "nature," as if there were something inherent in the constitution of humankind which predetermines the drives, wants, and needs of the masses. Both Beatty and Faber serve as Bradbury's mouthpiece here, and they depict a history in which the masses are portrayed as ignorant, greedy, and more interested in the comfort provided by technology than in creativity and humanistic communication. As we know, Beatty maintains that the different ethnic and minority groups had become offended by the negative fashion in which the mass media depicted them. Thus the machines and the mass media were compelled to eliminate differences and originality. The mass strivings of all these different groups needed more and more regulation and standardization by the state. Thus, individualism, uniqueness, and a critical spirit had to be phased out of the socialization process. Books had to be banned, and the mass media had to be employed to prevent human beings from critical deliberation and reflection.

This analysis exonerates the state and private industry from crimes against humanity and places the blame for destructive tendencies in American society on the masses of people who allegedly want to consume and lead lives of leisure dependent on machine technology. Bradbury portrays such an existence as living death, and only intellectuals or book-readers are capable of retaining their humanity because they have refused to comply with the pressures of "democracy" and the masses who have approved of the way in which the state uses technological control and provides cultural amusement. Faber makes this point even clearer than Beatty: " 'The whole culture's shot through. The skeleton needs melting and re-shaping. Good God, it isn't as simple as just picking up a book you laid down half a century ago. Remember, the firemen are rarely necessary. The public itself stopped reading of its own accord.' " (p. 87). Faber equates human beings with "squirrels" racing about cages (p. 87) and calls them the "solid unmoving cattle of the majority" (p. 107).

The dystopian constellation of conflict in *Fahrenheit 451* is not really constituted by the individual versus the state, but the intellectual versus the masses. The result is that, while Bradbury does amply reflect the means and ways the state endeavors to manipulate and discipline its citizens in the United States, he implies that the people, i.e., the masses, have brought this upon themselves and almost deserve to be blown up so that a new breed of book-lovers may begin to populate the world. (This is also suggested in *The Martian Chronicles* and such stories as "Bright Phoenix.") This elitist notion ultimately defeats the humanistic impulse in Bradbury's critique of mass technology and totalitarianism because he does not differentiate between social classes and their vested interests in America, nor can he explain or demonstrate from a political perspective—and essentially all utopian and dystopian literature is political—who profits by keeping people enthralled and unconscious of the vested power interests.

True, the quality of culture and life in the America of the 1950s had become impoverished, and machines loomed as an awesome threat since a military-industrial complex had been built during World War II and threatened to instrumentalize the lives of the populace. Nor has the quality been improved, or the threat diminished. But this deplorable situation is not due, as Bradbury would have us believe, to the "democratic" drives and wishes of the masses. Such basic critiques of society and technology as Herbert Marcuse's *One-Dimensional Man*, William Leiss's *The Domination of Nature*, and Harry Braverman's *Labor and Monopoly Capital* have shown that mass conformity has its roots in relations of private property and capital, not in the "nature" of humankind. In particular, Braverman provides an apt analysis of the degradation of work and life in the twentieth century. He focuses clearly on the problem which concerns Bradbury, yet which is distorted in the dystopian projection of *Fahrenheit 451*:

> The mass of humanity is subjected to the labor process for the purposes of those who control it rather than for any general purposes of 'humanity' as such. In thus acquiring concrete form, the control of humans over the labor process turns into its opposite and becomes the control of the labor process over the mass of humans. Machinery comes into the world not as the servant of 'humanity,' but as the instrument of those to whom the accumulation of capital gives the *ownership* of the machines. The capacity of humans to control the labor process through machinery is seized upon by management from the beginning of capitalism as the *prime means whereby production may be controlled not by the direct producer but by the owners and representatives of capital*. Thus, in addition to its technical function of increasing the productivity of labor—which would be a mark of machinery under any social system—machinery also has in the capitalist system the function of divesting the mass of workers of their control over their own labor. It is ironic that this feat is accomplished by taking advantage of the great human advance represented by the technical and scientific developments that increase human control over the labor process. It is even more ironic that this appears perfectly 'natural' to the minds of those who, subjected to two centuries of this fetishism of capital, actually see the machine as an alien force which subjugates humanity.'[12]

It might be argued that Bradbury has no sense of irony. Certainly his depiction of conformity and neo-fascism in America lacks subtle mediations, and thus the potential of his utopian vision wanes pale at the end of *Fahrenheit 451*. In fact, it is debatable whether one can call his ending utopian since it is regressive—it almost yearns for the restoration of a Christian world order built on good old American front porches. A group of intellectuals who memorize books are to serve as the foundation for a new society. There is a notion here which borders on selective breeding through the cultivation of brains. Moreover, it appears that the real possibility for future development is not in human potential but in the potential of books. That is, the real hero of *Fahrenheit 451* is not Montag but literature. This accounts for a certain abstract dehumanization of the characters in Bradbury's novel: they function as figures in a formula. They are sketchily drawn and have less character than the implied integrity of books. In essence, Bradbury would prefer to have a world peopled by books rather than by humans.

This becomes even more clear when we regard François Truffaut's film adaptation of *Fahrenheit 451*. Truffaut maintained that

"the theme of the film is the love of books. For some this love is intellectual: you love a book for its contents, for what is written inside it. For others it is an emotional attachment to the book as an object. . . . On a less individual and intimate level, the story interests me because it is a reality: the burning of books, the persecution of ideas, the terror of new concepts, these are elements that return again and again in the history of mankind. . . . In our society, books are not burnt by Hitler or the Holy Inquisition, they are rendered useless, drowned in a flood of images, sounds, objects. And the intellectuals, the real ones, the honest ones, are like Jews, like the Resistance; if you're a thinker in the world of objects, you're a heretic; if you're different, you're an enemy. A person who creates a crisis in society because he acknowledges his bad conscience— the living proof that not everyone has betrayed in exchange for a country house, for a car, or for a collection of electronic gadgets—he is a man to eliminate along with his books.[13]

Though Truffaut's interpretation of Bradbury's novel is informed by his French consciousness and experience of fascism and the Resistance, he extends the basic theme of the novel to its most logical, universal conclusion. From the very beginning of the film, the heroes are the books themselves, and all of Truffaut's changes highlight the significance of the books. For instance they are always prominent in each frame in which they appear, and the characters are dwarfed by them in comparison. The people are less human, sexual, and alive than

in Bradbury's novel. The divisions between good and evil become
blurred so that all human beings without distinction share in the guilt
for the mass degradation of humanity. The same actress plays Clarisse
and Mildred; Montag becomes more ambivalent as a moral protagonist while his adversary Beatty becomes more sympathetic. The de-
fenders of the books are not noble creatures, and, even in the last
frame where people actually become books themselves, they are less
significant than the literature and do not seem capable of communication. Annette Insdorf has pointed out that

> Truffaut's film explores the power of the word—but as a visual more than
> an oral entity. In a sense, the main characters are the books themselves.
> Truffaut even noted that he could not allow the books to fall out of the
> frame: "I must accompany their fall to the ground. The books here are
> characters, and to cut their passage would be like leaving out of frame the
> head of an actor." During the book-burning, close-ups of pages slowly
> curling into ashes look almost like fists of defiance. As in *The Soft Skin*, he
> suggests that the written word can capture and convey emotional depths,
> while the spoken is doomed to skim surfaces. The stylistic analogue to
> this sentiment can be found in the film's subordination of the dialogue to
> visual expression.[14]

While it is true that both Bradbury and Truffaut desire to show
that behind each book there is a human being, their obsession with
books and literature leads them away from exploring the creative
potential of people themselves, who are portrayed both in the novel
and film as easily manipulated and devoid of integrity. In the film, the
settings and costumes are both futuristic and contemporary, and they
evoke a suburban, anonymous atmosphere. Conformity is the rule,
and the landscape is frozen and sterile. Strange as it may seem, the
book-lovers or exiles do not seem capable of breaking through the
homogenized barren setting and congealed human relations. Again,
this is due to Truffaut's adherence to the basic assumptions of Bradbury's critique, which retains its elitist notions and can only display
frustration and contradictions. What is lacking in both novel and film is
a more comprehensive grasp of the forces which degrade humanity
and the value of literature. The dystopian constellation does not
illuminate the path for resistance or alternatives because it obfuscates
the machinations of the power relations of state and private industry
which hinder humans from coming into their own. Bradbury in particular exhibits no faith in the masses while trying to defend humanity,
and the dystopia which he constructs does not shed light on concrete
utopian possibilities.

In Ernst Bloch's study of concrete utopias reflected by literature, he discusses the important notion of *Vor-Schein*, or anticipatory illumination, which is crucial for judging the social value of the imaginative conception. The symbols and chiffres of a literary work must illuminate the tendencies of reality and at the same time anticipate the potential within reality if they are seriously concerned with projecting the possibility for realizing concrete utopias, those brief moments in history such as the French Revolution, the Paris Commune, the October Revolution in Russia, etc., when actual models for egalitarian government and non-exploitative social relations were allowed to take form. The latent possibilities for such concrete utopias must be made apparent through the work of art, and their truth value depends on whether the artist perceives and captures the tendencies of the times. In discussing Bloch's philosophical categories and their significance for science fiction, Darko Suvin discusses anticipatory illumination in terms of the novum, "the totalizing phenomenon or relationship deviating from the author's and implied reader's norm of reality."[15] Suvin maintains that "the most important consequence of an understanding of SF as a symbolic system centered on a novum which is to be cognitively validated within the narrative reality of the tale and its interaction with reader expectations is that the novelty has to be convincingly explained in concrete, even if imaginary terms, that is, in terms of the *specific* time, place, agents, and cosmic and social totality of each tale."[16]

Like Bloch, Suvin uses this notion of novum to clarify the political and ethical function of utopian literature. The artistic depiction of social tendencies and the novum always indicates willy-nilly the actual possibilities for putting into practice new and alternative forms of human comportment which might enable humankind to emancipate itself from alienating and oppressive conditions. Bloch regards both life and art as a process with utopia serving as a beacon, illuminating those elements and moments which can bring to life what-has-not-been-realized:

> The lonely island, where utopia is supposed to lie, may be an archetype. However, it creates a stronger effect through ideal figures of a sought-after perfection, as free or ordered development of the contents of life. That is, the utopian function should essentially hold to the same line as the utopias themselves: the line of concrete mediation with an ideal tendency rooted in the material world, as mentioned before. In no way can the ideal be taught and reported through mere facts. On the contrary, its essence depends on its strained relationship to that which has become

merely factual. If the ideal is worth anything, then it has a connection to the process of the world, in which the so-called facts are reified and fixed abstractions. The ideal has in its anticipations, if they are concrete, a correlate in the objective contents of hope belonging to the latent tendency. This correlate allows for *ethical ideals as models, aesthetic ones as anticipatory illuminations which point to the possibility of becoming real.* Such ideals which are reported and delivered through a utopian function are then considered altogether as the content of a humanely adequate, fully developed self and world. Therefore, they are—what may here be considered in the last analysis as a summary or simplification of all ideal existence—collectively inflexions of the basic content—the most precious thing on earth.[17]

Though Bradbury is idealistic, ethical, and highly critical of reified conditions in the America of the 1950s, the utopian function in *Fahrenheit 451* is predicated on a false inflexion of tendencies and contradictions in American society. The novum is not a true novelty allowing for qualitatively changed human relationships and social relations. Montag's learning experience reflects Bradbury's confused understanding of state control, education, private industry, and exploitative use of the mass media. Since he does not dig beneath the people and facts as they are, he cannot find the utopian correlate which points to realizable possibilities in the future. It is a far-fetched dream to have book-lovers and intellectuals as the progenitors of a new society, especially when they have an inaccurate notion of what led the "bad old" society to become fascist and militaristic. The ethical and aesthetic ideals in Bradbury's narrative are derived from an indiscriminate and eclectic praise of books per se. Despite his humanitarian intentions, Bradbury's hatred for the machine and consumer age, its effect on the masses, and the growing deterioration of the cultural level through the mass media led him to formulate romantic anticapitalist notions from an elitist point of view. Thus, what becomes significant about Bradbury's attempt to depict utopian possibilities for humankind individualized like a phoenix rising from the fire is his own contradictory relationship to America.

There is an acute tension between the intellectual and the majority of people in America. There is a disturbing element in the manner by which dissent and doubt are often buried in standard patriotic rhetoric in America. Yet, there are just as many intellectuals and book-lovers, often called mandarins, who upheld the formation of the military-industrial complex in the 1940s and 1950s, as there are those who dissented.[18] To love a book or to be an intellectual is not, as

Bradbury would have us believe, ideally ethical and humane. Writing at a time when the military-industrial complex was being developed and received the full support of the university system, Bradbury overlooked the interests of private corporations and complicitous network of intellectuals and book-lovers who have created greater instrumental control of the masses. Such an oversight short-circuits the utopian function of his books, and he remains blind to the intricacies of control in his own society. Books are not being burned with "1984" around the corner. Books are proliferating and being distributed on a massive scale. They are being received and used in manifold ways just as are the mass media such as television, film, radio, video—and not by a solid mass of cattle. The struggles of minority groups and women for equal rights and alternate technology and ecology point to certain massive contradictions which underlie the premise of *Fahrenheit 451*. If there is a utopian vision in Bradbury's novel, then it is based on a strange love of humanity and will surely never be concretized unless by books themselves.

Notes

1. A. James Stupple, "The Past, The Future, and Ray Bradbury," in *Voices for The Future*, ed. Thomas D. Clareson (Bowling Green: Bowling Green Univ. Popular Pr., 1976), p. 24.
2. Willis E. NcNelly, "Ray Bradbury—Past, Present, and Future," in *Voices for The Future*, pp. 169, 173.
3. Kingsley Amis, *New Maps of Hell* (New York: Harcourt, Brace, 1960), p. 110.
4. Joseph Blakey, *Fahrenheit 451* (Toronto: 1972), Coles Notes, pp. 90–91.
5. For good background material on this period, see Daniel Snowman, *America Since 1920* (New York: Harper and Row, 1968); I. F. Stone, *The Haunted Fifties* (London: Merlin, 1964); and Howard Zinn, *Postwar America* (Indianapolis: Bobbs-Merrill, 1973).
6. See Theodore Ziolkowski, *Fictional Transfigurations of Jesus* (Princeton: Princeton Univ. Pr., 1972). Like Jesus Christ, who went out preaching at age thirty, Montag has features of a Christ figure.
7. *Fahrenheit 451* (1953, rpt. London: Panther Books, 1976), p. 11. Hereafter all quotations cited in the text shall be taken from this volume.
8. See Richard Hofstadter, *Anti-intellectualism in American Life* (New York: Knopf, 1963).
9. *Science Fiction: History, Science, Vision* (London: Oxford Univ. Pr., 1977), p. 34.
10. Ibid., p. 174.

11. Quoted in William F. Nolan, "Bradbury: Prose Poet in the Age of Space,"
    Fantasy and Science Fiction 24 (May 1963):8. For similar statements by
    Bradbury, see *The Ray Bradbury Companion*, ed., William F. Nolan
    (Detroit: Gale Research, 1975), and the special Ray Bradbury issue of
    Rocket's Blast—Comicollector, vol. 131 (Oct. 1976), pp. 14–17, 28–29.
12. *Labor and Monopoly Capital* (New York: Monthly Review Pr., 1974),
    p. 193.
13. Quoted in C. G. Crisp, *François Truffaut* (New York: Praeger, 1972),
    pp. 81–82.
14. *François Truffaut* (Boston: Twayne, 1978), p. 49.
15. *Metamorphoses of Science Fiction* (New Haven: Yale Univ. Pr., 1979),
    p. 64.
16. Ibid., p. 80.
17. *Ästhetik des Vor-Scheins, vol. 1*, ed. Gert Ueding (Frankfurt am Main:
    Suhrkamp, 1974), p. 296.
18. The best depiction of this sad history is James Ridgeway, *The Closed
    Corporation: American Universities in Crisis* (New York: Random House,
    1968). See also G. William Domhoff, *Who Rules America?* (Englewood
    Cliffs, N.J.: Prentice-Hall, 1967); and Herbert I. Schiller, *Mass Com-
    munications and American Empire* (Boston: Beacon, 1971).

On Aggression:
William Golding's *Lord of the Flies*

Kathleen Woodward

The cheery morality of the popular children's adventure story requires at the very least a skeptical if not a cynical gaze. This is one of the points of departure of William Golding's meticulously crafted first book, *Lord of the Flies*, which was published in 1954 and was almost immediately heralded as a minor classic.[1] As a child, Golding had read enthusiastically R. M. Ballantyne's much beloved *Coral Island* (1858), a flag-waving tale about stalwart British lads who, shipwrecked on a remote and lovely Pacific island, brave adversity with high spirits and bring Christianity to the black natives. Golding found, however, that as an adult, the reading of this children's book had vastly altered for him. Its combination of staunch merriment, arrogance, and naïveté was offensive—worse, dangerous. Although the preface to *Coral Island* declares that the purpose of the book is "fun"—harmless and jolly entertainment—from our perspective in history it is clear to us, as it was to Golding, that this story for children served to rationalize the practice of colonialism and to reinforce the Victorian belief in the cultural, racial, and ethical superiority of the English. Shaken by the atrocities of World War II, the unthinkable mass slaughter organized by Hitler, Golding decided to model a fiction on *Coral Island* which underscored man's inherent capacities for cruelty, not cooperation. *Lord of the Flies*, he has said, is a "realistic" rendering of the hypothetical situation which Ballantyne had proposed one hundred years before.[2] I should also add that it departs radically from the tradition of the romance of survival established by Daniel Defoe's *Robinson Crusoe* (1719) and Johann Rudolf Wyss's *Swiss Family Robinson* (1812–13), which illustrate the enterprising courage of "civilized" man cast away on a deserted island.

    Just what Golding means by "realistic" is critical here. His vision of evil at the heart of man is violent and dark. When at the end of *Lord of the Flies*, the naval officer who rescues the schoolboys marooned in the midst of an atomic war, says ingenuously, it was like *Coral Island*, wasn't it, we know just how different it has been. The island is going up in flames. The twelve-year-old who had been elected chief is being hunted down in cold blood by the other children. One small child, mulberry-marked by a birthstain, has been lost to carelessness in an earlier fire. Another has been killed by a frenzied mob. A third has been deliberately murdered. In Golding's inversion of Ballantyne's successful survival story, conviviality and high jinks degenerate into shocking savagery as the island turns from a paradise into a fiery warground.

In the beginning, the island is so enchantingly beautiful, peaceful, utopian, that even a twelve-year-old schoolboy is sensitive to its poetic possibilities. As Ralph, the chief, thinks to himself, it is the "imagined but never fully realized place leaping into real life."[3] Uninhabited, rich with fruit, it is the locus of the mundane and the magical: the only limits are those of the imagination. Ralph delightedly perceives the shadows cast on his body by palm fronds as "really green" and the gulls which grace an offshore boulder are to him like "icing on a pink cake." Another central character, Simon, perceives the buds on evergreen bushes as "candles" redolent with spiritual significance. Yet the potential for evil also exists from the beginning, inherent not in the island but in man. In the very first paragraph we learn that the plane which carried the children here in a tragically ironic attempt to shelter them from war, left a "long scar smashed into the jungle." We further read that the first sound which Ralph hears he interprets as the "witch-like cry" of a red and yellow bird. And in the quick course of the story, the delicate pink spiral of the conch, a fragile shell which Ralph first uses to call the scattered kids together and which comes to stand for a democratic form of government and respect for the individual, is smashed, supplanted by the bloody, decaying head of a sow, matted with hungry flies, the emblem of despotism and the perverse desire for gratuitous violence.

I mention these few details because they suggest the care with which *Lord of the Flies* was constructed. It is a book which has the perfection of a miniature. The formal and structural elements—among them, the imagery of beasts, the recurring fires, the increasing tempo of violence—are artfully articulated with a clarity as transparent as that of the island's lagoon. These motifs have been scrupulously analyzed by critics of *Lord of the Flies*, and I refer the reader interested in this aspect of Golding's work to them.[4] But here I will not dwell on the

book's aesthetic dimension except to call attention to a general problem in much commentary which takes analysis of symbolism as its
point of departure: such criticism seems inevitably to falsify the character of *Lord of the Flies* by imputing interpretations to it whose
weighty significance the straightforward text cannot support. Even the
use of the term "symbolism" in regard to the book seems to me
misguided—pretentious and overweening. The refined techniques of
New Criticism, so responsive to the intricacies of symbolist and modern poetry and the psychological and symbolic depth of a Melville or
Faulkner novel, are inappropriate to the texture and scope of *Lord of
the Flies*.

For example, it is quite evident just what the conch and the sow's
head represent. There is a one-to-one correspondence between each
literary sign and the political system to which it refers. By dubbing the
sow's head "Lord of the Flies," which is a translation of the Hebrew
Ba'alzevuv or the Greek *Beelzebub*, Golding alludes directly to the
devil, or evil, in man. There is no mystery about this, no rich ambiguity
of intent. It is a plain reference, plainly stated. Thus, when E. L.
Epstein writes in notes to an edition of *Lord of the Flies* which is widely
used in classrooms around the country, "Golding's Beelzebub is the
modern equivalent, the anarchic, amoral, driving force that Freudians
call the Id, whose only function seems to be to insure the survival of the
host in which it is embedded or embodied, which function it performs
with tremendous and single-minded tenacity," we find no parity between his interpretation and the text.[5] The former is far more sophisticated in terms of complexity of thought than the latter. Furthermore,
Epstein's analysis allows him to inflate the significance of *Lord of the
Flies* and mistakenly judge it to be one of the most important texts in
the history of modern literature. He writes that in *Lord of the Flies*, "as
in few others at the present time, are findings of psychoanalysts of all
schools, anthropologists, social psychologists, and philosophical historians mobilized into an attack upon the central problem of modern
thought: the nature of the human personality and the reflection of
personality on society."[6] One would think Epstein were referring to
another text altogether, for there is a strange air of unreality, an
unmotivated profundity in his evaluation of *Lord of the Flies*. Although Golding's achievement is substantial, we must recognize that
Lord of the Flies in no way possesses the ambitious and darkly troubled
questioning of the human condition which we find in *Moby Dick* or
Heart of Darkness. Indeed, Golding's book is literally small in scope: it
is in reality a long short story rather than a short novel. And its

systematic machinery, which drives the plot, operates impeccably and deliberately in a single direction. The text simply does not invite multiple and meaningful symbolic interpretations, no more than does *Brave New World* or *Walden Two*. For, like the authors of these books, Golding has set up, as it were, a fictional laboratory experiment whose outcome can be predicted with accuracy.

This raises the important question of what form of fiction most accurately describes *Lord of the Flies* and therefore what approach (or approaches) to it might be most rewarding. Golding himself prefers the term "fable," which is the title of an essay included in his book *The Hot Gates*. In this essay, which was delivered originally as a lecture in the United States, Golding devotes himself to a matter-of-fact and lengthy discussion of *Lord of the Flies*. "The fabulist is a moralist," he asserts. "He cannot make a story without a human lesson tucked away in it. Arranging his signs as he does, he reaches, not profundity on many levels, but what you would expect from signs, that is, overt significance."[7] What is the lesson which Golding intends for us in *Lord of the Flies*? The purpose of the book is "to trace the defects of society back to the defects of human nature."[8] It is an argument against the optimistic notion, prevalent for many decades prior to World War II and shared by people of many persuasions, that violence done by man to man could be rooted out by the appropriate form of social machinery. *Lord of the Flies* provides blunt answers to the central and time-honored questions of political theory. Is man basically inherently good or selfish? Altruistic and peaceful, or aggressive and violent? To what extent is human nature fixed? To what extent can human nature be molded by society?

It is my understanding that the fundamental characteristic of utopian literature is social criticism: it embodies a critique of existing social organization. Utopian works make critical statements in fictional, or nonfictional, form about our social values, practices, and institutions. I agree with Howard Segal who has argued persuasively that the principal use of utopianism is theoretical, not practical.[9] A utopian vision is not a blueprint for erecting an alternative society but rather a heuristic device, as Darko Suvin calls it, for rethinking aspects of existing society.[10] The same could be said of dystopian fiction: it alerts us to the possible negative impact on society of certain practices, desires, and arrangements of power, and thus cautions us to proceed with care, altering our society's priorities. Viewed in these terms, dystopian literature advocates social change, just as does utopian literature. Aldous Huxley's *Brave New World* is an excellent example of this. Among other things, it asks us to consider the destructive effect that biological engineering, in many of its forms, might well have on the shape of society and the life of the individual. On balance, it argues that the mechanical reproduction of human life—a technology which in fact will soon be available—should be suppressed. And in a more general sense, Huxley calls attention to the ideological stranglehold of the technological imperative (the deterministic belief that what *can* be done technologically *will* be done) on twentieth-century industrial culture, and urges us to evaluate critically its implications for the future.

But if we define dystopian literature, like utopian literature, as primarily a vehicle for social criticism, in what way can we consider *Lord of the Flies* dystopian? Much of the book is devoted to politics, to the competing values of a totalitarian or democratic system. But Golding is not basically critical of the democratic form of government, which was of course his own when he wrote *Lord of the Flies*. Instead his vision is politically conservative, even reactionary. If both utopian and dystopian literature are moved by the impulse that social change is possible and necessary, *Lord of the Flies* is not. For Golding believes that the bottom line, the limiting factor, is human nature, of which he has a bleak and pessimistic view. Man is inherently evil and weak, and human nature is fixed, make no mistake about it. It is only in this sense that we could say that *Lord of the Flies* is dystopian: it is not self-consciously dystopian with regard to a historical moment of a social system, but rather pessimistic with regard to the nature of the human species. But a better term—and here I agree with Golding—would be "realistic." For essentially Golding is warning us that it *can* happen here, that the calculating aggression of a Hitler could erupt in England, or anywhere else or at any time, no matter what the shape of society. What can we do to avert such a tragedy? Golding explicitly counsels humility and self-knowledge as antidotes to the disease of cultural and personal arrogance. We must beware of those who assert, as does the petty tyrant Jack, "'We're not savages. We're English; and the English are best at everything,'" for such an attitude leads to colonialism, racism, and genocide. But as we will see, *Lord of the Flies* also suggests, implicitly, another means of containing such violence.

Although *Lord of the Flies* does not offer social criticism with the purpose of changing society, it does present a programmatic view of the relationship between human nature and the shape of society. Like utopian and dystopian writing, it demands that we think clearly and critically about our form of politics and the nature of the human animal; it requires that we move our thought beyond the work itself as literature, a fictional world that refers primarily to itself and the creative process, and into the real world of politics. Since it self-consciously presents us with a model of that world, we are both urged and obliged to test it against that world and other models of it in order to assess its use for us at our particular point in history. It is this approach, rather than a formalistic approach, which I believe will yield the best results if *Lord of the Flies* is considered first and foremost a fable.[11]

However, this does raise a thorny theoretical problem. In order to approach *Lord of the Flies* as a dystopian work, or a programmatic work, we must suspend its literary nature and treat it as if it were presenting us a model of society with the purpose of arguing a particular position with respect to it. How do we respond to argument? With argument. By asking if its claims are true or false. With *Lord of the Flies*, therefore, we would first question the adequacy of Golding's model and secondly the truth of his conception of human nature, just as if we were appraising a scientific experiment. This, however, may strike us as an odd way to approach literature. Yet if we think of *Walden Two*, such an approach seems perfectly appropriate. Skinner has cast his view of the relationship between man, behavioral engineering, and society in fictional form. But no one, to my knowledge at least, takes *Walden Two* seriously as literature. We regard it as a strategy which Skinner has chosen to present his theory. He might well have elected to write in the form of a discursive tract, and if he had, I suspect that our basic response would be fundamentally the same: we would first establish his theory on the basis of our observation of the text (but with our knowledge of his theory in hand), then discuss the correctness of his theory and its significance for our society. *Walden Two* has primarily an instrumental value, a utilitarian purpose, and it was clearly conceived with that in mind. Skinner intends to use the form of the novel in a certain way. But literature, which I for the moment oppose to utopian and dystopian work, does not first ask us to use it instrumentally. It in-forms our life differently. We "use" it differently. And this is our dilemma with *Lord of the Flies*: it is a piece of writing which has a programmatic intent—Golding intends to "prove" a hypothesis—but it is also an excellent piece of literature. Strangely enough, apart from the sheer literary talent of the author which cannot be denied, the way we seem to know this in Golding's case is that the work extends itself beyond the bare bones of its hypothetical intent.

But we must begin at the beginning. Golding is aware of course that the parallels between his literary world and that other world—our world—cannot be perfect. To my mind, it is not so much a question of perfection as it is the accuracy of his emphasis. Thus, we must ask, what are the limits of those parallels? What does Golding include? What does he omit? To what extent does his fictional analogy resonate meaningfully with the world as we know it? At what distance does it break down? I will turn first to these questions in terms of the quasi-anthropological primal scene which he presents as the origin of the "defect" in human nature. I will then consider the relationship between Golding's conception of human nature and recent research in biology, which will involve us for a few moments in the uneasy relationship between science and the humanities, and then conclude this essay with a few remarks on what I consider to be one of the most powerful themes of *Lord of the Flies* as literature.

The Tribal Community

Aptly described as an anthropological passion play,[12] *Lord of the Flies* is an inquiry into the politics of cohesion and conflict which attempts to show how the social bond disintegrates and eventually explodes into war. Golding's acute differentiation of the social roles of the four major characters invites comparison with the four-member hunting team of a primitive tribe as it is portrayed in John Marshall's classic ethnographic film *The Hunters* and analyzed by the cultural historian William Irwin Thompson.[13] According to this research, a successful hunting team in a tribal community requires four men, each of whom play different roles but all of whom work closely together. Thompson suggests that the team can be considered the anthropological germ cell, the primary human group, from which quantum leaps in cultural organization originated. He regards it as an ideal form of society whose existence in early human history was shattered by major advances in technological development. In Thompson we find a form of nostalgia for the harmonious interdependence and structural stability of the primitive community symbolized by the hunting team. He implies that politically it is superior because it encourages (indeed, demands) the development of individual talent in an atmosphere of cooperation, not competition.[14] Extreme division of labor is not institutionalized, information is shared equally, and the members of the team respect each other's skills. The four perform in a sophisticated and highly coordinated way as a set of complementary opposites, as mapped below with the corresponding characters from *Lord of the Flies*:

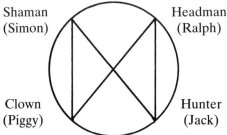

Shaman (Simon)   Headman (Ralph)

Clown (Piggy)   Hunter (Jack)

Left Side: Ideational   Right Side: Operational

—Ralph is the *Headman*, the leader who is the person best suited for the position but also the equal of the others. Once given the authority, he shows genuine leadership, learning to assess his limitations and to seek good counsel. As the plot progresses, his sense of responsibility and reality—that is, disillusionment—grows.

—Piggy is the *Clown*, the most intelligent of the four and the voice of common sense.

—Simon is the *Shaman*, whose religious sensibility and insight into the dark interior of man's nature are essential to the community. It is Simon who grasps both the literal and metaphorical meaning of the beast—the Beast from the Sea is a dead man who is feared, as we must fear our own potential for violence—and who tries to impart this to the others.

—Jack is the *Hunter*, intent, obsessive, skillful, and possessed of stamina.

Whereas Thompson views his model of the primitive community as utopian, Golding's fiction of the anthropological primal scene is pessimistic. The origins of human society, he implies, are rooted in conflict, because human nature is basically evil. The important point for us here is that while the spectrum of Golding's characterization corresponds to that portrayed in *The Hunters*, the *structuring* of their activity does not. What goes wrong? Must things break up? The problem is not that the psychological make-up of the four boys is deficient, that they each lack something essential. Rather, Golding's theory of the "essential illness"[15] in human nature which existed from the beginning and which inevitably erupts in violence can be submitted to a structuralist critique. The point is that in *Lord of the Flies* the social bond did not exist from the start (nor is there any real reason for it to exist) and that Golding presents us with a completely unrealistic model of the origins of human politics. Furthermore, Golding does not so much show us how a state of peace under a rational form of government breaks down, as he shows us how the conceivably pleasant condition of anarchy disintegrates under the pressure of aggression.

Thompson's model is completely inverted. On Golding's coral island, none of the four central characters is allowed to play his role properly. Unlike the situation in *The Hunters*, the four members of the elite in *Lord of the Flies* basically do not respect each other, do not share information appropriately, and do not divide labor in a beneficial way. Under these conditions, we should not be surprised that tension grows increasingly corrosive. While Piggy's essential role as the Clown is to make fun of the others, thus deflating their arrogance, they ridicule him instead, feeling superior to his ludicrously fat body and his school-marmish, no-nonsense attitude. Even Ralph, who comes to value Piggy's intelligence, feels that "Piggy was a bore; his fat, his ass-mar and his matter-of-fact ideas were dull, but," he admits to himself, "there was always a little pleasure to be got out of pulling his leg, even if one did it by accident." This is more destructive than simple dislike; on the part of the older boys, it is pure prejudice, for it is Piggy's physical nature—his debilitating asthma, his near blindness without his thick glasses, his pale fat body—which they despise. If Piggy is detested as an outsider, somebody who is "different," Simon is not esteemed for his mystical gifts. The role of the Shaman is to work magic when necessary, but Simon's vision into the meaning of things, which is quite accurate, is ignored. Worse, he is killed in the process of trying to reveal just what he does understand, and it is precisely his knowledge which would have delivered them from an unreasoning fear. He is misperceived as the Beast itself. Jack, the Hunter, hunts alone or only with his hunters (whom he completely dominates in a political hierarchy which he establishes) rather than with an interdisciplinary team, and thus inverts the process of hunting for the sake of survival to that of hunting to murder one of his own kind. And the Headman, Ralph, finds his leadership challenged from the very beginning. In addition, he makes several critical errors in judgment. He is wrong to delegate the responsibility for maintaining the fire to Jack and his hunters, and he is wrong to leave Piggy behind in the very beginning after the three of them decide to go off and explore the island.

It may seem less than generous to criticize Golding's fictional model. Many readers, and critics, are uncomfortable with such an approach, for generations of students have been taught that it is impolite, simply not good literary manners, to question an author's basic assumptions, his *donnée*, as Henry James called it.[16] But this is precisely what is at issue here—Golding's assumption, and conclusion, that human nature is evil. And we cannot be convinced that Golding's conclusions are well-founded unless we agree that his model is persuasive. If Golding's fable is brilliant in what it includes—his characterization is remarkably discerning—it is also ruthless in what it excludes. As a microcosm of the world at large, it self-consciously eliminates crucial aspects of society which create tension but, more importantly, provide purpose and generate binding social structures in the process.

First, Golding dismisses the basic problem of scarcity, which necessitates the organization of work. Fruit and fresh water are abundant, and the climate is tropical. The island is a leisure world where habits of discipline are superfluous. While the younger children play at the sea's edge, the older children play at being grown up. Voting and the right to free speech, the paraphernalia of democracy, are toys to them. The kids have only one urgent task—to keep the rescue fire going—and even this they are incapable of doing, for with few exceptions, their sense of the future gives way to instant gratification. Essentially they are playing a waiting game, and they invent dangerous games to pass the time.

Perhaps even more significant than Golding's bracketing of the problem of scarcity is his choice of a homogeneous group of middle-class white children, all of whom are boys, as a representative cross-section of society. There is no racial tension, no sexual tension, no tension of cultural difference. By populating his story with young boys only, all twelve and under, Golding removes the fundamental adhesive of society—the family. There are no kinship structures whatsoever, no bonds of love or even close friendship among these boys. It is tragically ironic that none of the boys are related by blood—and are eventually polarized by the desire to shed it. Thus the "society" which Golding portrays is *not* a society, but rather a collection of people. It has no objective (other than to prepare its own rescue, and not everyone agrees to that). It cannot even reproduce itself. It is small wonder that it turns pathological.

But this was not Golding's purpose. He intended to show that violence in society arises out of man's very nature, his instincts. Firmly believing that violence is congenital, "the terrible disease of being human" and not the result of faulty social organization, Golding makes no apologies for the parameters of his fiction. As he explains in

"Fable": "The boys find an earthly paradise, a world, in fact like our own, of boundless wealth, beauty and resource. The boys were below the age of overt sex, for I did not want to complicate the issue with that relative triviality. They did not have to fight for survival, for I did not want a Marxist exegesis. If disaster came, it was not to come through the exploitation of one class by another. It was to rise, simply and solely out of the nature of the brute."[17] These are strict limits indeed, and they limit the strength of Golding's argument. From our vantage point in history, we know that scarcity remains a basic source of conflict. We would be foolish to think it is not. The energy crisis is real and will only worsen in the future (but we must remember that Golding published *Lord of the Flies* in the fifties when the West was experiencing an efflorescence of consumer goods and the rebuilding of economies crippled during the war was proceeding at an astonishing pace). Whether we agree with Golding that the sexual drive is a "relative triviality" in terms of widespread violence is a more complicated issue to adjudicate, but we can certainly conclude that he does not approach it with sophistication, choosing instead to dismiss it summarily.

But what does Golding mean when he says violence arises "simply and solely out of the nature of the brute"? In part, Golding has misread the moral of his own fiction. The moral of the story, he has said, is that "the shape of society must depend on the ethical nature of the individual and not on any political system."[18] First, on the contrary, *Lord of the Flies* dramatizes, with power, how a society—like our own, not like a tribal community—can degenerate into lawlessness when there seems to be no apparent need to work with each other, no kinship ties binding people together, and no long-range social purpose but instead an emphasis on immediate satisfaction. Affluence, as we have seen, brings its own dangers. And secondly, it is more accurate, I think, to read *Lord of the Flies* as an argument for strict law and order within the democratic system rather than as a resigned plea that the shape of society depend on the upstanding ethical nature of a few individuals.

To the kids, it appears at first that the situation is ideal. They find themselves liberated from the constraints of their own culture—the adult world—and are able to invent, or so it seems, the form of law and order they wish. " 'No grown ups!' " exults Ralph, as "the delight of a realized ambition overcame him." But there is no longer any such thing as the origin of the state, or a clean cultural slate, or the noble savage, only another beginning. Neither cultural tradition nor the instinct for aggression (which is another form of human heritage that I will turn to later) is absent. The boys bring with them the knowledge of a democratic form of government, as they do a taste for violence. The conflict, which Golding so superbly articulates, is between the order of democratically arrived at rules and the expression of aggressive instincts.

There is no question that to Golding's mind democracy is the preferred form of government. He presents it as humane and wise, as infinitely preferable to the insanities of an authoritarian regime. Piggy, the spectacle-wearing intellectual, puts it neatly, and there must be no hesitation on our part about the answer: "'Which is better—to have rules and agree, or to hunt and kill? . . . Which is better, law and rescue, or hunting and breaking things up?'" In Golding's fable, furthermore, the electorate, uninformed as it is, makes the best choice after all, although the reasons for that choice are not the right ones. The kids vote for Ralph because he has a good image: he is tall, good-looking, and is the one who had sounded the beautiful conch which first brings them together. And sure enough, Ralph matures rapidly, coming to understand "the wearisomeness of this life, where every path was an improvisation and a considerable part of one's waking life was spent watching one's feet." And at the end of the story, he weeps "for the end of innocence, the darkness of man's heart, and the fall through the air of the true, wise friend called Piggy."

But what if Roger had been elected chief? Or Jack?

Golding's view of a democratic form of government is itself naive and innocent. It is clear to us that, unjust as it is, democracy in its "pure" form is not hardy enough to contain aggression. The moral to be drawn from the story is that the sweet persuasions of democracy must be sharpened by force. When Ralph asks Piggy midway through the narrative, "'What makes things break up like they do?'" Piggy's response is deadly accurate. "'I expect it's him,'" he answers, "'Jack.'" Although Golding suggests that everyone has the potential for letting blood—all of the children participate in the killing of Simon—Jack has a greater lust for it than the others. His regime is built on repression and violence. It cannot be combatted with the peaceful measures of democracy. Reason, indignation, and self-assertion, all of which Ralph try, will not work. Near the end of the story when Ralph goes up the mountain to demand Piggy's spectacles and to urge Jack and his band to help maintain the rescue fire, we know Ralph is being naive. He goes unarmed, underestimating the pathology of power.

Nor will the politics of isolation work. Piggy, Ralph, and the twins Sam and Eric try to hold down "civilization" and look after the little ones on the beach, but they are raided by Jack and his hunters, who have established a fort above them. The analogy to this is civil conflict or international war. One must fight back. Aggression requires aggression. But this Ralph never quite realizes. His form of government is constantly on the defensive, and thus he allows the situation to skid out of control. Ralph experiences a growth in moral consciousness—and this makes him sympathetic to us—but not a honing of his sense of *realpolitik*. A curtain flaps sporadically in his brain, as his hold on reality goes dumb and he loses the power of speech.

The only way that the *force* of reason can prevail is to smash Jack's political machine, which involves us in an unpleasant contradiction that Golding does not face (England was forced to go to war against Hitler, and Golding would certainly agree that such action was required). Thus, on Golding's coral island, it is not that the shape of society must depend on the ethical nature of the individual but that the ethics of the democratic system must be bent in order to perpetuate that system. Institutions of discipline and punishment must be erected. In the course of the narrative Jack turns into a Charles Manson or an Idi Amin who should be hunted down as a public enemy, assassinated by a CIA, or incarcerated in a penal colony. At one point, during a meeting, Ralph shouts in exasperation to Jack, "'You're breaking the rules!'" Jack responds, "'Who cares?'" And Ralph can only answer, "'Because the rules are the only thing we've got!'" He's right, but the problem is that there are not *enough* rules: a system of rules is necessary for when the rules are broken.

Those rules come from the adult world, which is absent. Without them and the power to enforce them, incipient democracy breaks down. Jack, the leader of the hunters, is the first to draw a knife to slice into animal flesh, but initially something holds him back—"the unbearable blood." This inhibition, this taboo, this remnant of custom, quickly fades. The second time around, Jack kills the pig with ease, with, in fact, triumphant abandon. "'You should have seen the blood!'" he exclaims. Likewise, another child, Maurice, takes pleasure in taunting the younger children, but still feels vaguely guilty about it. Why? Because he had internalized the rules of English society taught to him by his parents. The threat of punishment lingers with him. "In his other life Maurice had received chastisement for filling a younger eye with sand," the narrator tells us. "Now, though there was no parent to let fall a heavy hand, Maurice still felt the unease of wrongdoing." Roger's behavior is similar to that of Maurice, but more extreme. Early in the narrative, when he throws stones at a younger child, he hides in the foliage because he is afraid of being seen, of being judged by others. At the end, he kills Piggy, coldly, in the sight of everyone.

Ralph and Piggy, the two characters who steadfastly support democracy and refer to their upbringing in England positively, believe that the adult world provides appropriate models of behavior, and though they are partly naive about this too, they are basically right. Ralph's standard is "the memory of his sometime clean self." He invents a kind of fairy tale about adults *for* children, daydreaming of the cottage on the moor where he lived with his parents before he was sent away to school: there were wild ponies, cornflakes with cream and sugar, and good books to read. What sustained this "utopian" middle-class environment was discipline and English tradition, as well as love. "'Grownups know things,'" Piggy remarks elsewhere. "'They ain't afraid of the dark. They'd meet and have tea and discuss. Then things would be alright.'" It's possible. Realism and maturity might help one to see clearly, diplomacy might work. And we add, if they don't, institutions of punishment exist to repress undesirable behavior. It is in this sense that the political implications of *Lord of the Flies* are conservative, as they always are when someone believes that human nature is basically evil. Given the story, we are forced to conclude that law and order are the prime political issues and that it is better to impose and accept tradition than ever allow the rules to go slack.

On Aggression: Biology and Politics

Since Golding's vision of human nature implicitly sets a limit to political possibilities, we should not only look carefully at how his fictional world corresponds to the world as we know it, but also test it against scientific theory and research. But here I must add a note of caution. Given the limits of this essay and the complexity of research in ethology (the study of animal behavior), I do not intend to present a survey of such work, but instead will confine myself to sketching a basic model which will help us evaluate Golding's conception of human nature. Since I have argued that *Lord of the Flies* as programmatic fiction points beyond itself, my primary purpose here is to suggest a way we can approach the issue of the relationship between man and society which Golding raises.

Lord of the Flies, as I mentioned earlier, was published in 1954, and it seems therefore fitting that research in ethology made great progress in the fifties, soon afterward blossoming into a glamorous discipline whose development burst into the public consciousness in 1975 with the publication of Edward O. Wilson's stunning and controversial *Sociobiology*. Further, it seems all the more appropriate to examine some of the implications of this research since Golding uses the metaphor of the beast in man to convey our capacities for evil.

It may be that this metaphor is misleading, that it incorrectly suggests that man's animal origins are base, when on the contrary it is the human species which exhibits the most glaring exception to the rule of peaceful intra-species animal behavior. We may find it necessary, as has the esteemed biologist René Dubos, to readjust the metaphor in the context of what we know of the behavior of the human species as a whole. Impatient with what he considers to be currently the fashionable view that human nature was bad from the beginning and objecting to the inaccurate and negative connotations of the word "bestiality," Dubos made a point of entitling one of his many books *So Human an Animal*, which was awarded the Pulitzer Prize in 1969. In the more recent book *Beast or Angel? Choices that Make Us Human* (1974), Dubos balances the phenomenon of man's aggressive instincts against man's astonishing capacities for altruism:

> In view of the fact that human beings evolved as hunters, it is not surprising that they have inherited a biological propensity to kill, as have all predators. But it is remarkable that a very large percentage of human beings find killing an extremely distasteful and painful experience. Despite the most subtle forms of propaganda, it is difficult to convince them that war is desirable. . . . In contrast, altruism has long been practiced. . . . It certainly has deep roots in man's biological past for the simple reason that it presents advantages for the survival of the group.[19]

Dubos does not deny man's instinct for aggression, but he does find current emphasis on it misguided. It is also important for us to note that he regards altruism as an instinct.

Although the field of ethology has been enriched by the contributions of many prominent scientists, including Karl Von Frisch, Niko Tinbergen, and Wilson, and popularized in the writing of Desmond Morris and Robert Ardrey, here I will trace only some of the salient features of the theory of Konrad Lorenz, the famed and prolific Austrian ethologist.[20] Lorenz views the human species as subject to the same laws of causal behavior, that is, natural laws, as are other species

(I need hardly add that this is a position which is inimical and insulting to most humanists). Aggression is natural to man, not unnatural or irrational. This does not mean that Lorenz is sanguine about the increasing tempo of international violence. On the contrary, he regards it historically, as a pathological deterioration of behavior mechanisms which originally possessed survival value. From his point of view, what happened on Golding's coral island presumably would not have taken place in a simple tribal community, but only later, after the relationship between the biological basis of human behavior and cultural determinants of human behavior became unbalanced. Lorenz would argue that man was not born in "original sin," but rather that these aberrations of human behavior developed later. Indeed, he has undertaken the study of the relationship between the aggressive instinct, cultural development, and social behavior because he believes that if we understand the extent to which our behavior is innate, not learned, we may well be able to temper the expression of that aggression, which he regards as the greatest danger we face today.

What are the natural causes of the aggressive drive in the human species as well as in other animal species? How does this drive enhance survival? Lorenz advances several answers. The most important function of intra-species aggression is the calibration of the relationship between populations and resources (territoriality). Aggression also contributes to strengthening the defense of the young and furthering sexual selection (the fighting of sexual rivals helps promote selection of the best and strongest animals for reproduction). How is aggression expressed? Lorenz points out that in the course of evolution animal species have developed elaborate rituals—*signals* of dominance and submission—which function as analogues to morality, happily circumventing the need for actual physical combat and thus allowing populations to reap the benefits of aggressive behavior while avoiding its costs. Like other species, homo sapiens also has an innate aggressive drive toward its own members but, as Lorenz shows, our cultural and technological development unfortunately has permitted us to release that drive in ways which threaten our survival rather than enhance it. In particular, the invention of weapons long ago upset the balance between social inhibitions and the potential for killing, and as a consequence, it is only the human species that practices mass slaughter of its own kind for no apparent reason.[21]

In *Lord of the Flies* we see this enacted on a small scale. Had Jack and Ralph been limited to fighting out their battle with only their fists as weapons, the consequences of aggressive behavior would have been far less serious—a broken arm perhaps, or a black eye. But Jack and his hunters have introduced two deadly technologies into their war games—the military organization of men, a pentagon of power which Jack mobilizes to search the island for Ralph, and the fire-sharpened spear, which was first directed at the sow and is now intended for Ralph. The atomic war which serves as a backdrop to the manhunt reveals even more clearly the insane disproportion between man's aggressive instinct and his technology for expressing it.

Lorenz observes, however, that the development of weaponry, which made killing easier, has been paralleled by the development of rational responsibility, a specific inhibitory or compensatory mechanism whose purpose is to prevent the abuse of weaponry. Like the aggressive drive, these inhibitions also have an emotional, or instinctive, base. This is fortunate, Lorenz argues, for prohibitions based on logical, rational injunctions alone would be absolutely ineffective:

> Even the fullest rational insight into the consequences of an action and into the logical consistency of its premise would not result in an imperative or in a prohibition were it not for some emotional, in other words instinctive, source of energy supplying motivation. Like power steering in a modern car, sensible morality derives the energy which it needs to control human behavior from the same primal powers which it was created to keep in rein. Man as a purely rational being, divested of his animal heritage of instincts, would certainly not be an angel—quite the opposite.[22]

These instinctive, emotional reactions against intra-specific aggression we see in every member of the island's elite except Jack. When Jack starts to beat Piggy up, hitting him first in the stomach and then on the head, we read that "passions beat about Simon on the mountain-top with awful wings." And the memory of the crazed ritual dance of death, the murder of Simon, revolts Piggy and Ralph, and Simon and Eric too.

But why are their instinctual, emotional responses unable to contain Jack's violence? "Unless it is our innate feeling for these values," Lorenz writes, "under conditions of modern civilized life there is not a single factor exerting selection pressure in the direction of goodness and kindness."[23] Cultural mechanisms do not exist to encourage or channel their expression; on the contrary, conditions exist which cripple the natural sense of justice. I need hardly point out that in a society such as ours, fierce competition, not benevolence, possesses survival value. In addition, Lorenz singles out two other contemporary phenomena which discourage the expression of altruism, both of which are at work in *Lord of the Flies*—absolute tolerance of behavior and the lack of positive parental guidance. In part, what little order does exist on the island disintegrates because of the complete tolerance of destructive behavior: no one publicly assumes the responsibility for the loss of the mulberry-marked little boy, and no one publicly acknowledges the killing of Simon. And the "blessing," as Lorenz calls it, of "understanding, responsible, and above all, emotionally stable parents" is also lacking.[24]

Given this, Golding's fictional world does mirror the larger world. It conveys with literary power the pathological nature of contemporary aggression. For it is obvious to us that there is no natural need for Jack to hunt down Ralph. There are plenty of resources for all the kids, and no women to fight over. Thus, although Golding invites our disbelief by casting children as adults, this strategy does strengthen the theme of his fable in a very important way. The desire for instant gratification and narcissistic self-absorption we find normal in children, but reprehensible in adults, whom we expect to display a sense of responsibility for others and a concern for the future. Golding's point, and it is well-taken, is that the contemporary world of adults is in fact infantile and regressive, that there are no adults to guide and discipline the adults.

But from the perspective of Lorenz's theory of aggression, we can also critique Golding on two interrelated matters. Lorenz would argue that it is not only inaccurate but damaging to regard aggression as having a metaphysical dimension, for by doing so, we render it inexplicably inevitable. From the scientific point of view of Lorenz or Wilson, *Lord of the Flies* can be reproached for presenting aggression in terms of superstitious metaphor that serves to mystify rather than illuminate the phenomenon of violence (the objection that Golding did not have the benefit of such research is irrelevant here; we are interested in the correctness of his claim). "Human aggression cannot be explained as either a dark-angelic flaw or a bestial instinct," writes Wilson. "Human beings," he explains calmly, "are strongly predisposed to respond with unreasoning hatred to external threats and to escalate their hostility sufficiently to overwhelm the source of the threat by a respectably wide margin of safety."[25] The "essential illness" of mankind, the heart of darkness—just what phenomenon in the natural/cultural world do these metaphors refer to, the scientist asks, and how can it be explained. These are valid questions. Writers, and readers, cannot in good conscience ignore the claims of science when, as in Golding's case and in the case of much utopian and dystopian writing, their work proposes to make statements about the behavior of the human species. *Lord of the Flies* is in part guilty of mystification. Simon's silent colloquy with the sow's head, during which he realizes what Piggy had before guessed—that the beast is part of human nature—is routinely interpreted by literary critics as having mystical significance. According to the natural history of aggression, Simon's insight does not have a metaphysical dimension (we should remember also that Simon is just a kid who, although very sensitive, is subject to epileptic fits and was severely dehydrated prior to his interior monologue with the sow's head).[26] Nor is Simon's insight complete. It is partial: aggression is innate in man, but its pathological expression is not. At issue here is the origin and development of aggression, which leads us to a related point. According to Lorenz's theory, Golding's emphasis on man's inherent lust for blood is simply wrong. I'm not arguing that the "desire to squeeze and hurt" cannot be "overmastering," as it is in *Lord of the Flies* and as we read in the newspapers every day, but that the origin of aggression is not to be found here.

If we read Golding critically through the lens of scientific research, we can also submit biological theories of human behavior to the challenge of the humanities. Both movements of thought are required, for notwithstanding much rhetoric to the contrary, we live in a world characterized by distrust and disrespect between the sciences and the humanities—the two cultures, as C. P. Snow first called them in 1959. How do the humanities in general and *Lord of the Flies* in particular help us question science? The science of the limits of human behavior—whether rooted in the sociobiology of a Wilson or the behaviorism of a Skinner—has been criticized by humanists for the reductive, deterministic, and mechanistic nature of its thought. Many observations can be made in this regard, but I will limit myself to one only which invokes a traditional view of literature.

The methodology of modern science, as Hannah Arendt has shown, is to establish an Archimedean point from which we observe the world of nature as something distant from ourselves. In large measure the development of this methodology was dependent upon the invention of the telescope and the microscope. While we learned much about the world as a result, Arendt warns that we must be careful not to observe ourselves from this point. Yet this is of course exactly what has happened. In a passage in *The Human Condition* which can stand as a critique of the science of the limits of human behavior prophetic by some twenty years in the case of sociobiology, Arendt writes, "We look and live in this society as though we are as far removed from our own human existence as we are from the infinitely small and the immensely large which, even as they could be perceived by the finest instruments, are too far away from us to be experienced."[27]

This is precisely Wilson's strategy, as it is that of Lorenz. Wilson explains that "sociobiologists consider man as though seen through the front end of a telescope, at a greater than usual distance and temporarily diminished in size, in order to view him simultaneously with an array of other social experiments. They attempt to place humankind in its proper place in a catalog of the social species on Earth."[28] Lorenz uses the same metaphor. "Let us imagine," he writes, "that an absolutely unbiased investigator on another planet, perhaps on Mars, is examining human behavior on earth, with the aid of a telescope whose magnification is too small to enable him to discern individuals and follow their separate behavior, but large enough for him to observe occurrences such as migrations of peoples, wars, and similar great historical events."[29]

Viewing our own behavior as if from such a great distance allows us to make predictive statements about the behavior of the human species on a gross level which can indeed be quite correct. If, however, such deterministic theories of behavior are mistakenly applied to the arena of politics, which is concerned with another level of human behavior altogether, demagoguery can result. As we see in *Lord of the Flies*, as a consequence of a fatalistic view of man's nature, humans are perceived as less than human, as animals, to whom anything can be done. In the realm of recent human history, I need hardly point to the horrific actions of Hitler, who was heavily influenced by the theory of social Darwinism.

One of the achievements of *Lord of the Flies* is to alert us to this danger. The fable draws clearly the connection between deterministic theories of biology and politics. In *Lord of the Flies*, we see the *patterns of human behavior* as if from the Archimedean point which renders them visible, but which effaces the individual. We are also admitted into the *interior experience* of those who suffer as a result. The latter cautions us against the perils of the former. Piggy and Ralph engage our sympathy, perhaps at times even our empathy. Piggy's fearful insecurities, Ralph's hunted dread—what they are forced to experience at the hands of Jack we find monstrous. As the story rushes toward its conclusion, we are increasingly anxious for Ralph to escape, and our condemnation of Jack escalates. Thus, as literature, *Lord of the Flies* summons up precisely those instinctual, emotional responses which Lorenz asserts are the foundation for the prohibition of aberrant violence.

Childhood and Society

As a fable *Lord of the Flies* may be about the evil in the human heart, but as a novel it is about the frightening potential of children for violence. This is one of the complicated and fascinating effects of the book. The adult world may indeed be marked by extreme brutality— we remember intermittently that an atomic war is in process—but it seems for the moment infinitely preferable to the violent anarchy of children. For in the course of the narrative our suspension of disbelief is so perfectly manipulated by Golding that we temporarily forget that these characters are in fact children and respond to them as if they were adults. Thus, when they are rescued by a naval officer at the end of the story, and we recognize with a shock that they are children after all, we are willing to accept anything but this, even an atomic war, which now seems less savage than the violent obsessions of young Jack and his followers.

True, the conclusion of *Lord of the Flies* is ironic, a kind of frame which sets the fable in place. As Golding asks elsewhere, commenting on the ending of the story, "The officer, having interrupted a man-hunt, prepares to take the children off the island in a cruiser which will presently be hunting its enemy in the same implacable way. And who will rescue the adult and his cruiser?"[30] But this is not the only effect of the ending. We welcome with uncomplicated relief the figure of authority. We conclude that children require strict supervision and constant discipline, for without these, they pose a serious threat to the adult world.

Doris Lessing has written about this in her fine novel *Memoirs of a Survivor* (1975), which is also set in a future postwar period. As the narrator, who is an adult, admits, "At the sight of children, I was afraid. And I realized 'in a flash'—another one!—that I, that everybody had come to see all children as, simply, terrifying." The children form angry survival bands. How can they be dealt with? One character concludes that "the only way to cope with the 'kids' was to separate them and put them into households in ones and twos."[31] This is how to deal with the enemy—divide and conquer. In Golding's most recent novel, *Darkness Visible*, which is as sophisticated and phantasmagorical as *Lord of the Flies* is not, children also manifest this capacity for perverse behavior. The young Sophy, a beautiful child much admired for her angelic charm, reflects malevolently about killing her twin sister, whom she thinks receives more attention than she does. Both sisters grow up to be terrorists who not only fantasize about the politics of violence, but practice it. All of this resonates with our contemporary experience. In the newspapers we read of children not yet ten who beat up the elderly, of young babysitters who torture their charges in microwave ovens, of children who try to kill their parents, as the following newspaper clipping about an incident in Slidell, Louisiana, shows:

> Two girls discussed ways of killing their sleeping parents after a family argument, then set fire to their trailer home, police say.
> The parents were in a suburban New Orleans hospital Sunday with severe burns over 45% of their bodies.
> "They discussed shooting, stabbing, cutting their heads off and finally decided on fire," a sheriff's spokesman said.
> Deputies said the murder was planned after the girls, aged 9 and 13, got into an argument with their parents Friday.
> The girls were booked with aggravated arson and the attempted murders of Truett Simpson, 51, and his wife, Glenda, 42, who were rescued from their burning mobile home about 3 A.M. Saturday. It was first thought that the daughters died in the fire, but they were found later in New Orleans.[32]

This is evil, an action, like Jack's, so reprehensible that we cannot imagine a punishment for it. As our society grows more severely age-segregated, the generations come to regard each other as alien— the elderly are strangers to the middle-aged, children perceive their parents as belonging to another species, parents are threatened by their children. Much of the power of reading Golding's novel today rests here: the fear of the child as a violent other, virulent in itself, not a mere analogy for adult brutality (which we know better and accept more easily), but a potential enemy who turns, perversely, the screw.

Notes

1. Soon after the publication of *Lord of the Flies*, two other novels by Golding appeared: *The Inheritors* in 1955 and *Pincher Martin* in 1956. Within a few years of the publication of his first novel, literary critics (Frank Kermode among them) were hailing Golding as a writer of major stature. Most of their interest and praise centered on *Lord of the Flies*,

which Millar MacLure, for example, in "William Golding's Survivor Stories," *Tamarack Review* 4 (Summer 1957):60–67, acclaimed a "masterpiece." Paralleling the explosion of literary criticism on *Lord of the Flies* in the sixties and the appearance in 1964 of the movie directed by Peter Brook, was the immense increase of its popularity on college campuses. In 1962 it was reported that *Lord of the Flies* had sold more than sixty-five thousand paperbacks in less than three years. *Time* magazine dubbed it "Lord of the campus." But by 1970 it was clear that its popularity had peaked, as we read in James R. Baker's "The Decline of *Lord of the Flies*," *South Atlantic Quarterly* 69 (1970):446–60. As to the future visibility of *Lord of the Flies* on campus reading lists, I can only speculate here, but I do predict that it will surface again in large numbers as the threat of political authoritarianism and international power politics becomes increasingly evident to Americans in the decade of the eighties.

2. Quoted in Bernard F. Dick, *William Golding* (New York: Twayne, 1967), p. 18. For a discussion of the relationship of *Coral Island* to *Lord of the Flies*, see Carl Niemeyer's "*The Coral Island* Revisited," *College English*, Jan. 1961, pp. 241–45.

3. *Lord of the Flies* (New York: Capricorn Books, 1959). All references will be to this edition. Given the short length of *Lord of the Flies*, I will not refer the reader to the corresponding page numbers in this edition when I quote from the text.

4. See, for instance, Robert J. White, "Butterfly and Beast in *Lord of the Flies*," *Modern Fiction Studies* 1 (1964):163–70; E. C. Bufkin, "*Lord of the Flies*: An Analysis," *Georgia Review* 19 (Spring 1965):40–57; Bruce Rosenberg, "Lord of the Fireflies," *Centennial Review* 11 (1967):128–39; Eugene Hollahan, "Running in Circles: A Major Motif in *Lord of the Flies*," *Studies in the Novel* 2 (Spring 1970):22–30; and Jeanne Delbaere-Garant, "Rhythm and Expansion in *Lord of the Flies*," in *William Golding: Some Critical Considerations*, ed. Jack I. Biles and Robert O. Evans (Lexington: Univ. of Kentucky, 1978), pp. 72–86.

   For a review of the criticism on *Lord of the Flies*, see Maurice L. McCullen's splendid and exhaustive survey "*Lord of the Flies*: The Critical Quest," in *William Golding: Some Critical Considerations*, pp. 203–36. I refer the reader also to Jack I. Biles's excellent "William Golding: Bibliography of Primary and Secondary Sources," in the same volume, pp. 237–80.

5. "Notes on *Lord of the Flies*," in *Lord of the Flies*, p. 190.

6. Epstein, pp. 189–90.

7. "Fable," in *The Hot Gates* (New York: Harcourt, Brace and World, 1966), p. 85. Much commentary has been devoted to the question of genre, and most critics agree that the term "fable" is the most useful. I refer the reader to John Peters, "The Fables of William Golding," *Kenyon Review* 19 (1957):577–92; Margaret Walter, "Two Fabulists: Golding and Camus," *Melbourne Critical Review* 4 (1961):18–19; Millar MacLure

"Allegories of Innocence," *Dalhousie Review* 40 (Summer 1960):145–56; and Bernard S. Oldsey and Stanley Weintraub, "*Lord of the Flies*: Beelzebub Revisited," *College English*, Nov. 1963, pp. 90–99. For work on the fable, see Robert Scholes, *The Fabulators* (New York: Oxford Univ. Pr., 1967).

8. Quoted in Epstein, p. 189. Golding made this statement in a questionnaire which he filled out for the American publisher of *Lord of the Flies*.

9. "Utopianism as Ideology: A Defense," paper presented at the Second Annual Conference on Utopian Studies, Univ. of Michigan, Oct. 1977.

10. "Defining the Literary Genre of Utopia," *Studies in the Literary Imagination* 6, no. 2 (1973):135.

11. In "Two Fabulists," Margaret Walter argues that the purpose of a fable is to provide a dramatic analogy of the real world; my approach will be to critique that analogy. Juliet Mitchell's "Concepts and Technique in William Golding," *New Left Review*, May/June 1962, pp. 63–71, is one of the few essays which poses questions similar to mine and reaches, in some respects, similar conclusions. She reproaches Golding for not analyzing the problem of the origin of evil in man and accuses him of muddying the situation by casting adults as children.

12. Dick, p. 30.

13. "Values and Conflicts through History: The View from a Canadian Retreat," in Thompson's *At the Edge of History* (New York: Harcourt Brace, 1971), pp. 104–50.

14. However, Thompson also concludes that we are on the edge of exploding into another utopian organization of culture which he calls scientific-planetary civilization.

15. These are the narrator's words in *Lord of the Flies*.

16. In an otherwise thought-provoking essay entitled "Power and Authority: An Interpretation of Golding's *Lord of the Flies*," *Antioch Review* 30, no. 1 (Spring 1970):21–33, David Spitz succumbs at first to this line of reasoning:

> Now a novelist is not a historian; much less so is the author of a myth or fable. We cannot submit his work, therefore, to the standards and tests of historical or anthropological research. (For this reason I omit from consideration here what would otherwise be, I think, a telling argument: namely, that evil inheres not simply in man but also in collectivities, institutions, and social forces).

What a shame that a telling criticism must be relegated to the hushed enclosures of parentheses. Spitz then shows, persuasively, that Golding's characters were culturally determined and thus do not represent mankind as a whole; ultimately he does refer to actual cultural practice to press his point.

17. Golding, "Fable," p. 89.

18. Quoted in Epstein, p. 189.
19. *Beast or Angel? Choices that Make Us Human* (New York: Scribner's, 1974), p. 43.
20. In "*African Genesis* and *Lord of the Flies*: Two Studies of the Beastie Within," *English Journal*, Dec. 1969, pp. 1316–21, Richard Lederer and Paul Hamilton Beattie appear to take the same approach as I do here, but there is a major difference. Their primary purpose is to show how the two authors interpret the same questions about human nature. I begin from this point but also critique Golding from the perspective of science.

I draw my observations primarily from Konrad Lorenz, *On Aggression*, trans. Marjorie Kerr Wilson (1966; New York: Bantam, 1967) and *Civilized Man's Eight Deadly Sins*, trans. Marjorie Latzke (1973; London: Methuen, 1974). I refer the reader to three collections of essays which I have found very useful in this regard: Jonathan Benthall, ed., *The Limits of Human Nature* (New York: Dutton, 1974); Arthur L. Caplan, *The Sociobiology Debate: Readings on Ethical and Scientific Issues* (New York: Harper and Row, 1978); and Albert Somit, ed., *Biology and Politics: Recent Explorations* (The Hague: Mouton, 1976).
21. Edward O. Wilson takes issue with Lorenz in several areas but does concur that "the human forms of aggressive behavior are species-specific: although basically primate in form, they contain features that distinguish them from aggression in other species" (*On Human Nature* [1968; New York: Bantam, 1969], pp. 101–02).
22. *On Aggression*, p. 239.
23. *Civilized Man's Eight Deadly Sins*, p. 39.
24. *Civilized Man's Eight Deadly Sins*, p. 39.
25. *On Human Nature*, p. 122.
26. One of the major issues in Golding criticism is the religious dimension of his work. Many literary critics argue that Golding is a religious novelist. But this is not an issue of cool literary discussion only. Critics outside the literary establishment have attacked Golding for his religious views, among them Catholic priests, who have argued that *Lord of the Flies* might have a bad influence on undergraduates (see Francis E. Kearns, "Salinger and Golding: Conflict on Campus," *America*, 26 Jan. 1963, pp. 136–39; and John M. Egan, "Golding's View of Man," in the same issue of *America*, pp. 140–41). Notwithstanding such criticism and Golding's own statement in "Fable" that man is "a fallen being" who is "gripped by original sin" and that Simon is a "Christ-figure" (pp. 88, 97), it must be clear to the reader that I do not share this view in regard to *Lord of the Flies*. Golding's intent is one thing, the import of *Lord of the Flies* another. Golding's recent novel, *Darkness Visible* (1979), does, however, have a strong mystical dimension.
27. *The Human Condition* (Chicago: Univ. of Chicago Pr., 1958), p. 323.
28. *On Human Nature*, p. 17.

29. *On Aggression*, p. 228.

30. Quoted in Epstein, p. 189.

31. *Memoirs of a Survivor* (New York: Knopf, 1975), pp. 189, 181.

32. "2 Burned, Girls Held," *Milwaukee Journal*, 14 Jan. 1980, sec. 1, p. 2.

13
Robert Silverberg's *The World Inside*
Merritt Abrash

I

The World Inside (1971) is an engrossing novel. The extraordinary setting is compelling throughout. Characters are vividly drawn and sharply individualized, facing problems familiar enough to arouse sympathy yet fascinating in their twenty-fourth-century context. Cleverly interrelated plot elements sustain dramatic interest from beginning to end. For sheer readability, *The World Inside* ranks among the best utopian novels, even though rather less than a masterpiece is necessary to join that particular company.

At the same time, it is a description in detail of a futuristic society which clearly belongs somewhere in the utopian/dystopian spectrum. Characters in the book talk about the society's utopian qualities, and in the course of the narrative the author provides numerous commentaries of his own. Through ingenious devices, such as the research into the past by a member who happens to be a trained historian, the nature of society in A.D. 2381 is observed through a variety of perspectives and temperaments. Concern with the basic utopian dilemma of the individual's relationship to society is always present behind plot developments.

Furthermore, this close integration of idea with story is achieved within an unambiguously science-fictional context. Several of the works surveyed in this volume can be classified as science fiction, but *The World Inside* is the only one that first appeared in a science fiction magazine (*Galaxy*) in the hallowed serial form, and Robert Silverberg has described it (along with his *Tower of Glass*) as "closer to pure science fiction, the exhaustive investigation of an extrapolative idea, than anything else I have written."[1] As an exploration of an arguably utopian society, written by one of the best known names in the science fiction field and directed in the first instance toward precisely that audience, *The World Inside* has exceptional significance for students of utopian literature and thought.

The failure of science fiction novels to break into the ranks of widely studied utopian visions is interesting. Of course Ray Bradbury's *Fahrenheit 451* and Ursula K. Le Guin's *The Dispossessed* have gained extensive recognition, but considering the natural proclivity of science fiction writers to deal with exotic civilizations at various removes of time and space, it is clear that connoisseurs of utopia dismiss the overwhelming proportion of science fiction output. This deserves some explanation, the better to understand how Silverberg avoids falling victim to it.

The bedrock of science fiction, as of mysteries, westerns and other genres, is action rather than reflection. The story is the sine qua non, not to be interfered with or slowed down by ideas. Serious utopian literature, however, reverses the relationship: ideas are what count, and the story is meant to lend point to the ideas and not to distract from them. "The distinction," explained I. F. Clarke in a related context, "is that in *Brave New World* science is the situation; but in admirable stories like *The Day of the Triffids* science merely provides the opportunity for tales of action that are not very different from the adventures of Sinbad or Robinson Crusoe."[2] The near-absence of overlap between science fiction and utopian literature is attributable not to writers' skills or profundity, but to their priorities.

A case in point is Isaac Asimov's *The Caves of Steel*, a renowned novel which takes place in a future setting rather akin to Silverberg's world of 2381. Both societies occupy entirely enclosed spaces (a roofed-over New York City in *The Caves of Steel*) and have made elaborate technological adjustments to deal with population pressure. But there the similarity ends, because whereas Silverberg is seriously concerned with the nature of individual and group life under such constraints, Asimov uses the futuristic environment only as a prop for his detective story. He has written about so many different things during his career that he could no doubt write about utopia as well, but, appearances notwithstanding, serious utopian insights or commentary are almost entirely absent from this novel.

The rationale for and operation of the supercities in *The Caves of Steel* receive only two pages of summary and conventional treatment, concerned entirely with outward aspects. No perceptible psychological change can be detected in the inhabitants, whose conversations, relationships and daily rounds seem remarkably like those of non-

luxury apartment dwellers in a crowded late-twentieth-century metropolis. Even when novel mores or customs are described—"By
strong custom men disregarded one another's presence entirely within
or just outside the Personals [centralized lavatory-laundry chambers].
. . . The situation was quite different at Women's Personals"[3]—they
prove to be solely for plot purposes and lack significant connections
with the distinctive nature of the society. When a character speculates
on the consequences of a potential technique for beaming energy to
earth from space stations, the range of considerations is, in terms of
utopian thinking, pitifully narrow:

> Baley had the picture of an Earth of unlimited energy. Population could
> continue to increase. The yeast farms could expand, hydroponic culture
> intensify. Energy was the only thing indispensable. . . .
>   Earth's population could reach a trillion or two. Why not? . . . But
> they would be dependent on imported air and water and upon an energy
> supply from complicated storehouses fifty million miles away. How in-
> credibly unstable that would be. Earth would be, and remain, a feather's
> weight away from complete catastrophe at the slightest failure of any part
> of the System-wide mechanism.[4]

Not a word about *social* instability, or the consequences of failure
in the *organizational* mechanism. To be sure, such matters were less in
evidence in the science fiction mainstream when Asimov wrote the
book (1953) than they are now, but Silverberg's achievement in providing an absorbing plot and high level of action while remaining
reflective and sophisticated about ideas is still an uncommon one.[5] A
summary of the world of 2381 will show the breadth of his treatment
and how its science/technology features, while important, are kept
subordinate to human aspects.

In 2381 the earth supports seventy-five billion people, of whom
the overwhelming majority live in "urbmons," self-contained (except
for food) one-thousand-floor skyscrapers. A minute portion of the
population lives in food-growing communes. Urbmons and communes
are dependent on each other, but avoid direct contact and share no
common culture, not even language.

Each urbmon is divided horizontally into "cities" of between
twenty and forty floors, with about eight hundred people on each floor.
The cities (which are further broken down into villages) have strong
occupational identities and an undefined degree of control over their
own affairs. In the center of the urbmon is the service core, including

innumerable connections with a central computer, and underneath are facilities for "turning mass into energy"—recycling wastes, trash, the dead and, in the case of dangerous or persistent deviants, the living.

No one is allowed to leave the urbmon except to populate new urbmons or for professional requirements which cannot be satisfied by the gigantic data bank which is available to all. Maintenance outside the urbmons and the conveyance of products to and from the communes are carried out by robots.

Within the urbmon is a wide range of intellectual, recreational and spectator activities. Although formal religion still exists in attenuated forms, the dominant spiritual concept is the "blessworthiness" of maximizing human fertility. Most criteria of virtue, obscenity, etc., are related to this. Sexual activity is at the forefront of social interest, partly because of the pressures toward procreation and partly because urbmon society has, in consequence of population density, developed "post-privacy" norms which eliminate privacy in dress and behavior. All inhabitants agree that "the total accessibility of all persons to all other persons is the only rule by which the civilization of the urbmon can survive."[6]

The urbmon in which the novel takes place is administered by a privileged ruling class which co-opts fresh talent wherever it appears. There does not seem to be any political process involving the population at large. Police exist, with no apparent duty except throwing deviants from urbmon ideals "down the chute" into the recycling process. Less serious cases are referred by "consolers"—first-line therapists—to "moral engineers" whose techniques, although gentle, permanently change personality. "Blessmen" offer superficial assurances of oneness with the universe to those who undergo moments of alienation.

Everyone in the urbmon works, although for the less intellectual classes there is a good deal of makework. Outside of working hours, one's time is one's own, and family life and the pursuit of individual entertainment are similar to twentieth-century counterparts except for the sexual mores which result from the rule that no one can refuse a reasonable sexual request. Sexual activity, which is engaged in with spouses, friends and total strangers alike, is at a phenomenal level of frequency. Since jealousy is incompatible with a post-privacy culture, liaisons are not meant to be taken "personally" and traditional feelings of love and affection seem to play as full a role between husband and wife as in twentieth-century marriages. No mention is made of divorce or separation; almost all marriage partners are happy with each other and their family situations.

This information and a great many supporting details and statistics emerge without the use of much overt exposition in what is quite a short book—under two hundred pages. Silverberg manages this through a device rarely met with in utopian novels. Traditionally, a utopian plot line follows one character, usually a visitor or dissident, through a series of adventures which touch upon those features of the society important to the author. This can be unfortunate if the character is personally uninteresting (Julian West in Edward Bellamy's *Looking Backward*), the adventures are not very adventurous (a long list, on which such worthies as William Morris's *News from Nowhere* must be included), or the emphasized features are presented in rigidly schematic form (the "journalistic" sections of Ernest Callenbach's otherwise skillfully constructed *Ecotopia*). *The World Inside*, in contrast, consists of seven distinct episodes, each focusing on different combinations of characters, most of whom are in more than one episode but none of whom are in all of them. This arrangement permits Silverberg to portray a great variety of aspects of urbmon life as elements in the lives of nicely assorted inhabitants who become familiar to the reader.

Chapter 1

The convenient device of an outsider being introduced to the society is employed in this one chapter, in the form of a sociocomputator from a settlement on Venus (still underpopulated) who is shown around an urbmon by a fellow professional, Charles Mattern.

Chapter 2

A young woman and her husband are selected to be among the initial population of a newly-built urbmon. She resists leaving the urbmon she has always lived in, is sent to the moral engineers, and is then able to leave without regrets.

Chapter 3

A musician, Dillon Chrimes, participates in a spectacular concert, then takes a pill which gives him the sensation of merging with everyone in the urbmon. It is a fantastic high, followed by a dreadful low.

Chapter 4

A married couple find themselves trying to arouse jealousy and acting generally "unblessworthy" toward each other. Just before they become likely candidates for going down the chute, he (a historian) realizes they are emotional throwbacks to pre-urbmon society. They conspire to camouflage their feelings, and find themselves deeply in love.

Chapter 5

Siegmund Kluver, a rising specialist in the theory of urban administration, discovers that the urbmon's leaders are debauched, self-
aggrandizing and utterly cynical. At their orgy, to which his invitation is a
major step toward joining their ranks, Siegmund hesitates to show these
qualities in adequate measure and his prospects immediately fade.

Chapter 6

A computer primer, Michael Statler, becomes obsessed with the
desire to see the outside world and forges an exit pass. He comes to a
commune where he is charged with spying for the urbmon and almost
sacrificed to a harvest god by the puritanical, superstitious farmers. He
escapes back to the urbmon where he is immediately executed as a social
danger.

Chapter 7

Siegmund Kluver tries to regain his sense of purpose by visiting a
blessman, a consoler and various friends and strangers throughout the
urbmon. When nothing succeeds, he climbs to the roof and in a moment
of mystic exaltation jumps off trying to reach the sky.

The World Inside seems on first reading to have both the breadth
and depth, the drama and insight, of a major utopian novel. A study of
antecedents, internal consistency and implications will help determine
if this work, most of which originally appeared in science fiction
magazines, indeed belongs among the key visions in utopian
literature.

II

The World Inside is certainly a "hive" society, but it is not so certain
what a hive society should be. The only indisuputable characteristic
seems to be extreme crowding. But "hive" also implies an enclosed
space, and even though the dictionary definition does not require this,
the hive concept is not easily kept distinct from mere crowdedness
without it. The concept's source in insect societies also suggests that
hives should manifest a high degree of organization, especially a
drastic and wondrously efficient differentiation of functions between
members of the society, who are programmed or conditioned to keep
as busy as bees or as industrious as ants (or any other suitable
metaphor).

However, few fictional societies have met the criteria of crowding, an enclosed space and organization along the lines of insect
societies. H. G. Wells came close in *The First Men in the Moon*, where

the huge numbers of Selenites inside the moon are biologically specialized beyond the dreams of the most fanatical Director of Hatcheries
and Conditioning in Aldous Huxley's *Brave New World*. But since the
Selenites actually *are* insects (or more insect than anything else),
calling them a hive society doesn't quite come to grips with the issue.
The Caves of Steel meets the physical critieria of a hive, but the lives of
its characters bear no resemblance at all to those of ants or bees. They`
live instead like familiar human types who have had to make numerous
piecemeal adjustments to overburdened space facilities. Both Wells
and later commentators refer to *When the Sleeper Wakes* as a hive or
anthill society, but rather than envisioning distinctive hive characteristics it describes a late-nineteenth-century society, with some features
exaggerated, in a technologically visionary environment.

Silverberg's urbmons are completely enclosed and crowded to the
limit the society's standards of civilized living will allow. This is of
course a prescription for severe population pressure, which would
seem an inescapable fact of life (so to speak) in a hive yet plays no part
in Wells's novels mentioned above and is assumed to be under rational
control in *The Caves of Steel* ("their I.Q. rating, Genetic Values status,
and his position in the Department entitled him to two children, of
which the first might be conceived during the first year"). Silverberg
recognizes that population pressure in a hive environment will necessarily lead to social patterns unlikely in any *but* a hive society, and
accordingly goes much further than Wells or Asimov in exploring not
merely how a hive operates, but the effects of such operation on the
way of life and the psychology of the inhabitants.

On the other hand, there is nothing of bee- or ant-like regimentation in the urbmon. Organization is pervasive and unchallengeable,
yet no one seems to feel any urgency about their role in it. What little is
said about the atmosphere and relationships in daily work makes them
sound relaxed and even informal. No one has problems on the job
(except poor Siegmund Kluver), working hours are apparently quite
flexible, and specialization is no more intense than in any advanced
twentieth-century industrial society. Insect hives were never like this.

Since *The World Inside* is a unique blend of some elements
appropriate to a hive and others which are not, it cannot be expected to
owe much to previous hive stories. Curiously, its chief debt is to a
Wells story about a society which is neither fully enclosed nor rigidly
organized and in fact can be considered a hive only in the elementary
sense of crowdedness. But "A Story of the Days to Come" anticipates

key environmental features of *The World Inside*, and makes some of
its points about human consequences with plot developments very
similar to those in the later novel.

Wells describes England in the twenty-second century, with the
entire population concentrated in four huge cities.[7] Thirty-three million people live in London and no one in the countryside, which is
devoted exclusively to food production. The vertical orientation of the
city is as emphatic as in an urbmon: "The towering buildings of the new
age, the mechanical ways, the electric and water mains, all came to an
end together, like a wall, like a cliff, near four hundred feet in height,
abrupt and sheer."[8] And within the city, verticality provides the scale
along which class is measured, just as in *The World Inside*: "The
prosperous people lived in a vast series of sumptuous hotels in the
upper storeys and halls of the city fabric; the industrial population
dwelt beneath in the tremendous ground-floor and basement, so to
speak, of the place."[9] Farming is done by a distinct social group, but
instead of commune dwellers they are an enormous agricultural pro-
letariat which the Food Company conveys out of the city each day.
Production is so efficiently organized that weeds have almost dis-
appeared, and fertilizer is supplied by fountains sprinkling deodorized
urban sewage—a concept closely akin to the urbmon's distillation of
urine into pure water for the inhabitants and chemicals to be sold to the
communes. Moving roadways and widespread use of powered vehicles
have made walking "a rare exercise," and when Denton and Elizabeth, Wells's hero and heroine, walk from the city they soon find
themselves footsore, just as Michael Statler, the obsessed computer
primer in *The World Inside*, finds when he leaves the urbmon on foot
that "short horizontal walks along the corridors have not prepared him
for this."

Denton and Elizabeth, who have decided to live in the uninhabited countryside in order to marry without means, are, like Michael,
full of romantic imaginings about an outside world for which they are
wholly unprepared. The newlyweds are besieged by savage dogs, and
Michael narrowly escapes being sacrificed to the harvest god by the
commune people. All three are likable, eager and courageous, but do
not know how to live off the land or defend themselves against the
dangers there. "Ours is the age of cities," says Denton after the
encounter with the dogs; "More of this will kill us. . . . To each
generation, the life of its time. . . . In the city—that is the life to which
we were born."[10] "His conditioning asserting itself after all," writes
Silverberg of Michael's flight back to the urbmon, "Environment

conquering genetics" (p. 156). Denton, Elizabeth and Michael return to their cities defeated, the former to the harsh necessity of finding "means," the latter to execution. Later, in a moment of profound despair after becoming serfs of the Labor Company to avoid starvation, Denton and Elizabeth go to a high flying-machine landing stage on the outskirts of London and look at the stars. Denton has a mystical experience he can scarcely express:

> Down there it would seem impossible almost to go on living if one were horribly disfigured, horribly crippled, disgraced. Up here—under these stars—none of those things would matter. They don't matter. . . . They are a part of something. One seems just to touch that something—under the stars.[11]

Siegmund Kluver, disgraced in fact and not merely in imagination, climbs to the top of the urbmon and has a similar experience.

> Stepping out on the flat breeze-swept platform. Night, now. The stars glittering fiercely. Up there is god, immanent and all-enduring, floating serenely amidst the celestial mechanics. . . . Siegmund smiles. He stretches forth his arms. If he could only embrace the stars, he might find god. (Pp. 182–83.)

Denton, thwarted in his middle-class ambitions, subsides into the grim life of the lowest class; Siegmund, who had aimed much higher, leaps off the urbmon.

The points of resemblance do not extend past these matters of environment and plot into the natures of the two societies. Urbmon inhabitants sincerely contend that they are living in utopia, but no one could make such a claim for the society in Wells's story, where class differences have been hardened by technological advance and their effects compounded by the inequities of the economic system. Even considered as a dystopia, "A Story of the Days to Come" is confusing to analyze, since Wells provides little hard information about its economics and none at all about its politics. (These gaps are filled in *When the Sleeper Wakes*, which is a much more significant futuristic vision but, in the absence of the adventures of Denton and Elizabeth, less closely related to *The World Inside*.)

In contrast to "A Story of the Days to Come," *The World Inside* is crammed with details and statistics about urbmon society. Information about its economic life is plentiful, and its politics are seen through the eyes of a rising administrator who proffers convenient insights and analyses. The initial impression made by the two works considered together is that in this case Wells fell into the occupational hazard of simply telling a story, whereas Silverberg retrieved Wells's hints and fragments and constructed a genuine utopian vision around them. The question to be explored is the validity of that vision.

III

Utopian novels have traditionally been more specific about institutions (or lack of them) than about the corresponding individual and mass psychologies. In *Utopia*, More imparts all kinds of information about how Utopian society operates and its prevailing religious and philosophical beliefs, but little sense of the Utopians themselves aside from their relentless commitment to propriety and keen conviction of superiority to all other peoples. *Looking Backward* is notorious for the shallowness of its portrayal of personal and social life in A.D. 2000, in sharp contrast to the depth and passion of Bellamy's vision of a new economic and class order. No doubt this emphasis on how a society works is an occupational hazard of utopian novelists in the same way as science fiction writers give priority to narrative action, and it is a measure of Silverberg's skill that in *The World Inside* he avoids these particular tendencies of both types of writers.

Avoiding a tendency, however, is not the same as striking a balance, and Silverberg's penetrating exploration of the psychological consequences of urbmon society is accompanied by a strangely inadequate approach to institutions. This may sound like an unreasonable criticism, since *The World Inside* is replete with descriptions and explanations of the urbmon's operation, backed up with numerous statistics.* Yet from all this information no clear picture emerges of

---

*Despite his attention to most matters of detail, Silverberg's arithmetic suffers from a carelessness which lessens the impact of his "facts." The most serious case concerns world population. This is said (by both a sociocomputator and an administrative insider, so it must be assumed to be the correct figure) to total seventy-five billion. But consider the following points, all quite clear in the book:

1. The Chipitts constellation of fifty urbmons contains forty million people.
2. Chipitts is not the largest constellation but is larger than most.
3. Constellations cover large stretches of territory: from Chicago to Pittsburgh, Boston to Washington, San Francisco to San Diego, Berlin to Paris, Vienna to Budapest, Shanghai to Hong Kong, Bogota to Caracas, to list the ones actually referred to in the book. There is plenty of room between them, since no part of any other constellation is visible from the top of the three-kilometer-high urbmon in which the story takes place.
4. Michael Statler walks many miles from the urbmon without coming across a single house or person, and when he is flown even further away, the settlement he arrives

how the politics and economics of urbmon society actually work. The vagueness about politics is especially puzzling, since the character most in evidence throughout the novel is Siegmund Kluver, who is well on his way to becoming one of the ruling elite and lets the reader in on privileged information about how the urbmon is governed. But what his insights boil down to is that the leading men (apparently all the top administrators are male) are power-hungry, self-serving and cynical, and delegate all work except decision-making. Nissim Shawke, the thoroughly unpleasant possessor of vast administrative power, does, as far as Siegmund can tell, "nothing at all. He refers all governmental matters to his subordinates. . . . Shawke need not *do* but only *be*. Now he marks time and enjoys the comforts of his position. Sitting there like a Renaissance prince. . . . A single memorandum from him might be able to reverse some of the urbmon's most deeply cherished policies. Yet he originates no programs, he vetoes no proposals, he ducks all challenges" (p. 97). He also makes cruel fun of Siegmund's idealism and particularly any suggestions that urbmon life should live up to its utopian professions even if administratively inconvenient.

The other leading administrators are more amiable than Shawke but equally lacking in commitment and dynamism. Even the orgy at which Siegmund loses his nerve deserves no better than his disdain: "So common, so vulgar, the cheap hedonism of a ruling class." Yet Silverberg would have us believe that these decadent citizens and indifferent administrators, who in fact in his portrayal do not have a

---

at is a small town at best. The non-urbmon population is clearly a negligible part of the world total.

The conclusion from these points is that world population cannot be anywhere near seventy-five billion. If forty million is a more or less average figure for a constellation, it would take almost two thousand constellations to reach seventy-five billion; but since constellations cover such enormous swaths of land, it would be impossible to fit even five hundred of them on the earth's habitable surface.

Less significant in the novel but still indicative of carelessness with numbers is the calculation of the urbmon's midpoint, where Dillon Chrimes, for symbolic reasons, wants to be when he starts his transcendent drug experience. He has to settle for the 500th floor even though the "true midpoint" is "somewhere between 499 and 500." But of course the midpoint in a 1000-floor building is between 500 and 501.

Finally, when Charles Mattern is showing his visitor from Venus around the urbmon, they enter a newlyweds' dormitory where "a dozen couples are having intercourse on a nearby platform." Elsewhere in the book such a dormitory is described as shared by thirty-one couples (which, it is further explained, is eight more than it was meant to hold). The carelessness in the reference to "a dozen couples" lies simply in the failure to think about the implications of a number, since the possibility of almost half the couples having intercourse at the same daytime moment is, even in the supersexed urbmon atmosphere, exceedingly remote.

single redeeming quality among the lot of them, are allowed to possess power and privilege without a whisper of opposition, not even from the ambitious "rung-grabbers" rising in the official hierarchy. And this in a society where political standards are neither reinforced by the prevailing ideology nor imposed by formal conditioning!

Such an incongruity is possible because the book makes no effort to analyze the fundamental nature of urbmon politics. Siegmund cannot figure out which of the leaders is most important: "At the top level, power becomes an abstraction; in one sense everybody in Louisville [the topmost floors] has absolute authority over the entire building, and in another sense no one has" (p. 96). In the absence of further explanation, the "inside information" air of this statement merely disguises a complete lack of content. And what about the governmental level among or above the urbmons? One must exist, since decisions are made to build new urbmons and allocate resources for them, but it is never mentioned.

The nature of urbmon economics is even vaguer. No one buys things, gets salaries, handles money or is needy, so it is logical to assume that distribution is organized on communistic principles. However, there are occasional references to expense, and at one point Siegmund "authorizes a credit transfer to the blessman's account." The vast economic and social implications of "credit transfer" are so studiously ignored that the phrase seems to have wandered in from another book. Silverberg seems no more concerned with the economic than with the political functioning of urbmon society.

Of course the utopian writer gives unequal emphasis to different aspects of his or her imagined society. The areas perceived as most significant—in all likelihood the ones in which contemporary disharmonies stimulated the author to construct a utopia in the first place—will receive the most serious and detailed attention. Other elements will be treated less fully (or even, as in the case of the common people in Plato's *Republic*, ignored altogether) or simply settled arbitrarily. The outstanding example of the latter is the reaction of the hero of *News from Nowhere* to the "force vehicles" which convey heavy loads on land or water without noise, pollution or visible machinery: "I took good care not to ask any questions about them, as I knew well enough . . . that I should never be able to understand how they were worked."[12]

Just as Morris's "Nowhere" required an ideal form of mechanical power but his real interest was in entirely different aspects of the society, urbmons must have politics and economics but Silverberg's primary concerns lie elsewhere. The illusion he gives of having provided many answers obscures the fact that, like Morris's hero confronting the force vehicles, he takes care (but much more skillfully) to avoid asking serious questions about the less favored subjects. The social relations of urbmon society are what really interest him, and it is in that area, where he is most specific and consistent, that the essential utopian/dystopian quality is to be found. Sexual mores, of course, dominate urbmon sociology, but class considerations are surprisingly prominent. Although there is some relationship between material goods and class, the main indicator of status is vertical location in the urbmon, just as in "A Story of the Days To Come." Location is determined generally by occupation, with a ranking of rulers, professionals, minor officials, technical workers and manual workers similar to twentieth-century evaluations. Education, sophistication and even per capita living space decline as one descends in the urbmon, and classes have little contact with each other, which is not a surprise to the reader after the information that inhabitants of the upper floors label those of the lower with the term "grubbos."

If these attitudes toward class are reminiscent of Silverberg's own twentieth century, class characteristics are even more so. Top administrators and their families display arrogance and "cool" and are in no doubt of their superiority. In our only glimpse of them, industrial workers are described as "slumped and sullen human handlers." Artists live in San Francisco, rather low in the building but a tolerant place where "we don't push hard." The description by musician Dillon Chrimes of the inhabitants of Rome, which is located in the middling 500s, will be familiar to readers of modern European fiction.

> The people here are mostly minor bureaucrats, a middle echelon of failed functionaries. . . . Here they will stay in this good gray city, frozen in hallowed stasis, doing dehumanized jobs that any computer could handle forty times as well. Dillon feels a cosmic pity for everyone who is not an artist, but he pities the people of Rome most of all, sometimes. Because they are nothing. Because they can use neither their brains nor their muscles. Crippled souls; walking zeros; better off down the chute. (P. 44.)

Unlike class considerations, sexual mores have undergone drastic change, and this is Silverberg's real focus of interest in terms of pages devoted to it and depth of analysis. Mattern explains to his visitor from Venus that "each of us has access at any time to any other adult member of the community," and that means exactly what it says.

Access is institutionalized in the practice of nightwalking, whereby anyone (but almost always the male) can enter any room in the entire urbmon (but as a matter of good form people are expected to stick to their own cities) for any sexual purpose within reason. Nightwalking is at the core of "post-privacy culture," guaranteeing—so urbmon theory runs—that frustration, which would be explosive in a hive, will be forestalled. Since no one can withhold anything from anyone else, there is nothing to get frustrated about on the interpersonal level. The devaluation of the emotional intensity of sex in favor of sheer physical expertise reduces the danger of social strain that much further.

The World Inside's description of a stable and unregimented post-privacy culture is an original contribution to futuristic thought, a refreshing change from the usual population-pressure scenario of desperate social measures and totalitarian politics. However, imposing a radical new sexual code to enable people to live in hives, when hardly anyone would *choose* to live in a hive, seems a bit perverse. Wouldn't it make more sense to simply stop living in hives? But that cannot be done in the world of 2381, because the core of religion, morality and social planning is the absolute priority of unlimited fertility. Nightwalking is not only a mechanism for controlling frustration, but a tribute to the sacred duty to procreate. Sexual training and deliberate stimulation are not only aspects of society in which sex is fully open, but social aids toward the fulfillment of the most profound ethical obligation. The proliferation of human life in 2381 is perceived not as a population "problem" but as an exalted condition of things to which men and women, in their essential humanity, have discovered how to adjust their attitudes, behavior and institutions.

When the Venusian visitor happens to mention fertility control, Mattern, although a sophisticated sociologist, "clutches his genitals in shock at the unexpected obscenity. . . . 'Please don't use that phrase again. Particularly if you're near children.' " He then provides as provocative a formulation of utopian criteria as any ever written:

> "We hold that life is sacred. Making new life is blessed. One does one's duty to god by reproducing. . . . To be human is to meet challenges through the exercise of intelligence, right? And one challenge is the multiplication of inhabitants in a world that has seen the conquest of disease and the elimination of war. We could limit births, I suppose, but that would be sick, a cheap, anti-human way out. Instead we've met the challenge of overpopulation triumphantly, wouldn't you say? And so we go on and on, multiplying joyously, our numbers increasing by three billion a year, and we find room for everyone, and food for everyone.

Few die, and many are born, and the world fills up, and god is blessed, and life is rich and pleasant, and as you see we are all quite happy. We have matured beyond the infantile need to place layers of insulation between man and man." (Pp. 12–13.)

The power of this statement lies (as is the case with all significant utopian statements) in its self-sufficient quality, its invulnerability to refutation on its own ground. If life is better than death, if encouragement and support of new lives is better than prevention or suppression, if human ingenuity can find room and food for everyone, where is the opening for dispute? When Mattern says, "Can you deny that we are happy here?" his use of "happy" may not be the same as someone else's, but that is a different argument, as John Savage finds out in attempting to grapple with Mustapha Mond's self-sufficient argument in *Brave New World.* In any event, the Venusian does not even try to answer his host, and Silverberg's own response, while effective enough in literary terms, is deeply flawed in its character as serious utopian commentary.

IV

Silverberg's reaction to Mattern's claim of utopia is not in doubt. Every chapter in the novel ends on an ironic or negative note pointing up the diminished human quality of urbmon life. This gets rather heavyhanded toward the end. After alert, eager Michael Statler, whose expressions of initiative and curiosity closely reflect most twentieth-century readers' professed values, has been speedily executed upon his return from "the world outside," the chapter concludes: "The journey is over. The source of peril has been eradicated. The urbmon has taken the necessary protective steps, and an enemy of civilization has been removed." Siegmund's soul-tormented leap off the urbmon is immediately followed by the novel's final paragraph, in which dawn breaks over the urbmon and "God Bless! Here begins another happy day."

Michael and Siegmund have plenty of company in their disenchantment—namely, all the main characters in the book. Perhaps the most obvious evidence for Silverberg's determination to portray urbmon society as dystopia is his failure to allow a good look at contented members. Mattern, to be sure, is completely adjusted, but after serving as guide in the first chapter he scarcely appears again, and is not a particularly attractive character when he does ("sleek, fast-talking" and "tight-souled" are the adjectives attached to him). Even during the "happy day" in the first chapter he is "sickened and diz-zied" when he remembers his brother thrown down the chute many years before for antisocial behavior.

Dillon Chrimes, the musician, seems perfectly adjusted and at times filled with a positive delight about the urbmon. He enjoys a full life, has complete freedom to exercise his art, and toward the end of his ecstatic drug episode exults " 'Oh what a beautiful place. Oh how I love it here. Oh this is the real thing. Oh!' " But the net effect of the drug trip is negative—" 'You go all the way up, then you come all the way down. But why does it have to be so far down?' " (pp. 60–61)—and his creativity is temporarily blocked.

Dillon later admits to Siegmund, who has confessed his own feelings of alienation, that on the downside from the drug the urbmon " 'struck me as just an awful hideous beehive of a place.' " Neverthe-less, " 'what's the good of hating the building? I mean, the urbmon's a real solution to real problems, isn't it?' " Since it works most of the time, and there's no sensible alternative, " 'we stay here. And groove on the richness of it all' " (p. 169). So even Dillon, who has experi-enced that total identity with his fellows which is the ultimate fulfill-ment of a hive's inner nature, offers no better justification for the urbmon than utilitarian calculation.

Even nightwalking, which is universally recognized as indispens-able to post-privacy culture and also as a liberation from the "steriliz-ing" emotions of earlier societies, is not exempted from the disillusion afflicting all the main characters. Siegmund leaves his room because a nightwalker is visiting his wife there (although in a post-privacy culture no one cares if he stays), then realizes he is more interested in sleep than in sex. "Nightwalking suddenly seems an abomination to him: forced, unnatural, compulsive. The slavery of absolute freedom" (p. 174).

Silverberg does himself a disservice by concentrating on the dissi-dents and pointing up their plight with his own overt commentary. A mock utopia is most effectively exposed when it is shown at its best (by its own standards) and that best proves to be grotesque. Huxley does this superbly in *Brave New World*—Henry Foster, Lenina and Mus-tapha Mond are allowed to go through their usual paces on their own terms, and if the results appear ridiculous and appalling, it is not because Huxley says so, but because they are *inherently* ridiculous and appalling in the light of his readers' standards and need only be described to be condemned. Silverberg, in contrast, rarely lets his imagined civilization speak for itself.

A more serious flaw in *The World Inside* as a dystopian novel is that is strains the limits of utopian plausibility. Of course all utopian fiction involves a high degree of speculative "what if?," but the "if" should not be ruled out by the nature of things. If the lion has to lie down with the lamb, or telepathy become a common mode of communication, or a comet's gases transform human nature, the story should be classified as a fantasy rather than a utopian vision. The cult of maximum fertility in *The World Inside*—which demands positive action toward procreation, not merely the elimination of restraints (i.e., continence is as morally reprehensible as abortion), and does so as a permanent command, not merely as a temporary measure to offset some population deficiency—is so exceptional a departure in recorded human affairs[13] that readers need a plausible scenario of the events and attitudes which brought it about. Silverberg fails to provide this.

Historical developments from the twentieth century to the twenty-fourth are never described. A historian reflects that the twentieth century was the climax of the "ancient era," followed by a chaotic twenty-first and the arrival at modern times in the twenty-second, but the reader is left to guess what *happened*, and why New York's skyscrapers have been reduced to stumps and London is deep under water. Nearest to a causal explanation of the preoccupation with fertility is the remark, made in light conversation, that " 'a cultural imperative telling us to breed and breed and breed [is] natural, after the agonies of pre-urbmon days, when everybody went around wondering where we were going to put all the people' " (p. 25)—and that is not very near. Thus urbmon society, which could not have come into existence without extraordinary events in both the material and ideological realms, floats in mid-air as far as historical conviction goes.

The World Inside's most damaging shortcoming as a utopian novel—as a manifestation of serious visionary ideas in a persuasive fictional framework—is that too many of urbmon society's characteristics do not follow logically from its inner nature. The caste system in *Brave New World* mirrors perfectly the values and priorities of Fordian society, but the class system in *The World Inside* is simply arbitrary. Nothing in the organization of urbmon life makes class privilege and snobbery necessary or even probable. The only reason equality of sexual access does not produce the same social equality as equal income in *Looking Backward* or equality of refusal in Eric Frank Russell's . . . *And Then There Were None* is that Silverberg makes the outcome different. The same can be said about the political system. In *Looking Backward* it is a wholly logical outgrowth of socioeconomic priorities, but in *The World Inside* it is reduced to administration by a cynical elite for no stronger reason than that the author says so.

On a broader scale, all aspects of life on Le Guin's utopian planet Anarres flow persuasively from the society's ideological foundations, just as they did centuries earlier in More's Utopia. But many of the features of urbmon society do not survive the elementary question, "Why should they have taken these forms and not others?" Something as taken for granted as the rigid prohibition against leaving the urbmon is, when considered apart from story line, only one alternative among several. Sightseeing trips in land or air vehicles, for example, could hardly engender more restlessness than the frequent travelog shows on the "screen."

All of this suggests that *The World Inside* is a dystopia because its author uses his literary skill to make it sound like one, not because he demonstrates that a society organized like an urbmon will inevitably be a dystopian place to live. Instead of persuading his readers that the application of some principles which may seem obviously in the human interest will actually lead to diminished human qualities in the future, Silverberg portrays a future which is less human mainly because he imposes unattractive features on it. He loads the dice so consistently that the cautionary element (inseparable from all dystopian visions) is clearly intended to be taken seriously, but it is not easy to pin down just what is being cautioned against. On the assumption that the novel is concerned with something of greater scope than "permissiveness" or "hedonism," it seems to point to the loss of individualistic/romantic freedom under conditions of pervasive organization, even when that organization is not overtly oppressive and makes possible so estimable a goal as that propounded by Mattern after his visitor's reference to fertility control. The basic theme is hardly original, but is presented in an absorbing fictional framework and with some unusual variations.

But the classics of utopian literature do more (sometimes without even doing *that*): they weave so tight a bond between a society's inner nature and institutional and psychological manifestations that the reader cannot help thinking, "Yes, it would have to be like that." The urbmons, however, do *not* have to be as Silverberg describes them. What makes for literary effectiveness in a cautionary tale does not necessarily contribute to a fuller understanding of ideas. *The World Inside*, an outstanding achievement as science fiction, falls short of the more rarefied level of significant utopian thought.

Notes

1. In *Hell's Cartographers*, ed. Brian W. Aldiss and Harry Harrison (London: Weidenfield and Nicolson, 1975), p. 40.
2. *The Tale of the Future* (London: Library Association, 1961).
3. *The Caves of Steel*, in *The Robot Novels* (Garden City, N.Y. Doubleday, n.d.), p. 37.
4. Ibid., pp. 137–38.
5. Silverberg accomplished the same feat in his short story "Getting Across," in *Future City*, ed. Roger Elwood, (New York: Trident, 1973). The story features a suspenseful adventure in a highly original yet plausible dystopian setting, the origins of which are intelligently described.
6. *The World Inside* (Garden City, N.Y. Doubleday, 1971), p. 7.
7. In its description of the physical appearance and functioning of the twenty-second-century world, "A Story of the Days to Come" is like a trial run for *When the Sleeper Wakes*, in which Wells greatly expanded this aspect. Therefore several of the points in this and the following paragraph are identical, or nearly so, with material in the latter novel.
8. "A Story of the Days to Come," in *The Complete Short Stories of H. G. Wells* (London: Benn, 1948), p. 741.
9. Ibid., p. 737.
10. Ibid., p. 751.
11. Ibid., p. 771.
12. William Morris, *News from Nowhere* (London: Routledge and Kegan Paul, 1890), p. 140.
13. Societies have attached spiritual value to a high level of procreation, for example in obedience to the biblical injunction to be fruitful and multiply, but that is not the same thing as bending every effort to achieve the greatest possible number of births among the entire population. It has been suggested to me that nineteenth-century Mormon society might be a precedent for insistence on maximum fertility.

14

Chronosophy, Aesthetics, and Ethics in Le Guin's *The Dispossessed: An Ambiguous Utopia*

James W. Bittner

—*Beethoven*

There was a wall.
—*Le Guin*

I

The Dispossessed is an anachronism. By the time Ursula K. Le Guin set out to create her ambiguous utopia in the early 1970s, the positive utopia had been displaced in the system of literary genres available to novelists: as "new maps of hell" had become more numerous and more prevalent in the generations since Edward Bellamy's *Looking Backward* (1888), William Morris's *News from Nowhere* (1890), H. G. Wells's *A Modern Utopia* (1905), and Jack London's *Iron Heel* (1907), the form available in the literary system for constructing alternate worlds had changed "from utopia to nightmare." Two world wars and several colonial wars, the totalitarianism of the Soviet Gulag and the Nazi death camp, and the dehumanizing technology and domineering administration of capitalist life had nearly killed hope by eliminating the very ability to conceive utopia, let alone less radical alternatives. Thus Eugene Zamyatin's *We* (1924), Aldous Huxley's *Brave New World* (1932), and George Orwell's *1984* (1949) had evolved into the dominant genre models.[1] Utopian hopes, to be sure, experienced an explosive world-wide awakening in the late 1960s, in the Chinese Cultural Revolution, in the Prague Spring and in Paris in May 1968, in Miami and during the Siege of Chicago, at Woodstock and in communes, in the Black Power movement, in the women's movement, in

244

the ecology movement, and in the writings of Herbert Marcuse and others. But the literary utopia, said Robert C. Elliott, historian of the genre, was in the 1970s "all but dead."[2]

With this backdrop in mind—awakened utopian hopes and a dormant if not dying belief in the utopian novel—we might imagine a conversation in a publishing house in 1972 between Le Guin and a publisher, and the publisher, having read her manuscript, might have said to Le Guin what Keng says to Shevek in their discussion of the possibility of utopia near the end of *The Dispossessed*: " 'You are like somebody from our own past, the old idealists, the visionaries of freedom; and yet I don't understand you, as if you were trying to tell me of future things; and yet, as you say, you are here, now!' "[3] Just so: the substance of Le Guin's utopia is neither an obsolete and naive vision of social harmony and perfection from a more innocent age, nor is it a blueprint for the just society projected into the never-never land of the far future, though nominally it may be set "several hundred years" after "Ainsetain of Terra" in a solar system eleven light years from ours (pp. 63, 300). Rather, *The Dispossessed* is about the reality of the present moment, the "here, now." Le Guin uses the utopian genre to argue that the present is made real only as one com-prehends (grasps together) the internal relations, the complementary and di-alectical relationships of the past (memory and history, a promise made) and the future (intention and hope, a direction taken). As she remarked in an interview, *The Dispossessed* says "that there is no present without the presence of both the past *and* the future."[4] Thus Le Guin might have answered our imagined publisher, who doubts utopian possibilities, as Shevek answers Keng, who believes her world has forfeited its chance for utopia:

> "You don't understand what time is," he said. "You say the past is gone, the future is not real, there is no change, no hope. You think Anarres is a future that cannot be reached, as your past cannot be changed. [. . .] Things change, change. You cannot have anything. . . . And least of all can you have the present, unless you accept with it the past and the future. Not only the past but also the future, not only the future but also the past! Because they are real: only their reality makes the present real." (Pp. 307–8)

So if *The Dispossessed* is an anachronism, it is an anachronism about chronism, or, more properly, "chronosophy," the study of the "voices of time."[5] The reality of the present moment, here and now in 1983 or whenever we read Le Guin's novel is, according to the chronosopher Shevek, constituted by a chiasmatic relationship of times (past:future::future:past). Likewise, the form of the narrative in which he lives is itself a chiasmus: the first and last chapters are entitled "Anarres Urras" and "Urras Anarres" and as we read the novel from beginning to end, we criss-cross in space and time from one world to the other, between past and future, returning at the end to the beginning.[6] By making time a major theme in her narrative and by making her readers live that theme as they experience the form of her narrative, Le Guin reinvents and transforms the utopian genre. No longer is it just *u-topia* ("no place") and *eu-topia* ("good place"); it is also *u-chronia* ("no time") and *eu-chronia* ("good time; fulfillment of time"). Northrop Frye writes that "the question 'Where is utopia?' is the same as the question "Where is nowhere?' and the only answer to that question is 'here,' that non-spatial point at the center of space."[7] Le Guin's novel argues implicitly for a complementary temporal dimension: the question "When is utopia?" is the same as the question "When is never?" or "When is ever?" or, perhaps, "When is 'once upon a time'?" and the only answer to that question is "now," that non-temporal moment in the middle of time. Shevek and *The Dispossessed* are "here, now."

It is within this simultaneously multi-dimensional and non-dimensional field of space and time that the social-political themes and aesthetic structures of Le Guin's utopia should be examined. My aim is to explore some of the ways in which *The Dispossessed*, to a greater degree than just about any other utopia, fuses form and content. Le Guin has grappled, with remarkable success, with the nemesis that haunts literary journeys to utopia and back. Except for the drama of ironic clashes between a reader's actual world and an imagined utopian world, drama is otherwise missing from many utopian narratives because their static societies often make little room for the extraordinary individual. Dystopian writers, of course, can easily compose dramatic tales of individuals in conflict with their societies. Le Guin herself has done so in *The Lathe of Heaven* and in "The New Atlantis." In *The Dispossessed*, however, Le Guin has invented an anarchist utopian society, dynamic and revolutionary by definition, designed to operate *in* history, not outside of or at the end of history, created not only to make freedom an unalienable right of any individual, but also to make an exercise of that right of free choice in innovative and risk-taking acts a necessary condition for keeping alive the promise of freedom made when the utopian experiment began. Moreover, in order to move on from inherited dystopian visions and projections, Le Guin has written a palimpsest: she has superimposed the map of her utopian landscape over her map of hell, thereby absorbing, negating, and transcending dystopia to generate a utopian synthesis which, like the synthesis in any dialectical process, is no "epoch of rest" like *News from Nowhere*, but is on the contrary the beginning of another evolutionary stage. Rather than tell us, as Edgar does in *King Lear*, that we must endure our going hence, even as our coming hither, that "ripeness is all" (V.ii.9), Le Guin tells us that our lives should be a true journey, a voyage out and a return, a journey without an end separable from its means, in sum, that "process is all" (p. 294).

My aim, then, is to explore *process* in *The Dispossessed* by discussing first its story, then its plot. By "story" I mean the setting and the chronological course of Shevek's quest for a synthesis of Sequence and Simultaneity in a General Temporal Theory and the several personal and public walls he must unbuild to free himself to do physics, making his scientific quest at the same time an ethical-political quest. By "plot" I mean the arrangement of the story incidents, the designs of the image patterns, the configurations of symbols, the time-binding narrative techniques, the counterpointing of the Anarres and Urras chapters, all of which, I will suggest, are, in addition to being a formal analogue of Shevek's theory, a verbal analogue of a musical form: like the first four notes of Beethoven's Symphony no. 5 in C Minor, the first four words of *The Dispossessed* compose a motive, part of a theme which, when combined in an exposition, development, and recapitulation with other themes (linear and cyclic time, authority and freedom, possession and alienation, and exile and home), is the opening statement in a cyclical sonata form.[8] Shevek's science is temporal physics; music is "his Art: the art that is made out of time" (p. 140). Le Guin's science fiction fuses Shevek's scientific quest with her own fictional quest—both are quests in chronosophy—to create a landscape in which human acts, i.e., ethical acts and morally responsible choices, are possible. " 'It's true,' " says Shevek, " 'chronosophy does involve ethics' " (p. 199). Le Guin's means/end in *The Dispossessed* is a quest for an Archimedes point from which she can move the walls of our world to create an open landscape where loyalty, fidelity, and free choice are possible, where we can be at home. If, as H. V. S. Ogden says, More's *Utopia* is "at bottom a book on ethics," then Le Guin's ambiguous utopia is a legitimate child of the eponymous parent of the genre, for it too is at bottom a book on ethics.[9]

II

In his 1946 foreword to *Brave New World*, one satire on the Wellsian utopia which set the fashion for many nightmare visions of the future, Huxley remarked that if he were to rewrite the book, he would offer the Savage an alternative he did not give him in 1932. Instead of forcing him to choose between the "insanity" of utopia and the "lunacy" of a primitive Indian village, Huxley would offer this "sane" alternative:

> a community of exiles and refugees . . . [in which] economics would be decentralist and Henry Georgian, politics Kropotkinesque co-operative. Science and technology would be used as though . . . they had been made for man. . . . Religion would be the conscious and intelligent pursuit of . . . the unitive knowledge of the immanent Tao or Logos. . . . a society composed of freely co-operating individuals devoted to the pursuit of sanity. Thus altered, *Brave New World* would possess artistic and . . . philosophical completeness.[10]

Huxley never prepared an anarchist-Taoist new *Brave New World* based on this recipe, but the recipe stands as a rough pre-scription of *The Dispossessed*. Unlike Huxley, however, who understood his book to be about the future and judged its value in terms of the plausibility of its forecasts, Le Guin understands science fiction to be analogy, not extrapolation: she uses the devices of estrangement in fictional thought experiments to ask questions which, she says, are "reversals of an habitual way of thinking."[11] If she were extrapolating as Huxley was, then her novel would have been entirely about the "absolute regimentation" of "life in the ruins" on the burned-out and dusty Earth that Keng describes to Shevek (pp. 306–7), a fictional Earth which is, probably not by chance, contemporary with the fictional worlds of Zamyatin and Huxley. Moreover, Le Guin does not, as Huxley does, frame issues, choices, and possibilities in either/or terms, with a third possibility inserted between the horns of a dilemma; instead, as a Taoist, she regards binary relationships not as opposites but as interacting complements, and conceives of the Way as a balanced *and* dynamic synthesis of polarities.

Thus Anarres, a community of exiles and refugees from Urras (a community in which Shevek, Takver, and their friends in the Syndicate of Initiative may have to become internal emigres after he returns from Urras) is at once a product of "a very high civilization . . . and a highly industrialized technology" (p. 85) and at the same time a regression to a more primitive civilization, though not to "pre-urban, pre-technological tribalism" (p. 85)—a sane synthesis of Huxley's lunacy and insanity. Anarres is utopian not in its science and technology, economic abundance, and natural beauty, but in its freedom from authority, its basic moral assumption of mutual aid, and in the openness and lightheartedness of its people; Urras, on the other hand, is "Paradise" to Shevek and Keng (pp. 112, 306) not because of its secretive and walled-in people, its basic moral assumption of mutual aggression, and its authoritarian-bureaucratic administration of people in or out of the military, but because of the "complex wholeness" of life in its lush landscapes (p. 58), its economic abundance, and its well-financed scientific laboratories. In utopia, control of art and science, reminiscent of the dystopian thought control we associate with Zhdanovism and Lysenkoism under Stalin, is possible, as Shevek, Salas, and Tirin know only too well, while in dystopia among the profiteers, Shevek is granted utopian freedom to make his "immense exploration . . . into the extremes of the comprehensible" (p. 48). Not the level of material culture, but the level of moral culture is what distinguishes evolution toward utopia in Le Guin's novel: the normative evolutionary ethics of Peter Kropotkin, Joseph Needham, C. H. Waddington, and others is the substance (it stands under) of Le Guin's utopia.[12] Yet things change. The evolutionary process in a community of revolutionaries may turn into a devolutionary process ("Causative Reversibility") when individuals in the community cease being revolutionaries as they settle into positions of authority in an administrative network which has ossified into an authoritarian net that traps the new and denies any change that threatens the status quo. Le Guin's utopia, therefore, is ambiguous both in its reversal of traditional notions of what constitutes utopia, and in its very structure and texture: process is all.

Urras and Anarres are never still for a moment. Orbiting each other as planet and moon, moon and planet, together they orbit the star Tau Ceti. Although the dystopian image of Earth introduced late in the novel displaces the connections a reader would be making between Urras and Earth (thereby interrupting a too facile identification of real and fictional worlds, freeing attention from *things* so that it may concentrate on *processes*), the political divisions on Urras and the utopian settlement on Anarres are estranged versions of political realities on the Earth we know. A-Io, Thu, and Benbili are refracted images of the capitalist Euro-American states, the socialist Soviet state, and the economically undeveloped and politically volatile Third World; and the kibbutzim in the Palestinian deserts, settled by exiles and refugees from both capitalist and socialist states, are one model for the communities in the arid landscapes on Anarres, settled by Odonian refugees and exiles from A-Io and Thu. The armies of A-Io and Thu fight in Benbili for hegemony over the natural resources and over the survivors of civil wars there, while the scientists of A-Io and Thu serve their states by competing for scientific theories which will enable technicians to build new military-industrial hardware. By eliminating or co-opting dissent, Urrasti states survive, but do not resolve, the contradictions generated by an uneven development in material and moral conditions—Urras is progressive in bringing self-destructive exploitation of the ecosystem under control but has regressive and primitive relations between sexes and classes. Several generations before Shevek journeys from Anarres to Urras, Urrasti anarchists had brought down the Thuvian government and had emigrated, with the blessings of A-Io and Thu and the Council of World Governments, to Anarres. But in the 170 years between the Settlement and Shevek's trip, Anarres and Urras have been as active historically as they are astrophysically: the Urrasti, hoping to stop revolutionary change by buying off the Odonians with a world, cut themselves off from the future and insure the return of revolution; the Anarresti, hoping to eliminate authoritarian power by walling out the profiteers on Urras, cut themselves off from the past and insure the slow growth of authority. If Shevek and his friends can find no one in Wide Plains who knows enough history to explain obscurities in the *Life of Odo* (p. 30), Urrasti can find few signs of Odo, for Drio, where she was imprisoned for nine years, " 'was a moribund sort of town,' " explains Pae, " 'and the Foundation just wiped out and started fresh' " (p. 77). Shevek's goal is not to unite the two worlds; rather he wants to unbuild the wall the Anarresti have set between themselves and their past, to return to the roots of the struggle against authority in order to keep the revolution alive on Anarres. One inevitable by-product of his quest is that he opens the wall between Urras and its future and aids native Urrasti socialists. But his primary goal is to keep the Promise, to be a true and native Odonian. He would not like to see Odo's ideas so perverted that her spirit, should it return, would exclaim "Thank God I am not an Odonian!"[13]

Keng calls the Odonian community on Anarres an " 'experiment in nonauthoritarian communism' " (p. 301), alluding to the sources it shares with the authoritarian communism in Thu. Insurrection Day in *The Dispossessed* is an echo of the split at the 1872 Hague Congress when Marx ousted Mikhail Bakunin and the anarchists. In her headnote to "The Day Before the Revolution," the story of Odo's last day before the revolution that resulted in the mass emigration of Odonians to Anarres, Le Guin makes explicit what is already clearly implicit in *The Dispossessed*: "Odonianism is anarchism. Not the bomb-in-the-pocket stuff . . . not the social-Darwinist economic 'libertarianism' of the far right; but anarchism, as prefigured in early Taoist thought, and expounded by Shelley and Kropotkin, Goldman and Goodman, Anarchism's principal target is the authoritarian State (capitalist or socialist); its principal moral-political theme is cooperation (solidarity, mutual aid)."[14] In addition to separating nonauthoritarian from authoritarian communism, Le Guin distinguishes her pacifist anarchism from the anarchist violence expounded by Bakunin and Sergei Nechaev and criticized by Feodor Dostoyevsky in *The Possessed*: Le Guin's dispossessed are, as it were, saintly rather than diabolical anarchists (*The Devils* is the title of Dostoyevsky's novel in the United Kingdom). Although "anarchists" is a good enough "use name" for the Anarresti, "Odonians," their "true name" (to use a distinction from Le Guin's Earthsea trilogy), tells us more than Le Guin's explicit headnote does. Odo, revolutionary theoretician, organizer, and activist, did not live to cross to the Promised Land, but laid the foundation for the "Promised Man, the true and native Odonian" (p. 145), whose nature is embedded in the different meanings of the Greek word *odos*, a rough cognate of the Chinese *Tao* and the English *way*.[15] Applied to places, *odos* denotes a "way, road; course, channel of a river; the way to truth." Shevek and Takver think as Odonian chronosophists when they describe time as a river or a road laid out. With prepositions, *odos* means "further on the way; forwards, profitable, useful" (or, on Anarres, "functional"). All Odonians, says Sabul, must be functions analysts (p. 233), and a true Odonian would see his cellular, organic, holorganic, and ethical function as carrying Odonianism forward. Used to denote an action, *odos* refers to "travelling, journeying; journey, voyage." Heraclitus used it in this sense: *odos ano kato mia kai oute* ("the path up and down is one and the same"),[16] and Le Guin may have had Heraclitus in mind when she composed Odo's epitaph: "To be whole is to part; true voyage is return" (p. 74). Used metaphorically, *odos* has ethical and aesthetic implications: it can mean "way, manner; course of events foretold by divination; intent; way of doing or speaking; way of telling a story; course of action." The Promise (intent) "was deep in the grain of Odo's thinking" (p. 216); it is a direction taken, a course of action, the exercise of freedom. I will come back to Odonian ways of telling a story when I discuss the plot.

Odonianism, because of its similarities with Taoism—*Tao* means everything *odos* does and much more—is more than anarchism as prefigured by the early Taoists, for Taoism is not merely root, but root and branch of Odonian anarchism.[17] And because Odo was a woman, it includes as well a strong element of feminism, consonant with Emma Goldman's anarchism and the emphasis on the female in Taoism. One exchange in the novel reveals this anarchist-Taoist mixture in Odoanianism. " 'Wasn't it Odo,' " asks Chifoilisk, echoing Pierre Joseph Proudhon, " 'who said that where there's property there's theft?' "; Shevek answers with a quotation from Odo's *The Social Organism*: " 'To make a thief, make an owner; to create crime, create laws' " (p. 123), which sounds as much like the paradoxes in Lao Tzu and Chuang Tzu as it does like Proudhon. Above all, "Odonians" is the true name for the Anarresti because *odos*, unlike *an-arche* (without a ruler; contrary to authority), refers simultaneously to a thing (road) and a process (travelling), rather than to a state of being, and also because its similarities with *Tao* suggest the religious dimension of Anarresti life. Odonians, says Shevek to Kimoe, are not stones, but have a "religious capacity" (p. 13). Religious thought, the Fourth of Nine Modes of Odonian thought, considers "the profoundest relationship man has with the cosmos" (p. 13). The Nine Modes—the other eight are the metaphysical, ethical, philosophical, analogical, technological, economic, experiential, and physical modes—"are built of the natural capacities of the mind" (p. 13) and encompass circles of meanings from the material to the metaphysical as various and as wide as the meanings of *odos, Tao,* and *way.*

Without some capacity for religious thought and feeling, Odonians on Anarres would have suffered severe, perhaps fatal crises long before Shevek is born. Melford Spiro, applying a principle Charles Nordhoff derived from his study of communist societies in the United States—a harmonious commune "must be composed of individuals who are of one mind upon some question which to them shall appear so important as to take the place of religion, if it is not essentially religious"—suggested that Marxism-Leninism was the secular religion of the kibbutz, whose members had rejected the orthodoxy of ghetto Judaism only to develop another orthodoxy.[18] Le Guin's Odonians are not, in this respect, unlike the kibbutzniks. "Any religious person," said Le Guin while writing *The Dispossessed*, "would say, of course, that true freedom is gained by giving up things, possessions. And that's a very strong streak in human nature. We all know we're imprisoned by things, money, by buying and selling."[19] Le Guin's dis-possessed

Odonians are of one mind on the question of freedom and possessions and mutual aid, but their Odonianism, a nonauthoritarian and unorthodox secular religion existing without the props of an established church, as their morality exists without the props of law, comes out of crises with an ambiguous face. On the one hand, young Anarresti show an almost religious fervor in volunteering for emergency drought postings (p. 235); on the other hand, "anywhere that function demands expertise and stable institution," as during a drought emergency, "that stability gives scope to the authoritarian impulse" (p. 149), and orthodoxy creeps into the administrative apparatus. The Anarresti had begun their utopian experiment guided by principles similar to these:

> The strength of the kibbutz lies in its essential social nature which strives for the complete harmony of the individual and the group in every sphere of life, for the maximum development of each individual . . . and for the constant deepening of human ethical relations.[20]

and

> The kibbutz society has carried out a complete revolution of life, and has changed the ancient order of human social living. The property system, method of production, division of labor, foundation of the family, the character of human relations, the status of women, the foundation of education—all have changed in their fundamentals and are in the process of a permanent change.[21]

But Shevek discovers, when the Odonian community is a century and a half old, that his maximum development is stifled, human ethical relations are getting shallower, and the process of permanent change has hit a snag in its forward movement. Bedap, the novel's sharpest critic of counter-revolutionary trends, uses religious language when he says, " 'We don't educate for freedom. Education, the most important activity of the social organism, has become rigid, moralistic, authoritarian. Kids learn to parrot Odo's words as if they were *laws*—the ultimate blasphemy!' " (p. 149). A dialectical process sets in: as orthodoxy grows in theory, so it grows in practice. Administrative structures harden, giving the Sabuls on Anarres a sinecure from which they quash the unorthodox in art (Tirin and Salas), in science (Shevek), even in the individual mind, for reified social structures get reproduced as reified consciousness and consciences—"internalized Sabuls" (p. 292). The dispossessed are repossessed. Sabul, who seems to have lost his capacity to think in the Fourth Mode, rejects any physics that is not narrowly functional and utilitarian. On learning of Shevek's interest in Simultaneity principles, he dismisses it: " 'We're working on physics here, not religion. Drop the mysticism and grow up' " (p. 93). Shevek cannot do physics "cut off from the profoundest relationship man has with the cosmos" (p. 13), any more than his society, imprisoned by authority and orthodoxy, can maintain a process of permanent change. The ongoing betrayal of the true and native Odonian is a religious crisis as well as an ideological and political crisis.

Shevek's way (*odos, Tao*) of breaking out of these circles of orthodoxy and authority, his way of going ahead, his way through walls, is revolutionary in a radical (root) sense: a turning back, a return to the sources of the true and native Odonian, a return that is analogous with what one student of the kibbutz, David Sturm, calls the "recovery of the polarities of the theophanous event" needed to keep the kibbutz evolving (turning out, going forward) as an "influential moment in the history of human becoming."[22] " 'Revolution is our obligation,' " Shevek tells his brothers and sisters on Anarres: " 'our hope of evolution' " (p. 316). The four principles embodied in kibbutz life—the voluntary principle (free association), the communal principle (cooperation, mutual aid, collectivism), the equalitarian principle ("from each according to his abilities, to each according to his needs"), and the pioneering principle (valorization of labor, return to the soil, readiness to surmount obstacles)—will remain vital, says Sturm, only if they live as expressions of ultimate reality (religious pole) as well ideological principles subject to change in concrete history (secular pole). If the living kibbutz is a working out in history of the Zionist Myth of Return (Exile, Diaspora, Return), then living Odonian anarchism, *The Dispossessed* says, will be a working out in (fictional) history of "true voyage in return," the Odonian Myth of Return. Shevek's return to Urras may thus be seen as a recovery and reintegration of the religious and secular polarities in the true and native Odonian. In "his" room at Ieu Eun University Shevek formulates the General Temporal Theory, a "vision both clear and whole . . . a revelation" of the solid foundations of the universe (pp. 247–48), and in the streets of Nio Esseia he recovers "the world that had formed Odo's mind and had jailed her eight times for speaking it, . . . the human suffering in which the ideals of his society were rooted, the ground from which they sprang" (p. 251).

Like the heroes of the classical European novel, Shevek comes of age in a problematic society, and like those heroes, exists in what Georg Lukács calls a condition of "transcendental homelessness."[23] For Novalis, "Die Philosophie ist eigentlich Heimweh—Trieb überall zu Hause zu sein"; for Shevek, temporal physics (chronosophy) and Odonian anarchism are also actually homesickness—a desire above all to be at home.[24] The vision that comes to him with the General Temporal Theory is of "the way clear, the way home, the light. . . . There was no more exile" (pp. 247–48). The course of Shevek's quest to be at home takes him from Wide Plains to the Regional Institute at Northsetting to the West Temaenian littoral, back home to the Regional Institute, to Abbenay and partnership with Takver, to the Dust, then home to Takver and Sadik in Chakar, back to Abbenay to form the Syndicate of Initiative, then home to the mother planet Urras, and finally back home to Anarres, changed because of his leaving it, so that rather than going home again, his going creates the home he returns to. The course of Shevek's life—the spiral journey back home—follows the pattern of the quest in German and English Romantic literature and philosophy.[25] Each of Shevek's spiral journeys, from the learning center in Wide Plains to his encounter with the Hainishman Ketho (who represents home for all peoples in Le Guin's Hainish future history), is wider than the one that precedes it; each spiral is a process of unbuilding walls. The Romantic circuitous journey through alienation to reintegration, similar in form to the Zionist Exile, Diaspora, and Return, similar in shape to Beethoven's cyclical sonata form, is symbolized in *The Dispossessed* by the Circle of Life printed on the green covers of Anarresti books and drawn on the flags of Syndicalists and Socialist Workers on Urras. This two-hundred-year-old symbol of the Odonian Movement, a circle not quite closed, is an abstract version of the ouroboros, the snake with its tail in its mouth, a synthesis of linearity and circularity, as Shevek's journey is a circle not quite closed: the novel ends with him in the starship *Davenant* above Anarres Port. Shevek's story, then, is a sequence of spiral journeys to break out of imprisoning walls; the plot of *The Dispossessed*, juxtaposing chapters on Urras and Anarres, superimposes the spirals, so that we experience them simultaneously. Both the ethical imperatives of Odonianism—which give fullness to the here and now by integrating the past and the future, the future and the past—and Shevek's synthesis of Simultaneity and Sequency in a General Temporal Theory are expressions in the story of the plot's immanent synthesis of sequency and simultaneity in aesthetic forms.

III

The Simultaneity Principle. Principles of Simultaneity. One is Salas's music; the other is Shevek's science. Together they form a chiasmus,

their titles' inversions of each other just one instance of the ongoing
interplay of music and science in *The Dispossessed*. An awareness of
the internal relations between music and mathematics is as ancient as
the Pythagoreans and as recent as Le Guin's name for Cetian music,
the "Numerical Harmonies."[26] Significantly, the "harmonies of the
orchestra" are the background when eight-year-old Shevek shares his
discovery of Zeno's paradox with his speaking and listening group.
Exiled from the group, Shevek consoles himself with thinking of the
magic square

$$8 \ 1 \ 6$$
$$3 \ 5 \ 7$$
$$4 \ 9 \ 2$$

"a design in space like the designs music made in time" (p. 27). Years
later, Shevek and his friends talk of "the spatial representation of time
as rhythm, and the connection of the ancient theories of the Numerical
Harmonies with modern temporal physics" (p. 53), a connection Sabul
sneers at: " 'The universe as a giant harpstring, oscillating in and out of
existence! What note does it play, by the way? Passages from the
Numerical Harmonies, I suppose?' " (p. 103). Shevek looks to temporal physics and to music for "calm patterns," for the true and the
just, for the center where he can see "the balance, the pattern," the
solid foundations of the universe (p. 27). He would probably agree
with Adam Smith, who wrote that listening to a work of pure instrumental music is like contemplating a great scientific system.[27] But
Shevek learns from coming up against the walls of authority—Sabul
and the leader of Shevek's speaking and listening group are only two of
them—that scientific-aesthetic harmonies clash with social-political
realities. Shevek does not achieve his homecoming, his vision of the
solid foundations of the universe, until he gets through those walls to
integrate chronosophy in science and aesthetics with chronosophy in
ethics and politics: his partnership with Takver and his journey to
Urras are time-binding acts, acts which occur "within the landscape of
the past and the future" (p. 295), acts which affirm loyalty and fidelity
to personal and political promises and thus "assert the wholeness of
Time" (p. 223).

" 'A true chronosophy,' " Shevek says at Vea's party, " 'should provide a field in which the relation of the two aspects or processes of time
could be understood' " (p. 198). His General Temporal Theory, a field
theory in which the relation of the linear and cyclic processes of time
can be understood, is of course the most obvious "true chronosophy"

in the novel, a metaphor for the role time plays in constituting the ethical themes of loyalty, responsibility, fidelity, and the relation of means to ends.[28] But the real field in which the relations of succession and duration, being and becoming, or progress and promises can be understood is aesthetics: *The Dispossessed* is, after all, a novel, and a field theory inheres in the narrative process itself. The plot of the novel, a concatenation of Shevek's cyclic quests to break out of walls, is a verbal analogue of several musical forms, including Salas' *The Simultaneity Principle*,

> Five instruments each playing an independent cyclic theme; no melodic causality; the forward process entirely in the relationship of the parts. It makes a lovely harmony. (p. 155)

and the singing of the marchers in Nio Esseia:

> that lifting up of thousands of voices in one song. The singing of the front of the march, far away up the street, and of the endless crowds coming on behind, was put out of phase by the distance the sound mus travel, so that the melody seemed always to be lagging and catching up with itself, like a canon, and all the parts of the song were being sung at one time, in the same moment, though each singer sang the tune as a line from beginning to end. (p. 263)

and Beethoven's cyclical sonata form, whose three-part structure, like the dialectical triad in the traditional romance quest, takes us from home into exile and then back home again, but not to the one we left: instead, a new beginning.

The sonata form's three parts—exposition, development, and recapitulation—are often represented as A-B-A, but the form is not as static spatially as magic squares and palindromes are. Like all literary and musical forms, the sonata form exists only as it is performed or read; the sonata form does not yield time bound forever in amber: rather *the form is a process* of binding time. The essence of sonata forms, says Charles Rosen, is dramatic, a "clearly defined opposition . . . which is intensified and then symmetrically resolved."[29] The exposition, which begins on the tonic ("home"), states and defines the conflict between contrasting themes and harmonic totalities and key areas, and ends on the dominant or in the relative major or minor key. The development, characterized by tonal flux and modulations to distant keys, breaks the principal themes into smaller elements, combines them in new ways, and creates new contrapuntal relations. The recapitulation returns to the tonic ("home" again) and re-collects and re-presents the principal themes in a new equilibrium. One music critic describes the aesthetic effect as follows:

> the listener perceives the subjects in a new relationship—rather like a traveller who glimpses the constituent parts of a valley separately as he climbs a hill and then, when he reaches the summit, sees the entire landscape for the first time as a whole.[30]

The aesthetic goal of the sonata form is a vision of wholeness, comparable to that sense of wholeness Coleridge calls "the common end of all narrative":

> to convert a series into a Whole; to make those events, which in real or imagined History move on in a *strait* Line, assume to our Understandings a *circular* motion—the snake with its Tail in its Mouth.[31]

What I am proposing, then, is that Le Guin uses congruent musical and verbal narrative forms to constitute a field—the Circle of Life—in which ethical relations can be perceived properly, where it is possible, in Shevek's words, "to act rightly, with a clear heart" (p. 305). Ethical action is possible only in the present, in the presence of the past and future. If, as one musician puts it, "the proper perception of a musical work depends in the main on the ability to associate what is happening in the present with what has happened in the past and with what one expects will happen in the future,"[32] then ethical choices depend as well on the ability to associate part with whole, present with past and future, the "here, now" with the "there, then."

A key to the "process is all" philosophy at the center of Odonian anarchism is in the meanings of Odo's "true name"; her *literal* ("of letters") name is similarly a key to the process of Odonian storytelling, the plot structure of *The Dispossessed*. Like the letters that represent the sonata form, *Odo* is a palindrome.[33] If we use the letters A (Anarres) and U (Urras) to represent the chapters of Le Guin's novel, we get another palindrome, one of those designs in space that Shevek likens to the designs music makes in time:

AU	A	U	A	U	A	U	A	U	A	U	A	UA
1	2	3	4	5	6	7	8	9	10	11	12	13

In chapter one, the exposition, Le Guin states all the principal themes and defines the conflict between contrasting harmonic totalities or key areas. The exposition begins on Anarres (utopia; home; the tonic) and ends on Urras (dystopia; exile; the dominant/related key). Stated first on Anarres, "There was a wall" is a motive repeated throughout the development and recapitulation with a rhythmic insistence akin to

Beethoven's insistent repetitions of the four-note motive that opens his Fifth Symphony. We hear the motive not only when the word *wall* appears, but also whenever Le Guin sounds the related notes of prisons, locked doors, boxes, or wrappings; sometimes it is played pianissimo—Pae's "charm, courtesy, indifference" (p. 71), or Shevek's "hard puritanical conscience" (p. 154)—and sometimes fortissimo:

> And you the possessors are possessed. You are all in jail. Each alone, solitary, with a heap fo what he owns. You live in prison, die in prison. It is all I can see in your eyes—the wall, the wall! (p. 202)

and

> There is no freedom. It is a box—Urras is a box, a package, with all the beautiful wrapping of blue sky and meadows and forests and great cities. And you open the box, and what is inside it? A black cellar full of dust and a dead man. (Pp. 305–306)

And as Beethoven's four-note motive is not a whole theme or subject, but only part of a subject,[34] Le Guin's four-word motive is also part of a larger unit:

> There was a wall. It did not look important. . . . but the idea was real. It was important. For seven generations there had been nothing in the world more important than that wall.
> Like all walls it was ambiguous, two faced. What was inside it and what was outside it depended upon which side of it you were on. (p. 1)

The ambiguity is the continuing concern of the extended development section chapters two through eleven. All the themes and images presented in the exposition—the wall, the road, the rock, conflict between Shevek and his society, light, time, exile and home, commodity fetishism and reification (woman in the table), sexism, waste and profiteering, authority and freedom, marriage, and Beggarman, the Promise, choice and responsibility—all are recombined in the development in new contrapuntal relations as they appear in new key areas that modulate far from the tonic. The simple binary opposition between Urras and Anarres, defined by the wall in the exposition, becomes increasingly complex as it is redefined again and again: utopian themes are played in dystopian keys and dystopian themes are played in utopian keys. Shevek's conversation with Keng on Terran "ground" on Urras concludes the development and supplies the psychologically important modulation from the development section to the recapitulation, the final two chapters. The conflict between the

Syndicate of Initiative and the Import-Export Council of the PDC opens the recapitulation on the tonic (on Anarres); the exposition had opened with the ruckus at Anarres Port. The night forest on Urras (p. 19) reappears on the tonic, in Takver's eyes (p. 334). Although the last chapter is headed "Urras Anarres" we do not see Shevek on Urras after he gives Keng his General Temporal Theory. The Hainish starship *Davenant* provides a new tonic, a new set of harmonic relations in which Le Guin recalls those themes which she stated in keys away from the tonic in the second part of the exposition: Shevek feels at home on the *Davenant* as he did not on the *Mindful*, the name Kimoe has modulated to Ketho, the night garden on the *Davenant* recalls the night forest in a new key, and Shevek's imminent return to Anarres is his return to Urras in the home key.[35] From the harmonic ground established by the *Davenant*, Le Guin offers a perspective on the preceding journeys, the processes through which her themes have been developed, the movement toward integration and synthesis into a whole. The novel's concluding image, Shevek's empty hands, denotes possibilities alive in a present open to the past and the future, and resolves the conflicts between Anarres and Urras, past and future, that began with "There was a wall." Although Shevek faces the same stone wall, other walls are down; he has arrived at the "Anarres beyond Anarres, a new beginning" that Takver spoke of at the end of chapter twelve (p. 334).

A novel of 340 pages is not a symphony, and analogies are not identities; nevertheless, the narrative techniques Le Guin uses to bind time into a coherent whole serve the same goal served by Beethoven's or Berlioz's use of recurrent motives to integrate the movements of a symphony.[36] I have already mentioned two examples of her time-binding narrative techniques: the repetition in adjacent chapters of the same (or inverted) idea or image (ignorance of Odo's life on Anarres and Urras in chapters two and three), and the repetition of ideas or images in concentric chapters (Urras as "Paradise" in chapters three and eleven). A diagram will make the design of the plot clear:

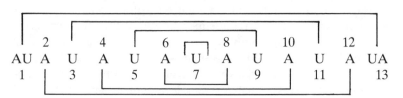

Any Anarres chapter (the "present," as we read it) occurs between Urras chapters (the future), which in turn stand within the chapters narrating the past and future of the "present" Anarres chapter; any Urras chapter occurs between Anarres chapters (the past), which stand within chapters narrating the past and future of the present Urras chapter. Any moment in a narrative, like any moment in music, takes its meaning from what has happened and what will happen; in *The Dispossessed*, however, any "now" is simultaneously past, present, and future.

Concentric chapters are centered on chapter seven, the spatial and thematic hub of the novel; in it, Shevek and Vea rehearse Thomas Huxley's and Kropotkin's debate over competition and mutual aid as laws of human evolution, and Shevek discusses chronosophy and ethics with Vea's guests. This central chapter is itself framed with a repeated image: it opens with Shevek finding a paper in his coat pocket and closes with Pae taking a paper from Shevek's desk. In chapters five and nine, Shevek discovers streets in Nio Esseia—first Saemtenevia Prospect, then Joking Lane. In chapter three, he hears someone practicing the Numerical Harmonies at Ieu Eun University, he discusses the practical application of a General Temporal Theory with Oegeo (faster than light travel), and he meditates on history and time in a four-hundred-year-old room; in chapter eleven, he discusses time and history and hope with Keng in a fourteen-hundred-year-old room in the River Castle in Rodarred, he describes the ansible, another application of his General Temporal Theory, and he hears the "insanely harmonious" bells of Rodarred ring seven o'clock. Chapters one and thirteen show us the *Mindful* and the *Davenant*; Kimoe and Ketho; and Anarres first as a "white stone falling down in darkness . . . his world, the world of the Promise" (pp. 6, 8), then Anarres as a "round white rock: moving yet not moving, thrown by what hand, timelessly circling, creating time" (p. 335). The symmetries, as these images demonstrate, are not perfectly balanced and static; they are, like everything else in the novel, parts of processes. At the same time the Urras chapters take Shevek from a four-hundred- to a fourteen-hundred-year-old room, backwards into Urras's "interminable history" (p. 68), from the gaudy exterior of Urras as Paradise, to Urras as Hell, the dusty cellar and death that are at its core, the Anarres chapters carry Shevek forward from a world of broken promises to "the fragile, makeshift, improbable roads and cities of fidelity" (p. 295). Rulag leaves Palat and Shevek in chapter two to pursue her career, and returns in chapter twelve to "deny the possibility of coming home" (p. 332); but Shevek, at home with Takver in chapter twelve, remembers Tirin, "a natural Odonian—a real one!" (p. 291), who first played "the Beggarman" in chapter two, and whose play Shevek will invert by going to Urras. And in chapter twelve Shevek comforts Sadik, practicing the theory he formulated at the end of chapter two: "brotherhood . . . begins in shared pain" (p. 55). Chapters four and ten both begin with Shevek travelling (to Abbenay in a dirigible; to Chakar on a train and in a cargo dirigible); both show him struggling with his conscience and with Sabul; and both end with reunions: Rulag visits Shevek in hospital, leaving "the sense of the breaking of promises, the incoherence of time" (p. 110), and he joins Takver and Sadik in Chakar, finding completeness of being, . . . fulfillment, a function of time, . . . [and] loyalty, which asserts the continuity of past and future, binding time into a whole" (pp. 294–95). Finally, the central Anarres chapters, six and eight, are another hub. Besides including *The Simultaneity Principle* and *Principles of Simultaneity*, they show the Odonian promise operating in Takver's and Shevek's partnership, a process more central, probably, than any event in the novel, even Shevek's General Temporal Theory. "Marriage," says Le Guin, is "the central, consistent theme" of her work.[37]

Within the aesthetic and temporal field created by these dynamic symmetries, Le Guin uses other time-binding narrative devices. Most obvious are ironic juxtapositions like Shevek's walking tours of Abbenay and Nio Esseia in chapters four and five, and the contrasts between Vea, woman in dystopia, and Takver, woman in utopia, in the three central chapters.[38] At least once, Le Guin even repeats the same phrase in adjacent chapters. In chapter eight, Shevek crumples up a note from Sabul "and then brought his hands down clenched against the edge of the table, twice, three times, in his passion seeking pain" (p. 228); in chapter nine he sits at his desk the morning after Vea's party, and "in the bright morning sunlight he brought his hands down against the edge of the desk deliberately and sharply, twice, three times; his face was calm and appeared thoughtful" (p. 241). We perceive sequence in Shevek's life—here, from pain and passion to thoughtful and calm perception—only when we have a sense of simultaneity that comes with recurrence. Besides connecting adjacent chapters with echoing scenes or ideas or images, Le Guin integrates the whole narrative with several image patterns, among them strands of light imagery, no surprise in a story about a theoretical physicist written by a novelist influenced by landscape painting.[39] Shevek looks at the gleam of firelight on the rim of his water glass at the end of chapter one and sits in sunlight at the beginning of chapter two; he holds moonlight in his empty hands at the end of chapter three and looks into the westering sun at the beginning of chapter four. As sunlight shifts across the papers on his desk, he works on *Principles of Simultaneity* in chapter six, and also lies naked in the moonlight with Takver talking of beauty, patterns, and wholeness. His General Temporal Theory gives him a vision of "the home, the light"; he feels like a "child running out into the sunlight" (p. 247). Le Guin collects the several strands in light imagery—I have mentioned very few of them—with an authorial comment in the final chapter: "The sunlights differ, but there is only one darkness" (p. 340). Then she concludes the novel with "the blinding curve of sunrise over the Temae" on Anarres (p. 341). "The sun," said Thoreau at the end of *Walden*, "is but a morning star."[40]

Although symmetries, juxtapositions and echoes, and patterns of imagery are important narrative devices in *The Dispossessed*, Le Guin's most significant technique for connecting chronosophy, aesthetics, and ethics is the continuing dialectic between her characters' and her readers' senses of past and future, anticipation and memory. The plot is a contrapuntal process of returning and going forward; Shevek's recollection and recovery of his Odonian roots on Urras accompany the development and reintegration, in his partnership with Takver, of Odonian principles on Anarres. This is anamnesia, and works in two ways.[41] In the early chapters on Urras, Shevek remembers events that happened (to us, will happen) in the later chapters on Anarres; and in the later chapters on Anarres, Shevek, Takver, and Bedap remember events from the early Anarres chapters. Shevek's past tense is often the reader's future tense: memory and anticipation are fused. When in chapter three Shevek accepts Atro's handkerchief,

> an importunate memory wrung his heart. He thought of his daughter Sadik, a little dark-eyed girl saying, "You can share the handkerchief I use." That memory, which was very dear to him, was unbearably painful now. (Pp. 61–62)

That unbearably painful memory stays in our memories, directing our anticipation toward chapter ten, when we see Shevek coming home to Sadik and Takver after a four-year separation. With everyone crying in a swirl of pain and joy, four-year-old Sadik breaks through walls of uncertainty and fear of the stranger to offer mutual aid:

[Shevek] wiped his eyes with the backs of his hand, and held the knuckles out to show Sadik. "See," he said, "they're wet. And the nose dribbles. Do you keep a handkerchief?"

"Yes. Don't you?"

"I did, but it got lost in a washhouse."

"You can use the handkerchief I use," Sadik said after a pause.

"He doesn't know where it is," said Takver.

Sadik got off her mother's lap and fetched a handkerchief from the drawer in the closet. (P. 278)

This narrative device is used often—on Urras in chapter one, for example, Shevek has a "vivid memory" of walking in Triangle Park in Abbenay (p. 21); he walks in the park in chapter four (p. 89). Thus do literary devices figure forth Odonian Causative Reversibility, whose significance is primarily ethical, the "handling of the problem of ends and means" (p. 41). More than connecting aesthetics and ethics, though, this technique binds ethics in a field created by aesthetics and chronosophy: the "obscure concatenations of effect/cause/effect" (p. 163) in narrative time connect the concentric Urras chapters with the concentric Anarres chapters, a linkage of times into homeostatic processes symbolized by Takver's mobiles "Occupation of Uninhabited Space" (pp. 162, 168, 227, 286) and "Inhabitation of Time" (p. 324).

Finally, one set of concatenations of memory and event in the text may be read as a paradigm for the aesthetic experiences we have when we read Le Guin's novel. Sleeping in Oiie's house on Urras, Shevek dreams of Takver and himself crossing a snowy landscape, walking toward "a hardly visible barrier" (pp. 135–36). Shevek has already remembered Takver several times in his early weeks on Urras, but we have not yet, at this moment in the narrative, really met her. She was at Shevek's party at the Northsetting Institute, "her lips . . . greasy from eating fried cakes" (p. 53), and she had appeared briefly in Abbenay, "that girl . . . the one with the short hair," Shevek remembers, "who had eaten so many fried cakes the night of the party" (p. 104), but he cannot remember her name. In the chapter following the one that ends with Shevek's dream, he meets her on a hiking trip in the Ne Theras, recognizes that "he had committed an unforgivable fault in forgetting her" (p. 157), is forgiven, and agrees to bond with her for life. Ten years after the Northsetting party, at another going-away party— Shevek has accepted an emergency posting to Southrising—Takver asks,

"Do you remember . . . all the food, the night before you left Northsetting? I ate nine of those fried cakes."

"You wore your hair cut short then," Shevek said, startled by the recollection, which he had never before paired up with Takver. (P. 220)

Recollection (anamnesia) pairs things up, indeed, "pairing up" may be the best name we can find for all the processes at work in Le Guin's novel. It describes what Shevek's chronosophy does with Sequency and Simultaneity; what Shevek and Takver do in their partnership, what Odonian ethics does with ends and means; what Shevek's journey and return do with the ambiguous wall on Anarres; what Le Guin does with aesthetics and ethics; what the narrative process in *The Dispossessed* does with utopia and dystopia, past and future, future and present, present and past, beginning and end. Recollection creates wholes. Anamnesia in *The Dispossessed* points the arrow of time in two directions at once to create the reality of a "here, now," a design in space like the designs music makes in time; it is as fully ambiguous as the utopian experiment on Anarres is. Without revolution, reversion (*ana-*) in time (*chronos*), time (*chronos*) has no progression (*ana-*), no evolution; without memory and history, the future is without hope. Without hope, there is no utopia; without utopia, there is no hope. *The Dispossessed* is an anachronism.

Coda

Is it not, to say the least, untimely to be casting around for a code of laws for the aesthetic world at a moment when the affairs of the moral offer interest of so much more urgent concern, and when the spirit of philosophical inquiry is being expressly challenged by present circumstances to concern itself with that most perfect of all the works to be achieved by the art of man: the construction of true political freedom? . . . I hope to convince you that the theme I have chosen is far less alien to the needs of our age than to its taste. More than this: if man is ever to solve that problem of politics in practice he will have to approach it through the problem of the aesthetic, because it is only through Beauty that man makes his way to Freedom.

—Friedrich Schiller[42]

Notes

1. On the system of literary genres, see Claudio Guillén, *Literature as System* (Princeton, N.J.: Princeton Univ. Pr., 1971); on genre evolution and dominant forms, see Robert Scholes's discussion of Eichenbaum and Jakobson in *Structuralism in Literature* (New Haven: Yale Univ. Pr., 1974), pp. 87–91; and on dystopias, see Kinglsey Amis, *New Maps of Hell*

(New York: Harcourt Brace, 1960); Chad Walsh, *From Utopia to Nightmare* (New York: Harper and Row, 1962); and Mark Hillegas, *The Future as Nightmare* (1967; rpt. Carbondale and Edwardsville: Southern Illinois Univ. Pr., 1967). The dystopia was not entirely dominant, for in the last forty years utopias have appeared periodically. Four are Austin Tappan Wright's *Islandia* (1942), which Le Guin read when she was thirteen, "and so of course," she writes, "its influence is generic in all my work" (letter from Le Guin, 15 Sept. 1976); *Walden Two* (1948) by B. F. Skinner, who behaviorism Le Guin pilloried in *The Lathe of Heaven* (1971); Ivan Yefremov's *Andromeda* (1957); and Huxley's *Island* (1962). Le Guin's comments on Zamyatin are in her "The Stalin in the Soul," *The Future Now*, ed. Robert Hoskins (Greenwich, Conn.: Fawcett, 1977), pp. 11–20; and in her "Science Fiction and Mrs Brown," *Science Fiction at Large*, ed. Peter Nicholls (London: Gollancz, 1976), pp. 13–33, which includes Le Guin's account of the genesis of *The Dispossessed*.

2. "Literature and the Good Life: A Dilemma," *Yale Review* 65 (1975):37. Elliott, author of *The Shape of Utopia: Studies in a Literary Genre* (Chicago: Univ. of Chicago Pr., 1970), discovered *The Dispossessed* shortly after writing his premature obituary of the genre. Le Guin's theme, he wrote in a review, is "anachronistically positive" ("A New Utopian Novel," *Yale Review* 65 [1975]:256).

3. *The Dispossessed* (New York: Harper and Row, 1974), p. 308. Subsequent references are to this first hardcover edition. *The Dispossessed* is one of six novels in Le Guin's Hainish future history. Different assessments of the place of *The Dispossessed* in the design of the whole future history are Ian Watson, "Le Guin's *Lathe of Heaven* and the Role of Dick," *Science-Fiction Studies* 2 (1975):67–75; and "Le Guin's Hainish Future History" in my "Approaches to the Fiction of Ursula K. Le Guin," (Ph.D. diss., Univ. of Wisconsin, 1979), pp. 226–362.

4. Quoted in Gene van Troyer, "Vertex Interviews Ursula K. Le Guin," *Vertex* 2 (Dec. 1974):96.

5. "Chronosophy" is a neologism coined by J. T. Fraser, whose collection *The Voices of Time* (New York: Braziller, 1966) is one of the most important sources for Le Guin's ideas in *The Dispossessed*. Fraser defines "chronosophy" as "the interdisciplinary and normative study of time *sui generis*" (p. 590). Shevek asks about "chronotopology" (p. 92), and refers to himself as a "chronosophist" (p. 182); Sabul delivers the party line on "chronosophical thought in the Odonian Society" (p. 211); and Shevek discusses "chronosophy" at Vea's party (p. 195 ff.). Asked by an interviewer how she "came up with" Shevek's General Temporal Theory, Le Guin answered,

> There are shelves of books about space and space-time, but there's *one* main reference for thinking about time, either from a physics point of view or from philosophy. It's called *The Voices of Time*. . . .

> Sequency and Simultaneity seem to be the basic question. As well as I understood it, I tried to work it into the book. (Barry Barth, "Ursula Le Guin Interview," *Portland Scribe*, 17–25 May 1975, p. 8.)

It would take a long essay to show how Le Guin did just that. In lieu of such an essay, I would mention Friedrich Kümmel's important piece in Fraser's book, "Time as Succession and the Problem of Duration," and one of many echoes: in "Time and Synchronicity in Analytical Psychology," the Jungian psychologist Marie-Louise von Franz writes, "Number forms an ideal *tertium comparationis* between what we usually call psyche and matter" (p. 231) In *The Dispossessed*, Le Guin, whose interest in Jung is well known, writes, "Ainsetain had used *number*, the bridge between the rational and the perceived, between psyche and matter" (p. 246).

6. I propose a theory of chiasmus as a deep structure in science fiction narratives in "Chiasmus, Dialectics, and Archimedean Points: Toward a Rhetoric of Science Fiction," presented at the Annual Convention of the Popular Culture Association, Detroit, Apr. 1980.

7. "Varieties of Literary Utopias," *Utopias and Utopian Thought*, ed. Frank E. Manuel (Boston: Beacon Pr., 1967), p. 49. One of Frye's phrases is transposed.

8. On the cyclical sonata form in Beethoven, see *Encyclopedia Britannica: Micropaedia*, 1974 ed., s.v. "cyclic technique"; and Hugo Leightentritt, *Musical Form* (Cambridge, Mass.: Harvard Univ. Pr., 1951), pp. 327–54. Le Guin concluded her "Response" to the special Le Guin issue of *Science-Fiction Studies* with these words on literary influences: "I doubt that any of those writers, even Tolstoy, has helped me make a world out of chaos more than Beethoven, or Schubert, or J. M. W. Turner" (*Science-Fiction Studies* 3 [1976]:46). When she participated in a seminar on science fiction at the University of California at Berkeley in 1977, Le Guin spoke of "the tension between the musical structure of her work and the political content" (letter from John Boe, seminar organizer, undated).

9. "Introduction," *Utopia* by Thomas More, trans. and ed. Ogden (Northbrook, Ill.: AHM Publishing Corp., 1949), p. viii.

10. *Brave New World* (New York: Harper and Row, 1969), pp. viii–ix.

11. "Is Gender Necessary?" in *Aurora: Beyond Equality*, ed. Susan Anderson and Vonda McIntyre (Greenwich, Conn.: Fawcett, 1976), p. 132.

12. Le Guin openly acknowledges her debt to Kropotkin, whose influence on the novel is ably discussed by Philip E. Smith II, "Unbuilding Walls: Human Nature and the Nature of Evolutionary and Political Theory in *The Dispossessed*," in *Ursula K. Le Guin*, ed. Joseph D. Olander and Martin H. Greenberg (New York: Taplinger, 1979), pp. 77–96; and Victor Urbanowicz, "Personal and Political in Le Guin's *The Dispossessed*," *Science-Fiction Studies* 5 (1978):110–17. See also A. G. N. Flew, *Evolutionary Ethics* (New York: St. Martin's Pr., 1967). Le Guin's em-

phasis on ethics in utopia is a structure of feeling specific to the early 1970s, and is defined with characteristic clarity by Raymond Williams, "Utopia and Science Fiction," *Science-Fiction Studies* 5 (1978):203–14.

13. As Marx is reported to have said "Thank God I am not a Marxist!" (J. Hampden Jackson, *Marx, Proudhon and European Socialism* [New York: Collier, 1962], p. 147).

14. *The Wind's Twelve Quarters* (New York: Harper and Row, 1975), p. 285.

15. The following on *odos* grows from Samuel R. Delany's parenthetical remark on Odo ("To Read *The Dispossessed*," *The Jewel-Hinged Jaw* [Elizabethtown, N.Y.: Dragon Pr., 1977], p. 274), and the Liddell-Scott *Greek-English Lexicon*.

16. G. S. Kirk and J. E. Raven, *The Presocratic Philosophers* (Cambridge: Cambridge Univ. Pr., 1957), p. 189. Heraclitus is in Shevek's thoughts as he returns to the Regional Institute: "You shall not go down twice to the same river" (p. 48).

17. On Le Guin's Taoism, see Elizabeth Cummins Cogell, "Taoist Configurations: *The Dispossessed*," in *Ursula K. Le Guin*, ed. Joe De Bolt (Port Washington, N.Y.: Kennikat Pr., 1979), pp. 153–79; and "Le Guin's Taoism, the Romance and Utopia" in my "Approaches to the Fiction of Ursula K. Le Guin," pp. 363–434.

18. *Kibbutz: Venture in Utopia* (Cambridge, Mass.: Harvard Univ. Pr., 1956), pp. 168–200. Bruno Bettleheim, *Children of the Dream* (New York: Macmillan, 1969), helped Le Guin construct her Odonian community's family structure and educational principles.

19. Quoted by Charles Yost, "Ursula Le Guin: What's Wrong with Our New Left . . . ," *Northwest* (magazine section of the [Portland] *Sunday Oregonian*), 13 Feb. 1972, p. 8. Herbert Read writes, "Anarchism, which is not without its mystic strain, is a religion itself" ("The Philosophy of Anarchism," *Anarchy and Order* [Boston: Beacon Pr., 1971], pp. 47–48). If I discuss religion in *The Dispossessed*, I by no means deny the important Marxist approach to themes of alienation, reification, and commodity fetishism, treated already by Darko Suvin, "Parables of De-Alienation: Le Guin's Widdershins Dance," *Science-Fiction Studies* 2 (1975):265–74.

20. From a kibbutz statement of principle, quoted by Spiro, p. 10.

21. Speech by a kibbutz leader, quoted by Spiro, p. 60.

22. "The Kibbutz and the Spirit of Israel," in *The Family, Communes, and Utopian Societies*, ed. Sallie TeSelle (New York: Harper and Row, 1972), pp. 118–19. Like all thought experiments, *The Dispossessed* simplifies: Le Guin's Odonians do not have to displace another people, as the State of Israel has removed Palestinians from their land and driven them into exile.

23. *The Theory of the Novel*, trans. Anna Bostok (Cambridge, Mass.: MIT Pr., 1971), p. 41.

24. Quoted by M. H. Abrams, *Natural Supernaturalism* (New York: Norton, 1971), p. 195.

25. To read Abrams (pp. 141–324) on the Romantic circuitous journey with Le Guin in mind is to be impressed with the depth of her roots in Romanticism.
26. For a survey, see Claude V. Palisca, "Music and Science," *Dictionary of the History of Ideas*, ed. Philip Wiener, 5 vols. (New York: Scribner's 1973), 3:260–64; and James Haar, "Pythagorean Harmony of the Universe," ibid., 4:38–42.
27. Charles Rosen, *Sonata Forms* (New York: Norton, 1980), p. 12.
28. See M. Teresa Tavormina's fine essay "Physics as Metaphor: The General Temporal Theory in *The Dispossessed*," *Mosaic* 13 (1980):51–62.
29. *Sonata Forms*, p. 12.
30. Bernard Jacobson, "Sonata," *Encyclopaedia Britannica: Macropaedia*, 1974 ed., vol. 17, p. 6.
31. *Collected Letters of Samuel Taylor Coleridge*, 6 vols., ed. Earl Leslie Griggs (Oxford: Clarendon Pr., 1956–71), 4:545.
32. F. E. Kirby, "Musical Form," *Encyclopaedia Britannica: Macropaedia*, 1974 ed., vol. 12, p. 725.
33. As are *Oegeo*, the name of the engineer at the Space Research Foundation in A-Io who illustrates Causative Reversibility by proposing an application for Shevek's theory before the theory is in hand, and *Salas*, whose music might very well sound the same if performers read from a mirror image of his score.
34. Donald Francis Tovey disposed of the " 'short figure' heresy" in his *Essays in Musical Analysis*, vol. 1 (London: Oxford Univ. Pr., 1935), pp. 38–44; reprinted in *Symphony No. 5 in C Minor*, ed. Elliott Forbes (New York: Norton, 1971), pp. 143–50.
35. The name *Davenant* comes from the French *avenant* ("comely, prepossessing") and *avenir* ("future") (letter from Le Guin, 21 Apr. 1978). It is the Terran name for Hain. There is some truth in Nadia Khouri's charge that Le Guin, "stuck in her own aesthetic project, is forced to resort to a contrived and non-functional ending—a *deus ex machina*" ("The Dialectics of Power: Utopia in the SF of Le Guin, Jeury, and Piercy," *Science-Fiction Studies* 7 [1980]:53. Might we not say the same thing about the last movement of Beethoven's last symphony? I see my approach as complementing Khouri's ideologico-political approach.
36. Berlioz further developed Beethoven's cyclic sonata form by using the *idée fixe* in pieces like *Harold in Italy*, whose viola part Belle plays in Le Guin's "The New Atlantis," another story that pairs music and mathematical physics.
37. Introduction to the 1978 edition, *Planet of Exile* (New York: Harper and Row, 1978), pp. xii–xiii.
38. Note that Takver's name is like a palimpsest written over the letters of Vea's name, as Le Guin's utopia is a palimpsest written over the dystopian visions she inherited, as chapter seven is enclosed in chapters six and eight.

39. On Le Guin's "landscape painting," see my "Persuading Us to Rejoice
and Teaching Us How to Praise: Le Guin's *Orsinian Tales*," *Science-
Fiction Studies* 5 (1978):215–42.

40. *Walden and Civil Disobedience*, ed. Owen Thomas (New York: Norton,
1966), p. 221. Two sentences from "Civil Disobedience" distill into a
concentrated form much of *The Dispossessed*: "Action from principle—
the perception and the performance of right,—changes things and relations; it is essentially revolutionary, and does not consist wholly with any
thing which was. It not only divides states and churches, it divides families;
aye, it divides the *individual*, separating the diabolical in him from the
divine" (pp. 230–31).

41. Le Guin speaks of anamnesis and narrative in "It Was a Dark and Stormy
Night; or Why Are We Huddling about the Campfire?" *Critical Inquiry* 7
(1980):191–99, originally delivered to a symposium on narrative at the
University of Chicago.

42. *On the Aesthetic Education of Man*, trans. Elizabeth M. Wilkerson and
L. A. Willoughby (Oxford: Clarendon Pr., 1967), pp. 7, 9.

Index

271